VIOLENCE AND
GENDER RELATIONS

VIOLENCE AND GENDER RELATIONS

Theories and Interventions

edited by
Barbara Fawcett, Brid Featherstone,
Jeff Hearn and Christine Toft

SAGE Publications
London • Thousand Oaks • New Delhi

First published 1996

 SAGE Publications Ltd
6 Bonhill Street
London EC2A 4PU

SAGE Publications Inc
2455 Teller Road
Thousand Oaks, California 91320

SAGE Publications India Pvt Ltd
32, M-Block Market
Greater Kailash – I
New Delhi 110 048

British Library Cataloguing in Publication data

A catalogue record for this book is
available from the British Library

ISBN 0 8039 7649 6
ISBN 0 8039 7650 X (pbk)

Library of Congress record available

Typeset by Photoprint, Torquay, Devon
Printed in Great Britain by The Cromwell Press Ltd,
Broughton Gifford, Melksham, Wiltshire

Contents

Contributors

Barbara Fawcett
Lecturer in Social Work, University of Bradford
Barbara Fawcett has worked in a variety of social work settings for the past 12 years as a practitioner, manager and systems researcher. Her experience includes working with homeless families, children and families, people with disabilities and people experiencing mental distress. She is currently carrying out research into the interaction and interrelationship between carers and those perceived to require 'care'. Barbara lectures in social work in the Department of Applied Social Studies at the University of Bradford. Her publications include articles in *Social Work Education, Care in Place: International Journal of Networks and Community* and *Critical Social Policy*; she co-edited *Women, the System and Mental Health* (University of Bradford, 1994).

Brid Featherstone
Lecturer in Social Work, University of Bradford
Brid Featherstone is a qualified social worker and has worked in the area of child protection as a social worker and a manager. She is currently researching the subject of women's violence towards their children. Her publications include articles in *Social Work Education, Care in Place: International Journal of Networks and Community*, and *Critical Social Policy*; she co-edited *Women, the System and Mental Health* (University of Bradford, 1994). She is currently co-editing a book on mothering, with Wendy Hollway, to be published by Routledge.

Jalna Hanmer
Professor of Women's Studies, University of Bradford
Jalna Hanmer is convenor of the Violence, Abuse and Gender Relations Research Unit; and was Director of the ESRC Project on Violence, Abuse and the Stress-coping Process, Project no. 1; Co-convenor of the ESRC Research Strategy Seminars on Violence, Abuse and Gender Relations, Department of Applied Social Studies; and Evaluator, Leeds InterAgency Project (Women and Violence): projects on health, education and civil and criminal justice (Home Office/Programme Development Unit). She has written extensively on women, violence and agency responses; she is co-author of *Well-founded Fear* (Hutchinson, 1984) and *Women, Violence and Crime Prevention* (Avebury, 1993); and co-editor of *Women, Violence and*

Social Control (Macmillan, 1987) and *Women, Policy and Male Violence, International Perspectives* (Routledge, 1989).

Elizabeth Harlow
Lecturer in Social Work, University of Bradford
Elizabeth Harlow has seven years' experience as a social work practitioner. Since 1989 she has been employed as a lecturer in social work at the University of Bradford, and is currently researching, for a PhD, the question of gender and the progression to management within Social Services departments. Her publications include articles in *Gender, Work and Organization* and *Social Work Education* and chapters in *Changing Social Work and Social Welfare* (Open University Press, 1992) and *Gender and Organizational Change* (Routledge, 1995).

Jeff Hearn
Senior University Research Fellow, University of Manchester
Jeff Hearn has researched and written on violence, sexuality and sexual harassment, child abuse, and men and masculinities. He is co-author of *'Sex' at 'Work'* (rev edn, Prentice-Hall, 1995); and co-editor of *The Sexuality of Organization* (Sage, 1989) and *Taking Child Abuse Seriously* (Unwin Hyman, 1990). He is the author of *The Gender of Oppression* (Wheatsheaf, 1987) and *Men in the Public Eye* (Routledge, 1992); and co-editor of *Men, Masculinities and Social Theory* (Unwin Hyman, 1990). He was formerly Reader in Sociology and Critical Studies on Men; Co-convenor of the Violence, Abuse and Gender Relations Research Unit; Director of the ESRC Project on Violence, Abuse and the Stress-coping Process, Project no. 2; and Co-convenor of the ESRC Research Strategy Seminars on Violence, Abuse and Gender Relations, Department of Applied Social Studies, University of Bradford.

Wendy Hollway
Reader in Gender Relations, University of Bradford
Wendy Hollway trained as a psychologist and did her PhD in understanding the construction of gender difference and identity in relations among adults. She has been involved in teaching, training and consultancy in group and team relations, organizational change, equal opportunities, women and work and women in management training. Her current research and teaching applies psychoanalytic theory to gender and sexuality. She is the author of *Work Psychology and Organizational Behaviour: Managing the Individual at Work* (Sage, 1991); *Subjectivity and Method in Psychology: Gender, Meaning and Science* (Sage, 1989); and (with others) *Changing the Subject: Psychology, Social Regulation and Subjectivity* (Methuen, 1984). She currently holds an ESRC grant (with Professor Tony Jefferson) on gender difference, anxiety and the fear of crime and is co-editing a book on mothering (with Brid Featherstone).

Elizabeth Lancaster
Lecturer in Social Work, University of Bradford
Elizabeth Lancaster worked for the West Yorkshire Probation Service for 13 years, initially as a welfare rights adviser and then as a probation officer, latterly specializing in working with people who have committed sexual offences. She took up a post as a lecturer in social work at the University of Bradford in the summer of 1994, and is currently using her practice experience as a basis for developing her research around issues concerned with the 'treatment' of perpetrators of sexual crime.

Judith Milner
Senior Lecturer in Social Work, University of Huddersfield
After 14 years' social work practice, Judith Milner took up a post as senior lecturer in social work at the University of Huddersfield where she has responsibility for teaching on child protection and probation practice on diploma. She recently returned to practice in a northern authority as a member of a child protection team. Currently, she provides training on risk assessment in child protection and probation practice. Her recent publications include articles in *Critical Social Policy*, and *Surviving Childhood Adversity: Issues for Policy and Practice* (Dublin Social Studies Press, 1993). She was a member of the Violence against Children Study Group that produced *Taking Child Abuse Seriously* (Unwin Hyman, 1990).

Melody Mtezuka
Lecturer in Social Work, University of Manchester
Melody Mtezuka is a black South African born woman who now works as a lecturer in social work at the University of Manchester. Her social work practice background is in child guidance/child psychiatry where her critique of Western models of the assessment of troubled children was initially developed. She continues to look analytically at the theoretical frameworks used in social work education and training and offers the students opportunities to broaden their appreciation of particular issues which face other cultural groups, especially within the context of predominantly white value systems. Her recent publications include 'Towards a better understanding of child sexual abuse among Asian communities', *Practice*, vols 3 & 4, 1989–90; and (with B. Hughes), 'Social work and older women', in *Women, Oppression and State Social Work* (Unwin Hyman, 1992).

Christine Toft
Conference Organizer and Departmental Administrator,
Department of Applied Social Studies, University of Bradford
Christine Toft has organized a number of major conferences for the Department of Applied Social Studies, and has contributed to previous conference publications. She is a qualified social worker and has recently

co-edited the conference volume *Women, the System and Mental Health* (University of Bradford, 1994).

Terri Whittaker
Director of Postgraduate Social Work Studies, University of Liverpool
Terri Whittaker is currently a lecturer at the University of Liverpool where she teaches in the areas of ageing, disability and community care. She was previously a specialist social worker with older people and has written extensively in this area. Recent publications include a training manual relating to anti-racist social work practice with black elders and various articles focused on women, ageing and social work practice. A book, *Working with Elder Abuse*, was published by Arena in 1995. Current research includes a major study of the elder abuse systems within two local authority Social Services departments and worker/user experiences of these.

Acknowledgements

We are grateful to Plenum Publishing Corporation, New York, for permission to reproduce the following article: J. Hearn, 'The Organization(s) of Violence: Men, Gender Relations, Organizations and Violences', *Human Relations*, 47 (6), June 1994, pp. 707–30 as Chapter 3 of this volume.

We also wish to thank Karen Phillips of Sage for her support throughout the project and to record our indebtedness to Pauline Brier for her patience and hard work.

During the production of this book the tragic death of Melody Mtezuka occurred, and we would like to dedicate this book to her.

Introduction

Barbara Fawcett, Brid Featherstone, Jeff Hearn and Christine Toft

Violence is always with us. It is both historically persistent and immediately topical. It exists in the very structure of society and it repeatedly surprises. Violence also takes many forms: physical, sexual, emotional, verbal, representational, cognitive. It includes men's violence to women and children, violence between men and between women, women's violence to children and men, and indeed children's violence to each other and to adults. Violence can be directly from one person to another and can be between people; it can be interpersonal or institutional, local or global, between known others or between strangers. It is a clearly multifaceted set of actions and activities.

Violence also raises complex questions of theoretical analysis, policy development and practice. Theories of why violence occurs are many and various: biological, psychological, social psychological, sociological, political, economic. More precisely, specific theories have attempted to explain violence through individual pathology; psychodynamic developments; stress, frustration and blocked goals; socialization and learning theory; family system processes; societal structures and sociopolitical critique.

Furthermore, such various explanations may be feminist, non-feminist, or anti-feminist. While feminist work has tended to emphasize the importance of men's social and structural power over women and children, this has not necessarily been at the expense of explanations that also consider psychological, psychoanalytic and social psychological questions.

The overall and major theme of this book is the examination of violence through a focus on gender relations. All the chapters consider, albeit in very different ways, violence through the lens of gender. This means in practice a primary concern for men's continuing violence to women and children. However, a gendered approach to violence does not mean a neglect of women's violence. Neither does a central concern with gender lead to a lack of attention to other social divisions, such as class, race, age and generation. These and other social divisions are considered throughout this book.

Clearly, violence is not just a question of theory and theoretical analysis. Violence and its reduction and elimination is also a question requiring urgent policy and practical responses. Changing policy and practice is necessary in all spheres of life. Organizations act as contexts of violence, as initiators of violence, as institutions responding to violence and as agencies employing professionals who work on and against violence. Professional interventions to violence include those by lawyers and criminal justice professionals, doctors and health workers, social workers, probation officers, counsellors, and housing officers. This book explores key areas, demonstrates the interrelationship between research, theory, policy and practice and suggests innovative courses of action. It is organized in four broad sections: current issues and debates; gendered organizations; the problem of men's violence; and generation and gender.

In Part I, the current issues and debates are investigated, with particular reference to men's violence to known women. Chapter 1, by Jalna Hanmer, explores recent research on violence to women from known men, including women's understandings of such violence. Building on this earlier research, she reviews the evidence accumulated from recent in-depth interviews with women whose personal and/or family origins are from Pakistan, Bangladesh, India, the Caribbean and with white British women whose migratory roots have been lost in time. Sixty women living in refuges or in the community were interviewed. Interviews were also carried out with agencies about the contacts they had had with the women's struggles to alter their lives. A major emphasis throughout this chapter is the importance of recognizing commonalities as well as diversities between women experiencing violence.

Chapter 2, by Jeff Hearn, analyses men's understandings of violence to women, particularly known women. These are examined in three major ways: as changing historical constructions, as everyday constructions by men, and as constructions through theoretical explanations of violence. These three approaches are closely interconnected, and have further implications for both practical and policy interventions and the development of social theory.

In Part II, the focus is on violence and gendered organizations. First, Jeff Hearn (Chapter 3) considers some of the changing ways in which gender and sexuality have been approached, or indeed avoided, within organizational analyses. He goes on to explore the connections between gender, sexuality, violence and organizations. His examination is elaborated through the identification of significant analytical questions, a case study of organizational responses to men's violence to known women, and an evaluation of the potentials and limitations of a 'violence' perspective for organizational analysis. Throughout, special attention is paid to men's power as a major element in the structuring of sexuality, violence and organizations.

Chapter 4 by Elizabeth Harlow reviews some of the ways in which social work organizations are concerned with violence on a day-to-day basis. While the most overt kinds of violence between organizational members and their clients is acknowledged, it is to the more covert and taken-for-granted forms of violence occurring within the organization that most attention is given. Again, the main focus is on men's violence against women, and the chapter is explicitly concerned with social work organizations. Harlow argues that violence need not always be overt. Covert violence can also be said to occur as part of daily routine practices and, indeed, may be fundamental to the very nature and structure of all organizations to a greater or lesser extent.

Wendy Hollway's chapter (Chapter 5) differs in focus and style. Through a case analysis, she shows the effects of using a concept of gendered power relations which sees power as relational, potentially productive as well as potentially oppressive, and as multiple and contradictory. Accordingly, a view of the systematic and asymmetrical nature of men's power in organizations is shown. This chapter is in contrast to the others because it takes as its central theme power and its relation to gender, rather than violence and its relation to gender. The purpose in talking about gendered power relations in a relatively non-violent setting (that is, in a setting where inequality and discrimination are usually reproduced without the use of what would be called violence, in common-sense terms) is to provide a perspective on power which identifies its multiplicity and resulting contradictions and examines the differing potential for change in specific circumstances.

In the final chapter of this section (Chapter 6) Barbara Fawcett shares with Hollway a concern with the application and development of feminist post-structuralist theory to the problem of violence and gender relations. This is, however, pursued in a different way and with contrasting implications. The chapter extends the analysis of violence and gender relations into new terrain, including the impact of organizations and organizational definitions on the categorization and indeed violation of women and women's experience. It also relates the notion of gendered organizations to formal organizations, informal organizations, networks and communities. The chapter specifically explores the implication of these themes in the areas of mental health and community care for women from public and private perspectives.

In Part III, the emphasis is on the problem of men's violence. This involves attention to research findings on men, as well as professional considerations and interventions from both social work and probation. Chapter 7, by Jeff Hearn, draws on recent research on men's experience of their own violence to women they have known, most usually wives, partners and girlfriends. This involved in-depth interviews with 60 men about their understandings of their own violence; what they had done and why they had done it; as well as the nature of reactions from friends, family and social agencies.

Judith Milner's chapter (Chapter 8) is located in social work practice and addresses current criticisms of feminism in terms of knowledge related to child protection interventions. She argues that such criticisms are a further part of the process by which men seek to construct child abuse in a way which diminishes their responsibility for the management of their own violence. She describes strategies which social workers could use to respond to this situation.

The section is concluded with Elizabeth Lancaster's chapter (Chapter 9) on responses to male sex abusers within the Probation Service. She charts the development of this work within the service and outlines a range of practice initiatives. In the context of current debates about the future of the Probation Service and the criminal justice system, this chapter is a timely reminder of possible strategies and initiatives.

Part IV explores issues related to violence, generation and gender. Terri Whittaker begins this with an examination of the nature and extent of the relationship between gender, violence and elder abuse (Chapter 10). She argues that the discourse around elder abuse is based on United States' research from the field of 'family violence' and is therefore problematic in that it obscures the real issues which are ones of gender and power, rather than pathology and 'problem families'. The chapter concludes with an attempt to chart the beginnings of a feminist analysis and practice in relation to elder abuse and asks why feminists have been so slow to take an interest in this area. She suggests that this is due in part to ageism within the movement.

The final three chapters all explore aspects of generation and gender through a focus on violence to children. In recent years, the initial questions raised by 'individual' sexual abuse cases appear to have been complicated by the discovery of forms of abuse which include large numbers of adults and children and/or involve strange rituals or ceremonies. In the wake of each 'case' of such abuse, fast and furious debates have ensued in the popular and social work press. Such debates have been at their sharpest when suggestions of ritual or satanic abuse have been aired. Brid Featherstone and Elizabeth Harlow (Chapter 11) explore what has become known as the phenomenon of 'organized abuse', including, in the first instance, definitional issues. The key themes which have emerged from the debates, themes of silence and disbelief, are identified. Such themes are, of course, familiar to all who have worked with children who have been subjected to sexual abuse and are related to fundamental questions about families, sexuality and power. The issues for practice and the lessons that workers in a variety of settings appear to have learnt, particularly in relation to therapeutic interventions, are explored.

This is followed by Melody Mtezuka's examination of some of the issues raised in work with black children who have been sexually abused (Chapter 12), which poses questions about the appropriateness of current assessment models for black families based on 'Eurocentric' notions of family organization. As a result of these inappropriate assessment models, interventions are frequently unhelpful and misinformed. The chapter argues for the development of work in this area which would ensure that theories, policies and practices are based on an understanding both of racism and of culture.

In the final chapter, Brid Featherstone explores the paradoxical position of women's violence in that it is simultaneously over-scrutinized and neglected. She argues that this is scarcely surprising given how often women are either idealized or denigrated in contemporary Western society. Ambivalent and contradictory processes operate to position women, particularly mothers, on the one hand as the source of all the harm children suffer or as their only source of protection, and, on the other, as powerless victims themselves. She argues that attempts to understand women's violence towards children reflects such a counter-position, frequently investing the women concerned with total power or total powerlessness, and that men, by contrast, are either invisible or the source of all violence.

The range of perspectives contained within this book illustrates the strength and diversity of current debates, particularly among feminists and those influenced by feminisms. It also relates research findings and theoretical perspectives to practice situations, demonstrates interrelationships and explores connections and distinctions between institutional and interpersonal violence. These debates, because of their significance, must continue. This volume seeks to re-stimulate interest and re-focus attention on issues around violence and gender relations which remain so important for theory, policy and practice.

PART I

CURRENT ISSUES AND DEBATES

1

Women and Violence: Commonalities and Diversities

Jalna Hanmer

In the UK, research on violence has developed from a theoretical perspective that is based on oppression, exploitation and the dominance of men over women in marriage and society (Dobash and Dobash, 1979). Force and the threat of force are described as elemental factors holding together social structures and social processes based on the subordination of women (Hanmer, 1978). These ways of understanding violence to women by men developed from the Women's Liberation Movement's involvement in creating services for abused women. New questions could be asked and explored and statutory agency provision could be examined afresh. A parliamentary Select Committee was set up in 1974 to gather evidence on the problem of violence in marriage and to recommend appropriate responses (Select Committee on Violence in Marriage, 1975). Social policy issues of housing, health, social work and welfare were immediate issues to be explored (Binney et al., 1981; Borkowski et al., 1983; Maynard, 1985). Women's Aid (the refuge movement) was studied as part of research funded by the Department of Health and Social Services (Pahl, 1985). Later, the Home Office began to take an interest in altering the police response to violence to women in the home, and several policy documents were issued and a research overview report was published by the Home Office Research Unit (Smith, 1989). Policing, too, received attention (Hanmer and Saunders, 1984, 1987, 1993; Edwards, 1989). It was reported that women frequently found the law problematic (Atkins and Hoggett, 1984; Smart, 1984; Edwards, 1989; Smart and Sevenhuijsen, 1989). Research studies were also conducted on areas of the law which commonly impinge on women's lives such as divorce (Bottomley, 1984), custody bargaining (Wertzman, 1991), residence and contact (Hester and

Radford, 1992) and domestic violence (Freeman, 1984; Radford, 1987). The statutory and voluntary agency responses to black women's issues were addressed separately (Mama, 1989).

Raising the issue of rape and the responses of the state followed a similar pattern (Toner, 1977; Adler, 1987; Smith, 1989), as did that of the sexual abuse of girls (Nelson, 1982; Kelly, 1988) and children generally (Campbell, 1988). These types of violence are part of the experiences of women and girls, and can be those of women's children. Pornography, too, can be an aspect of abuse as can physical attacks (Itzin, 1993). In terms of personal experience, there is no necessary sealing off of one type of violence and abuse from another (Hanmer and Saunders, 1984, 1987, 1993), although the response of the state may involve attention to different aspects of the experience or the same aspects in different ways.

Some of this perspective on violence originates from research in the United States (in particular, Brownmiller, 1975; Dworkin, 1981; Russell, 1982; Bart, 1985; Chapman and Gates, 1987; Scully, 1990). Interestingly, though influential worldwide, this work is not mainstream in its country of origin. Nevertheless, the literature on violence against women, and agency responses to it, has been fundamentally important in making issues of violence and abuse visible, although in a highly restricted way, within the social sciences. The focus has generally been on women's experience of violence from men and the way state and related systems have responded. Attention to men's part in violence has often been indirect, or at least less direct. Thus, many of these studies can be read as also about men, men's violence and masculinities. In some cases, for example Scully's (1990) study of rapists, the question of men is addressed directly through interviews and/or other analyses.

Women's Views on Violence

Among the many important concerns and insights of this literature, there is the question of women's perceptions and definitions of violence. Women's perceptions of violence differ greatly from that of men (see Chapter 2); this violence reflects women's social position relative to men in society generally. The most general expression of women's definition of violence in relation to individual men is being unable to avoid becoming involved in situations and, once involved, being unable to control the process and outcome. With strangers, this definition covers behaviours that are visual only (for example, chasing, flashing), verbal (for example, abusive and threatening language), physical (including sexual attacks) and any combination of these elements (Hanmer and Saunders, 1984).

While violence both from known men and from strangers can be described as behaviours designed to control, dominate and express authority and power, the precise behaviours used may vary. With known men, a combination of forms of abuse is always present, although these can be merged or separate, sporadic or constant. For women, violence includes emotional, sexual and physical forms, including threat. How these controlling behaviours are expressed affect women's responses to the relationship. When violence is sporadic and connections with other forms of control and domination are not obvious, or perhaps not always present, women may describe violence as interspersed through an otherwise happy relationship so that, for example, 'He is alright when not drinking.'

Interlocking behaviours of control and domination can be physical, sexual, emotional and economic. Thus known men, unlike strangers, can exert economic control so that a woman has no access to money, even her Child Benefit, or she may not be allowed to work outside the home. Food can be restricted so that women may fear starvation and death for themselves or their children, and a woman may be forced to find others to feed her and her children. This can be family, friends or public agencies. Lack of adequate control over money needed for survival of the household is widespread among women who are being abused in other ways. These may include forced sexual intercourse following physical violence, or women may be required to engage in unwanted sexual practices more frequently than desired, or both together. Emotional abuse coexists with these more physical forms which further undermine women's sense of personal worth and competence. The way that forms of violence and abuse suffuse every aspect of women's lives makes it difficult for women to emerge from what are best understood as abusive systems of social relations.

Known men may demand and achieve through physical violence complete obedience to every order. This includes psychological denigration both when the woman is alone with the man or in front of others. Humiliation is an important strategy in obedience training. The forms this takes can appear to be almost whimsical. For example, one woman was told to get up from her chair, cross the room, pick up the man's trainers and hand them to him when he could touch them without moving from his seat on the sofa. This type of behaviour was understood by the woman as a test of her obedience. In achieving this degree of control, a man can successfully make other demands on the woman, such as insisting she vacate the marital bed for his mistress, refusing to allow her to leave the house, timing her when she goes shopping, cross-examining her if she dares to speak to anyone, refusing to allow her to see a doctor or go to a hospital for treatment or to remain in hospital if she is already receiving treatment.

These forms of violence damage women's relationships with significant others, including workmates and friends. Women's relationships with family and children may even be ended. Women may give up children for a variety of reasons; the man may not want a particular child around, he may be abusive to one or more children, and on ending the relationship she may continue to defer to him by surrendering children. Men may force women to have abortions or attack them when they are pregnant which results in miscarriage. Women may also undergo abortions because the quality of life is so low that women fear for the future of another child. Alternatively, men may force women to have children that the women do not want. At the extreme, women can dissociate, speaking of their earlier self before the violent relationship began, as someone else, a lost personality, a person of worth and abilities who no longer exists. This is not a simple psychological problem but a transformation of the self.

The Research

This chapter draws on research that builds on this background literature. The research, funded by the Economic and Social Research Council and part of the Initiative on the Management of Personal Welfare, was conducted in Leeds, Bradford, Keighley, Halifax and other nearby places in West Yorkshire during 1991–93.[1] The focus was on women's experience of violence within the family from known men. Thirty women were interviewed in depth from a number of communities, whose personal and/or family origins were from Pakistan, Bangladesh, India, and the Caribbean, and 30 white British women were interviewed whose migratory roots have been lost in time. Women were interviewed in languages that they felt comfortable with, that is, Punjabi, Urdu and English. Women were living in refuges and in the community. With the women's permission, we also interviewed agencies from social services, housing, health, the criminal justice system and the voluntary sector about the assistance they gave to these women in their struggle to alter their lives.

Commonalities and Differences

The discussion begins by focusing on commonalities between women. It then moves on to consider differences between women and between women and men and the role of agencies and society more generally in creating these differences. Commonalities and differences, both from the point of view of women and from those who provide services to women, are readily evident in the interviews. There is always a difficulty in discussing commonalities and differences. To speak of commonality immediately raises difference as an issue and to speak of difference questions commonality. And then there is the issue of which difference and which commonality is to be given priority. Some differences which relate to how women were obtained for interview and in what languages these interviews took place have already been mentioned. For the organization of the research these are important differences between women. But what of the women concerned? Which differences affect them in relation to how and why women experience violence and the solutions they and others develop?

Across ethnic groups, what women experience and how they define their experience are marked by similarities. There are common themes, whatever the women's origin and background, that are relevant to understanding and placing both individual and structural differences in a context that enables agencies to provide good quality services. The first similarity is in how women understand violence. The second similarity that continually surfaced in interviews is the importance of family, whether women were married or yet to be married and whatever ethnic or cultural group women come from. There are three important aspects:

1 Women live within a web of relationships through which family members and others intervene in women's lives.
2 Women struggle against domination, control, coercion and violence directed at them through the web of relationships in which their lives are located.
3 The boundaries that specify correct family behaviour for women are not those that bind men to society and cultures, however diverse cultures may be in other ways. This is the most basic factor of all and constitutes the framework that either fully or partially legitimates violence against women in their homes.

Thus women's attempts to deal with violence involve personal struggles, the involvement of others, and cultural boundaries that are not the same for women as men. Women exist within their own cultural domain. Women live within a culture within a culture.

In looking at the lives of women who were married, such women's experiences were partly shaped by socially structured differences in their marriage or marriage type arrangements. Women's marriages were of three types and involved two factors: who arranged the marriage and how kinship was involved. Marriages were arranged either by families or by the individual marriage partners. Marriages arranged by families were between those related by kinship, particularly cousins, or they were arranged by families between women and men who were not kin. These differences are important to the lives of women, but domination, control and violence against women and their children occurs whatever the preferred form of marriage, and, whatever the preferred form of marriage, families attempt to mediate relationships characterized by violence. The pattern of marriage within white British society which is seen as freely entered into by both parties and based solely on their choice is no more likely to produce violence-free marriages than those that are arranged, whether between family relations or strangers.

A Web of Relationships

Because of the intensely negative and debilitating situations experienced by women, they struggle to find ways to improve their position through their relationships with others. These may include the woman's family of origin, and if married or in some other relationship with a man, his family.

These relations typically include four generations if grandparents are living, and three if not, and can include mothers and mothers-in-law, fathers and fathers-in-law, brothers and brothers-in-law, sisters and sisters-in-law and their children; and they extend laterally to include mother's and mother-in-law's brothers and sisters, father's and father-in-law's brothers and sisters, and their children, and more distant relations, including on occasion friends of these relations.

Many or few people can be involved in the area of struggle where women are fighting for their lives – sometimes literally and always in the sense of the quality of their lives. Over time, the involvement of others ebbs and flows. Over time, women learn about who can help and how. They learn about the others they are tied to through marriage and/or kinship and their knowledge of the outer world expands. Their behaviour changes, as do their views of the world that they were brought up to believe they would unproblematically inhabit.

Violence: Themes and Effects

The specific situations around which violence occurs involve all aspects of shared residence and life. For married and cohabiting women, major themes are money, housing, sex and reproduction including abortion, divorce and remarriage, employment, his and her friends, food, clothing, children, domestic cleaning, wife's behaviour, her independence, husband's behaviour, and fidelity. Women's vulnerability to violence and risk of being treated violently increases with pregnancy and children. This is because women bear children and, once born, assume responsibility for them.

There are other similarities between women that cross cultural borders. For example, women from any culture may be treated violently because their husbands wish to be rid of them. Violence to women can begin with marriage, with pregnancy, with the birth of children, and can include violence against children. It can continue for many years and involve sexual, physical and emotional attacks and traumas. Women leave to protect their children and themselves. This is more than a question of direct attack; life can also be threatened through material deprivation: no food in the home because the woman has no control over money, not even her Child Benefit. Both she and her children may be forced to leave in order to eat.

There are many immediate effects of violence on women and children. Women may be terrified. As one woman said, 'I was very frightened of him, I had a great fear of him in my mind, it was like a beast had come, not a husband. I would shake if he came into the room. I would go to one side of the room and stay there and shake.' Babies and very young children are physically abused, 'He took her upstairs and down hitting her, on the floor, everywhere hitting her, after hitting her he threw her behind his feet.' And children, too, are terrified, 'She was that frightened of him upon seeing him she would start to shake and start making distressed noises.'

There are many different responses. Women spoke of not going to the hospital or involving anyone else after particularly violent attacks because, in the words of one woman, 'I think I was just totally broken. I was still, I think, locked into the relationship. I thought if I start going down that road, going to the hospitals and the police it would be the end of us, and I really didn't want that.' Women want to feel positive and hope that men will change, 'I suppose I was excusing him, thinking, blaming myself I suppose, thinking eventually he'll realise that I'm not to blame and he'll stop doing it.'

There are many long-term effects of violence on women and children. For example, living with violence can create depression and despondency. As one woman explained, 'As time has gone on over the years I've lost a lot of my strengths.' Another long-term effect of violence less often discussed is abortion. Because women are primarily responsible for children they may decide not to proceed with a pregnancy given the way that their other children are being treated and the violence and abuse directed towards themselves. Women consider the future because they assume responsibility for their children.

Families Intervene

In violence against women in their homes, there is variation in who is or becomes involved in a woman's situation. For all the women interviewed, families are deeply implicated, both positively and negatively. Women can be in situations where they have no contacts outside the family, but many also have friends: her friends, his friends, and her workmates and employers whose responses to her may also be either positive or negative. The involvement of others is not necessarily fixed over time as either positive or negative. Individuals may vacillate between these two responses. Negative responses include both active and passive support of her abuse and for her abuser. Others may collude and encourage her abuser or refuse to intervene, thereby conveying a message of support for the way things are. For example, women were told by close family members from all communities either that they should not make a fuss because married women are always hit, or else they were told the opposite, that they should not stand for it. Within families, different members could take both positions.

Families or members of families can decide that nothing can be done to change the man's behaviour, and turn to offering help to the woman. Power is differentially distributed in families and it can be others with little power who offer the crucial assistance, such as younger women members of the same family, his or hers. This may be done in secrecy as it is an act of courage and involves danger for a family member with little power and prestige.

Families can go to considerable lengths in their attempts to protect their daughters and to provide them with a socially correct future. For example, among Muslims the tradition is cross-cousin marriage and especially favoured is marriage between father's brothers' sons and daughters. More than one daughter may be married into the same family and both sons and daughters may be exchanged between two families. At its best, this creates an interrelated network of family obligations. This is a sophisticated system of marriage relations controlled by men but where women are the guardians of the system. In Britain, women protect the family against the external threat of racism and the internal threat of assimilation. When, however, this type of marriage does not work, the problem for women is particularly acute as they are breaking up extended families and the community, not just the married pair. In this type of extended family, brothers have a special responsibility for sisters. When these obligations are not met, women can be plunged into continuing problems of violence and domination.

Strategies and Cultural Boundaries

Everyone involved has strategies and these relate to the boundaries set by culture. The roles and expectations of others in relation to the woman are influenced, if not determined, by kinship. She is daughter, sister, aunt, granddaughter, niece, mother. Everyone has strategies: her, him, her family, his family (and within families different people have different roles and strategies). Strategies relate to boundaries set by culture, religion, education, class, economic circumstances and language.

Through interactions with others, women's views of themselves, their marriages, their families, their futures, change over time. Women live in a world where we know what is expected of us as women, and while our relationship to that knowledge may be ambivalent, many women do not question their destiny as defined by the group with which they identify until they personally experience progressively greater difficulties in living the expected kind of life. This, however, is not to say that culture is uniform and that all women within the same cultural group interpret cultural expectations and boundaries in the same way. These can be contested areas.

How women negotiate within and across cultural boundaries by re-formulating their relationship to cultural expectations is part of the decision radically to alter their lives. Women must mentally negotiate the change before it becomes a possibility that is more than a few days' rest and recuperation before returning. Crossing cultural boundaries takes place both in terms of the structure of ideas that locate the self in relation to others and in terms of leaving behind, challenging, and restructuring the web of relationships that make up daily life.

Women adopt various ways of resituating themselves in relation to cultural boundaries:

1   Women may eventually conclude that, 'I have not given up cultural ideals, others have.' The importance of this formulation is that 'I am not guilty of bringing dishonour or shame onto the family, he is or they are.' The ideals remain intact and unquestioned.
2   Or women may decide that there are other cultural ideals that come into play: 'My honour, too, is important.' 'He or they have gone too far.'
3   Or women may be between conflicting cross-cutting cultural boundaries and conclude that 'My demand for independence takes precedence over the demands of others for particular types of bonds of relationship.'
4   Or women may find themselves thrust out of the boundaries: 'My survival physically and emotionally and/or that of my children takes precedence over my/our destruction.'
5   Or women may decide that the quality of their lives is too minimal to continue: 'My future requires a better life for myself and my children.'

It can take women many years and agonizing emotional trauma to reach the point where they reformulate and resituate themselves in relation to cultural boundaries. But once this process begins women are freer to consider leaving and moving back into the community as a one-parent family. Having done this, women can describe their new lives in less or more positive terms. For example, one woman described her new life as half a life. She had to give up that half which was about meeting cultural expectations for wives in order to secure safety for herself and her children. This is experienced as a loss which involves emotional pain. Another woman, however, described her life as a single parent as half way up. This woman is not looking back; around being a wife she has crossed the cultural boundaries of her ethnic group.

Men and Cultural Boundaries

The strength of cultural boundaries for women raises the issue of what are the boundaries for men? In individual situations women recount how the involvement of other people both supports and perhaps even actively encourages the behaviour of their men, but other people also criticize this behaviour. The outstanding overarching impression given, as women explain the detail of their lives, is that their men appear to stand outside community and family accountability as understood by and applied to women.

Others do move to restrain a husband and/or other family members who may be abusing an individual woman. While these interventions may work for some women, the research interviews were with women for whom the traditional and individual family modes of intervention were not effective.

As the interventions were ineffective, one is led to ask not just how, but why do others attempt to restrain husbands, as there appear to be other cultural values that take precedence for men.

Women describe men's relationships with members of the man's family of origin, with her and the children, with his and her friends, with work colleagues, and with other women. In the last analysis, while there may be objections, the reality is that men can place their affections, loyalties, income and time elsewhere and still maintain their position as husband and father in the eyes of others. The reverse situation is not possible for women. Women who place their affections, loyalties, income and time elsewhere are inevitably defined by others as bad wives and mothers against whom social sanctions must be introduced and enforced. Although not all women are equally affected, there is a clear double standard in operation that impacts on women regardless of their cultural group.

In all cultural and ethnic groups husbands have cultural and family advantages that come both from being male and from being husbands. This may partly explain why men are often so loath to give up the women they abuse. They lose the gendered social advantages gained by being a husband and have only those of being male to fall back upon. When women establish themselves as single parents, men who are not immediately moving on to another woman become single and itinerant; a lowly social position especially as men age. To be part or head of a family carries considerable power and status in the community for the male.

The Roles of Agencies and the State

The result of this community-held double standard is that if an individual woman decides to leave a relationship where a man demonstrates a lack of loyalty, affection and care for his wife and their children, she may find herself on her own without family support, or this may be very limited or grudgingly given. If there are no friends as well, a woman can be in a very isolated position. The importance of agencies for immediate and long-term social support then becomes particularly acute.

There are several problems which women who become single parents face; in particular, women usually have to begin again, dislocated from their community, placed somewhere where they and their children know no one. As one woman who was able to stay within her own community explains, 'If we had moved, my child wouldn't have known a soul. I thought of all the people she knows at her school and how far back they go. In the neighbourhood you're a fixture, you and others whose names you may not know but see everyday is part of being alive and rooted.' People have views on women on their own that can be more difficult to negotiate for the woman as stranger than when they know her from the past. For black women, being uprooted is aggravated by the daily racism they face. Racism makes it more difficult for women to achieve independence in a new community. But over time, by living independently, women can restructure the cultural demands by which they live. By struggling to establish independent lives women can build new personal strengths. In this process agencies can be helpful.

The state plays a complex role in relation to women and children. Its various agencies have responsibility for recognizing harm, providing care and protection, and for controlling the lives of women and children. Somewhere embedded in all these activities lies the notion of equal treatment between women and men within the family, and between women from different cultures and communities, but what stands in the way of this always being delivered? Unfortunately, women's experiences of agencies are very mixed.

First, I would like to look at the treatment of women and children which may not be equitable *vis à vis* their ethnic or community background. There are crucial differences between the women interviewed that relate to the response of the dominant culture to ethnic minorities; for example, services for girls who are sexually, physically and emotionally abused and generally to women without British or European citizenship.

One of the most significant differences between the women is that single women were interviewed only from communities originating in the Asian sub-continent. Young single women are in women's refuges because there is no other place for them. As well as violence, which can take the form of sexual as well as physical assault, young women's struggles within their families involve continuing with their education, marriage plans, taking up employment, their friends and social life, the clothing they wear or wish to wear, the desire or decision to leave home, and relationships with men. Violence is also associated with domestic cleaning, cooking and money. White women often escape violence and sexual abuse in the family by leaving to live with another man, which may not end their abuse but it does enable young women to leave their family home. This escape route is less easily available in cultures with a strict moral code for women. All the white women interviewed were in refuges or had been rehoused because of abusive adult relationships with men. Some also had physical, sexual and/ or emotional abuse in their childhoods to recount. Some had multiple partners where similar problems had arisen. But none was in a refuge directly because of abuse while a child.

We interviewed young women whose abuse had not been noticed by agencies with responsibilities for children or, if noticed, no further intervention had taken place. Their struggles to end their abuse were successful only when old enough to leave home. This is a complex issue because girls from the dominant culture are also being overlooked by agencies, but the issue is not simply one of degree but of qualitative difference in responses by agencies. Agencies can be reluctant to intervene in the families of ethnic minorities.

Another major difference centres around nationality and citizenship. Nationality is not an issue for women with British citizenship who marry

British men, whereas it is a major issue for women when their nationality or that of their husbands is not British. For women who are not British nationals there are issues of control exercised by their husbands and his family over citizenship, residence, and documents regarding nationality, visas and other papers. These affect both women without British nationality and women married to men with other passports and countries of origin. There are also issues of leaving home and settling in another country and of having to stay with the man for one year in order to gain residence rights in Britain.

To return to the similarities between women's experiences of agencies whatever their ethnic or community group, women were interviewed who were forced out of their homes and localities by the indifference of agencies to whom they finally turned for help. There were issues of communication in that women sometimes thought that their general practitioner or social worker, for example, knew all about their situation, but this could be denied or no records found. Women sometimes meet responses from agencies that are similar to those they meet in the family in that some will offer assistance and some will not and some will intervene in ways that worsen a woman's position.

Women were also interviewed who managed to stay in their homes because of the help they received from agencies as well as being offered safety and assistance by leaving their homes and settling elsewhere. There were many examples of positive agency intervention, beginning with women's refuges. The state sector, too, can intervene positively in the lives of the interviewed women. The help received has enabled some women to survive with their children when no, or very little, support was available from anywhere else.

A primary issue about agencies is that the same agency can help, be indifferent, and be hostile to women. The inconsistency in response from staff is a major issue for the police, housing, social services, health, indeed all the state agencies. Staff can lack information about other agencies, so that women may not receive the most appropriate referrals, in particular to services provided by women's groups in the voluntary sector.

The double standard I referred to earlier can continue to operate after a woman sets up an independent home if the man does not want her to have this. This double standard that allows men to be considered good enough husbands and fathers whether or not they invest their affections, loyalties, income and time in their families, enables men to make demands that are not regarded as reasonable or desirable if made by women in similar situations. Children are used and abused in order to regain entry into the woman's new home and/or to continue to harass women. Women's descriptions can make professional interventions sound as irresponsible as the actions of the men they are attempting to assist or regulate. There can be a lack of urgency and appreciation of the views and needs of the parent with greater responsibility for children by agency staff.

One woman explained, 'Here I am, I'm on the front line battling to keep him at bay, and to do the job that the social worker or the probation officer should be doing, which is to say to him, "Look calm down, listen to what's happening to your children, how they feel. Respect their feelings and you can build a relationship." I shouldn't be the one who has to say that to him. Legally speaking, he shouldn't even ring me up.'

Women with multiple contacts with agencies can conclude that 'People say there's this agency, that agency, and when it comes to us, there's nothing.'

Involvement of Others

The involvement of others in areas of struggle in which women, and often children, are primary targets, both contributes to patterns of dispute and of resistance. How others are brought in and by whom, what they do, how cultural forms are used (beliefs, norms, etc.) and why others intervene (the nature of the relationship with the woman or the function of the agency/ state) are major contributory factors in creating differences between women and in women's individual situations when facing violence in the home. This is why it matters so much how others respond. Like the old adage, if you are not part of the solution, you are part of the problem; there is no neutral ground to which one, whether agency or individual, can withdraw. The concept of the level playing field to guide professional intervention has to include knowledge of the different position that women, as against men, occupy in relation to family, children and community in order to provide equal treatment.

Conclusion

We need to move forward in ways that give women real choices. This means developing services that are culturally sensitive. Agencies need to be confident in intervening in families from a variety of backgrounds. Women need well-funded women's services in the voluntary sector. Appropriate housing that looks to the needs of women with respect to location, size and condition is needed, as are neighbourhood-based services and support for women. Women who succeed best in establishing a new life are able to take up employment that is fulfilling and reasonably paid. Women need education and training for employment. Women need advocacy and, where appropriate, interpretation services that assist in representing their points of view. Women need consistency in agency responses. To support women is not to treat them more favourably than men, but to recognize the responsibilities women carry and their need for a decent life.

Note

1. ESRC Research Project No. L206 25 2003, 'Violence, Abuse and the Stress-coping Process, Project no. 1' (April 1991–March 1993).

References

Adler, Z. (1987) *Rape on Trial*, London: Routledge and Kegan Paul.

Atkins, S. and Hoggett, B. (1984) *Women and the Law*, Oxford: Basil Blackwell.

Bart, P. (1985) *Stopping Rape: Successful Survival Strategies*, New York: Pergamon.

Binney, V., Harkell, G. and Nixon, J. (1981) *Leaving Violent Men*, London: Women's Aid Federation.

Borkowski, M., Murch, M. and Walker, V. (1983) *Marital Violence: the Community Response*, London: Tavistock.

Bottomley, A. (1984) 'Resolving family disputes', in R. Freeman (ed.), *State Law and the Family*, London: Tavistock.

Brownmiller, S. (1975) *Against our Will: Men, Women and Rape*, New York: Simon and Schuster.

Campbell, B. (1988) *Unofficial Secrets: Child Sexual Abuse – The Cleveland Case*, London: Virago.

Chapman, J.R. and Gates, M. (eds) (1987) *The Victimisation of Women*, Beverly Hills, CA: Sage.

Dobash, R.E. and Dobash, R.P. (1979) *Violence against Wives*, New York/Basingstoke: Free Press/Macmillan.

Dworkin, A. (1981) *Pornography: Men Possessing Women*, London: Women's Press.

Edwards, S. (1989) *Policing 'Domestic' Violence: Women, the Law and the State*, London: Sage.

Freeman, R. (ed.) (1984) *State Law and the Family*, London: Tavistock.

Hanmer, J. (1978) 'Violence and the social control of women', in G. Littlejohn, B. Smart, J. Wakeford and N. Yuval-Davis (eds), *Power and the State*, London: Croom Helm.

Hanmer, J. and Saunders, S. (1984) *Well-founded Fear: a Community Study of Violence to Women*, London: Hutchinson.

Hanmer, J. and Saunders, S. (1987) 'Women, violence and crime prevention', Report of a Research Study Commissioned by West Yorkshire Metropolitan County Council, November.

Hanmer, J. and Saunders, S. (1993) *Women, Violence and Crime Prevention: a Community Study in West Yorkshire*, London: Avebury.

Hester, M. and Radford, L. (1992) 'Domestic violence and access arrangements for children in Denmark and Britain', *Journal of Social Welfare and Family Law*, 1: 57–70.

Itzin, C. (1993) *Pornography*, Oxford: Oxford University Press.

Kelly, L. (1988) *Surviving Sexual Violence*, Cambridge: Polity Press.

Mama, A. (1989) *The Hidden Struggle: Statutory and Voluntary Sector Responses to Violence against Black Women in the Home*, London: The Runnymede Trust.

Maynard, M. (1985) 'The response of social workers to domestic violence', in J. Pahl (ed.), *Private Violence and Public Policy: the Needs of Battered Women and the Response of the Public Services*, London: Routledge and Kegan Paul.

Nelson, S. (1982) *Incest: Fact and Myth*, Edinburgh: Stramullion.

Pahl, J. (ed.) (1985) *Private Violence and Public Policy: the Needs of Battered Women and the Response of the Public Services*, London: Routledge and Kegan Paul.

Radford, L. (1987) 'Legalising woman abuse', in J. Hanmer and M. Maynard (eds), *Women, Violence and Social Control*, Basingstoke: Macmillan.

Russell, D.E.H. (1982) *Rape in Marriage*, New York: Macmillan.

Scully, D. (1990) *Understanding Sexual Violence: a Study of Convicted Rapists*, London: Harper Collins.

Select Committee on Violence in Marriage (1975) *Report, together with the Proceedings of the Committee. Volume 2: Report, Minutes of the Committee and Appendices*, London: HMSO.

Smart, C. (1984) *The Ties that Bind*, London: Routledge and Kegan Paul.

Smart, C. and Sevenhuijsen, S. (eds) (1989) *Child Custody and the Politics of Gender*, London: Routledge.

Smith, L. (1989) *Domestic Violence*, Home Office Research Study 107, London: HMSO.

Toner, B. (1977) *The Facts of Rape*, London: Arrow. Rev. edn 1982.

Wertzman, L. (1991) 'Women and custody bargaining', in L. Wertzman and M. Maclean (eds), *Economic Consequences of Divorce: the International Perspective*, London: Oxford University Press.

2

Men's Violence to Known Women: Historical, Everyday and Theoretical Constructions by Men

Jeff Hearn

Feminist practice, research and theory demonstrate the extent and importance of men's violence to known women. The fact that women are most at risk of violence from men with whom they have a heterosexual relationship is a matter of great personal, political, policy and theoretical concern. It is also a social phenomenon that challenges much conventional 'malestream' sociological wisdom (O'Brien, 1981), in particular around the separation and interrelation of agency and structure of primary and secondary social relationships, and the pervasive idea of the ungendered individual in 'the family'. In exploring theory and research on violence, these issues are highly interrelated.

Recent research on men has developed from a number of directions: from feminist scholarship, from gay scholarship and from men's diverse responses to feminism. In a variety of ways, it has attempted to make the social construction of men and masculinities explicit. The focus is explicitly 'men', whether it is men 'who rape' (Beneke, 1982; Scully, 1990), men who are 'behind bars' (Wooden and Parker, 1982) or men who 'confront pornography' (Kimmel, 1990). However, the majority of this work, and particularly that which has come to be known as 'men's studies' (especially in the United States), has generally not explored the question of men's violence to any large extent. This lack of attention to violence in many of these studies, and particularly those conducted by men, has been noted (Hanmer, 1990) as one of their major shortcomings. It is partly for this reason that more critical studies on men and masculinities are being developed.

In this more critical tradition the focus on men's power and domination is seen as a central problem. Violence is located as one element of that power and domination, even though there are major discussions and debates about the explanation of those violences (for example, Kaufman, 1987). Accordingly, different accounts of violence – psychoanalytic, learning theory, structural/patriarchal – give different accounts of men and masculinities (Hearn, 1990). This perspective therefore engages with the variety of ways in which violence and masculinities interrelate with each other – for men in general, for particular types of men (for example, by economic class, age and so on), and for individual men.

Additionally, the focus on men has been stimulated by a variety of policy and practical developments around men's violence both within and outside the state. These include redefinitions of police policy towards men's violence to women and children in the home (Hanmer, 1990), more specific work with rapists and sex offenders (Wyre, 1987), and the growth of group-based counselling, self-help and educational programmes for men who have been violent (Gondolf, 1985). The major initiative for the last of these developments has been in North America. Considerable debate is in process around the appropriateness of different styles, practical methods and philosophies of such programmes (see p. 112).

This chapter draws on a variety of previous research. This includes critical theoretical and practical work on child abuse conducted with the Violence against Children Study Group (Hearn, 1988, 1990); historical research on men's power in the public and private domains (Hearn, 1992); and recent Economic and Social Research Council research on men's experience of violence to known women, which has been in process since April 1991.[1] This last project is one of two linked, yet separate, projects on violence; the linked project directed by Jalna Hanmer addresses women's experience of violence from known men (see Chapter 1).

Both projects also examine the policy and practices of agencies, their management and workers, in the area of men's violence to women. These were examined through interviews on policy, and, where the individual gave permission, the follow-up of individual contact with agencies. Initially, 60 women and 60 men were interviewed, and follow-up agency interviews, examination of records and other individual contacts took place in over 200 cases (Hanmer, forthcoming; Hearn, 1995, 1996).

In conceptualizing this research, issues of power and politics permeate throughout the research process. These apply to the subject matter of the research – men's violence to known women – the disciplinary location of the research work and the relation of the research to existing paradigms. The conceptualization of this research involves the recognition that gendered power relations are basic to the study of violence. It is because of this that there are different projects on women and men. The two studies are located in relation to feminist research/women's studies, and pro-feminist research/critical studies on men, respectively.

The state of knowledge is very different in the two fields of women's experiences of violence from known men, and men's experience of violence to known women. There is a considerable amount of work, both practically and theoretically, on violence against women and there has been relatively little on men's violence. Accordingly, different research questions and research agendas have operated in the two projects.

In addition to different organizational perspectives, this research also illustrates that agencies are gendered and present gendered understandings of violence which are directly related to policies and practices. Indeed most formal agencies operate from men's definitions, men's constructions, and men's definitions of violence. In the case of state organizations, men's control and definitions, both in general and of violence, are particularly dominant. This applies in both state bureaucracies and the legal system. Challenging these, women's definitions, policies and practices have been developed through women's organizations in relation to violence against women. Such contestations of definitions and meanings of violence, implicit and explicit, apply not only to agencies and their policy development, but also to academia and social theory.

Not only are agencies important in the development of actual and potential policies on men's violence to women, but they also have the effect of structuring the social lives of women and men. Agencies structure the meaning of violence by both omission and commission in policies and practices. The historical and cultural construction of violence may specifically shape the personal circumstances and future courses of actions for women and men in relation to violence.

This chapter explores some selected aspects of men's constructions of men's violence to known women – historical, everyday and theoretical. These three aspects exist in constant and complex interrelation. The first main section charts the process of historical recognition of the problem of men's violence to women. The emphasis here is on the formal recognition of that problem in state law and policy. This emphasis is not meant to suggest that state law is necessarily effective (McCann, 1985). Rather it is presented as a series of changing formal definitions of the problem that influence the constructions by both state agencies and individuals within and outside those agencies. The second section focuses on men's everyday definitions and perceptions of what is meant by violence to known women. This section draws most directly on the ESRC research referred to above. The third section examines the diversity of theoretical constructions, particularly men's theoretical constructions, of men's violence to known women. These in turn feedback to both agency and individual understandings. The chapter concludes with some comments on the implications of these questions for social theory more generally.

Historical Recognition

In attempting to 'make sense' of men's violence to women, it is necessary to consider the problem in a clear historical context. This is especially important in understanding how such violence has been accepted, condoned, normalized and ignored by both individuals and institutions. It has been seen as a 'private matter'. Individual men's perceptions of violence to women are themselves affected by the definitions and constructions produced and reproduced in agencies. The recent increase in recognition of the problem by state agencies has arisen from the action of the Women's Movement, and particularly Women's Aid.

Men's violence to women was an important focus of attention in both 'first-wave' feminism (see, for example, Cobbe, 1878, 1894; Pankhurst, 1913) and 'second-wave' feminism (see, for example, The British Women's Studies Group, 1979; Coote and Campbell, 1982). The basic Act of Parliament that defines violence to the person is the Offences against the Person Act of 1861. The relevant sections are 42 (common assault), 47 (assault occasioning actual bodily harm), 20 (unlawful wounding), and 18 (grievous bodily harm). However, this Act could not be said to have operated in relation to men's violence to known women until subsequent reforms in the nineteenth and twentieth centuries.

Significantly, the reform of the legal treatment of men's violence to women within marriage that was made in 1878 followed shortly after the Cruelty to Animals Act of 1876. The latter Act extended to all animals the provision of the Cruelty to Animals Act of 1849 which had made it illegal to 'cruelly beat, ill-treat, over-drive, abuse or torture' any *domestic* animal (c.92, s.2) (James, 1986: 601). Prior to 1878, the 'rule of thumb' had operated in the courts, whereby husbands were not permitted to use a stick broader than a thumb. The 1878 Matrimonial Causes Act allowed women to use cruelty as grounds for divorce. Magistrates were given powers to grant swift and cheap separation orders to women who could prove a *specific* incident of physical assault. In this way, state law had begun to claim, if only in word, some theoretical jurisdiction over men's violence in marriage, and so to recognize, if only implicitly, a distinction between violence and sexuality in marriage.

A number of other legal reforms were introduced towards the end of the nineteenth century. These included the Married Women's Property Act of 1870, which gave wives the right to keep their own earnings; the Married Women's Property Act of 1882, which introduced women's rights to keep property they owned in marriage or acquired later, even though no criminal proceedings could be taken against a husband while the 'partners' were cohabiting; the Maintenance of Wives Act 1886, which empowered magistrates in local courts to grant and enforce maintenance orders of no more than £2 per week; and the Summary Jurisdiction (Married Women) Act 1895, which made it easier for women to gain protection of the court following persistent physical cruelty rather than a specific physical assault. Additionally, in 1891, a husband lost his 'right' forcibly to imprison his wife in the matrimonial home to obtain his 'conjugal rights' (*R. v. Jackson*, Court of Appeal, 1891).

Despite these reforms, and the formal equalization of women's and men's property rights in marriage, by the end of the nineteenth century in practice there had been little shift in the nature of men's authority over women in marriage. Men's day-to-day domination was routinely reinforced by the state, for example, in the avoidance of intervention in 'marital disputes' by the police. The position of women was also generally weak in terms of divorce proceedings and the award and receipt of maintenance.

Julia Brophy and Carol Smart (1982: 210) have summarized this situation as follows:

> She had no right to leave her husband without his permission and if she did he could physically restrain her. She had no right to maintenance if she could not prove her husband had committed a matrimonial offence . . . he could divorce her on a single act of adultery whilst she had to establish adultery combined with another matrimonial offence . . . Any challenge by a wife to his authority, or to the principle of sexual monogamy resulted in the courts refusing to grant her maintenance. The magistrates courts . . . treated adultery as an absolute bar to maintenance for wives.

Thus while the picture was, to put it politely, mixed, the late nineteenth-century reforms did at least clarify the situation in terms of criminal law. Thus it is the Offences against the Person Act of 1861 which is the most relevant for the prosecution of physical violence to known women.

'Second-wave' feminism has led to the reappraisal of legal responses to violence. However, even in 1967 when the first Matrimonial Homes Act was passed 'matrimonial violence was a non-subject' (Freeman, 1987: 38). The Act was designed to preserve the rights of occupation of the non-owning and non-tenant spouse rather than to respond to violence. Following the establishment of the Women's Aid Federation in 1974 and the Parliamentary Select Committee on Violence in Marriage (Select Committee on Violence in Marriage, 1975), the Domestic Violence and Matrimonial Proceedings Act was passed in 1976, giving additional powers of injunction, including for the unmarried, and of arrest. Subsequent reforms, such as the Matrimonial Homes Act 1983, which strengthened the power of the ouster order, still, however, failed to produce a fundamental reform of state intervention in favour of women's freedom from violence (see Binney et al., 1981; Atkins and Hoggett, 1984).

Richard Collier (1995: 284) has summarized the aftermath of the 1976 Act as follows:

> Cases since 1976 have tended to focus on the housing of the parties, the circumstances in which men may be excluded from the home and the need to reconcile a woman's need for protection with the laws respecting a man's rights of property (for example see Davis v Johnson [1979] AC 164; Spindlow v Spindlow [1979] 1 All ER 169; Richards v Richards [1984] AC 174; Myers v Myers [1982] 1 WLR 247). What emerges from much research is a commonly held belief that domestic violence is a 'crime' only in the most serious of cases and a judicial antipathy to the view that the interests of husband and wife may not in all instances, be the same (see Hoskyn v Metropolitan Police Commissioner [1979] AC 474 per Lord Wilberforce p. 448, also Lord Salmon, p. 495; Boyle, 1980). Furthermore domestic cases would appear to often receive lower sentences than in other cases of violence (Binney et al., 1981; note R v Cutts [1987] Fam Law 311).

In this context it is perhaps not so surprising that Alan Bourlet, then Assistant Chief Constable of South Wales Constabulary, wrote in 1990:

> In his annual report for 1988, Her Majesty's Chief Inspector of Constabulary (Home Office, 1989) does not once mention marital violence in his review of the year's events, traditionally considered of importance to the police. Public order

situations, crime, drugs misuse and terrorism are all touched upon, but the allocation of resources for marital violence is not featured under the headings of crime or social factors, indicating the low priority attached to marital violence by the police service. (Bourlet, 1990: 21)

In the past few years, there have been uneven attempts to reform policy and policy implementation within particular state organizations. Reform has occurred most directly in police forces with the enactment of 'domestic violence' pro-arrest policies; the treatment of violence equally seriously regardless of its location or the relationship of the parties; and the creation of special units. In 1988 the Chief Constable of West Yorkshire issued a Policy Statement on Domestic Violence to all members of the Force, pledging a commitment to treat violence in the home as seriously as violence in the street and elsewhere. Other state agencies, notably the Probation Service and the Crown Prosecution Service, have also given more attention to this problem.

What we have here is a series of concessions from the state, and particularly state agencies controlled by men, in response to individual men's violence to women. The state has thus sponsored particular social forms within the private domain. Increasingly, but rather gradually, the private powers of men – individual husbands and fathers – have been brought into the control of the state. Most importantly, legal and other state constructions of violence have generally served to play down its significance and to constrain its definition, while at the same time there has been a gradually increased awareness and recognition of the problem in law, policy statement and, to an extent, in policy implementation.

Men's Everyday Constructions of Violence

It is only by considering the dismal historical context of men's violence to women that it becomes possible to understand the way in which men generally perceive and define violence in everyday contexts. This question has been addressed through the recent research on men's experiences of violence to known women that has been funded by the Economic and Social Research Council as part of the Initiative on the Management of Personal Welfare (also see Chapters 3 and 7).

Women's views of men's violence are wide ranging and include emotional, sexual and physical elements, including threat (see Chapter 1). They also encompass women's experience of being unable 'to control the initiation of the behaviour [of men] and the subsequent interaction'. Furthermore, '*the greater the uncertainty about the outcome the more terrifying the encounter*' (Hanmer and Saunders, 1984: 33, emphasis in original). Thus women's views of violence include an awareness of the uncertainty and potential of men's violence (Stanko, 1994).

Men generally define violence in much narrower terms than do women. The paradigm form of violence for men is physical violence. But even here certain kinds of physical violence are often excluded or referred to in passing. Thus, for men who are violent to women, the construction of what is meant by violence is itself part of the problem. Features of physical violence that are often excluded include pushing, holding, blocking, the use of weight or bulk, throwing things (like food or furniture or crockery), damaging property (like doors). Physical violence is reduced to the use of a relatively fleeting part of the man's body, or an object (weapon) held by the hand, onto a part of the woman's body. It is for this reason that holding or blocking, or even throwing the woman, is not necessarily constructed as (physical) violence. Physical violence is included when the extent of the violence is greater than the exclusions described above, when there is visible damage, when the damage is relatively lasting, when the police arrest.

There are two other important forms of violence that are usually talked about by men only indirectly, in terms of violence to known women. First, there is the question of 'sexual violence'. For most men, what is usually called 'sexual violence' is not included in accounts of violence to known women. Except for the special case when a man has been arrested and charged for rape, men rarely define coercive sex and pressurized sex as violence to women. On the other hand, 'sex' and 'sexuality' do figure strongly in men's accounts of violence to women, but more usually as a 'reason' for their violence. In particular, suspected or known infidelity ('messing around') is often seen as a justification for violence, to the woman herself or to the 'other man' in question, or to both. Sex figures in another way in the exact correspondence between the heterosexual relation and the violence of men to known women (Hearn, 1994a).

Secondly, there is the question of violence to children as a form of violence to women. While some men do acknowledge that children witnessing violence to women, usually their mothers, is relevant, it is more usual for the men not to see this as part of the violence. Indeed, the two forms of violence – to women and to children – are generally seen as unconnected by men. This is to some extent reinforced by the way in which agency responses to child abuse are separated off from those to violence to women through the child protection system. The only time that Social Services departments become involved in responding to violence to women is when there is a question of child protection. No men described their own violence to children and young people as a form of violence to women.

Having said this, a few men did articulate very explicitly the processes of the complex interrelations of sexuality and violence in their intimate heterosexual relations with women. One man spoke of 'intensity of feeling, therefore intensity of action and reaction will be the greater. Exactly what I mean'. As a way of explaining sexual assaults to each of several women he argued 'violence really is an emotionality backed by perhaps a certain form of personality which might consider itself passionate . . . or insecure . . . .' In his own case, he explained, 'I've got a sexual bent for the emotional and dramatic side with women . . . if I was gay I think it would be the same, the male would take over the more interior life.'

Another man described the way in which he had been consciously able to humiliate the woman. This included not only making her stand in the corner of the room and stay upstairs, but something more about his definition of her sense of her appearance and her worth. As well as describing about 30 physical assaults, he also explained how he would tell the woman 'You're not attractive and nobody will fancy you and I could get better than you and what did I need her for.' He continued 'of course this was so that she wouldn't think she was interesting to anybody else, so I had like a hold.' This was reinforced by his refusal to allow her to visit him in prison to avoid his supposed embarrassment at being seen with her.

Men's generally narrower definitions are partly a product of men's structurally dominant social position and partly a consequence of the form of the particular social relationship with the woman in question. They show that the process of violence involves how violence itself is constructed. Thus naming and definitions of violence are themselves a social, not a natural, process. It depends on perspective: as violator, violated, observer or commentator. While definitions of 'battering' may include physical, sexual, psychological violence, as well as destruction of property and pets (Gondolf, 1985), attempts at all-inclusive definitions have to be treated with caution, as they themselves are located in gendered social processes. In particular, there are great dangers in separating violence off from the rest of social relations between men and women. This separation can be a major way in which men reproduce violence, both as individual violators (Jukes, 1993) and as definers and constructors of violence, through state and other agencies (Hearn, 1994b). These processes of contesting definitions of violence are thus central to welfare and other social interventions against violence.

Theories and Explanations of Men's Violence

Having surveyed the historical recognition and men's definitions of violence, we now move on to another contested area: the theorizing and explanation of men's violence (Hearn, 1990). There is a vast range of possible theories available, not just from across the social sciences, but also from the biological sciences. Some theories have attempted to explain men's violence in terms of biology, innate physical and/or psychological aggression. This may include explanations based in sociobiology, functionalism, and psychological essentialism. These may be open to criticism for neglecting questions of power, cultural and historical relativity, and morality. In his survey of practical and theoretical responses to 'wife abuse', Gondolf (1985: 27) identifies, drawing on the work of Gelles (1983) and Bagarozzi and Giddings (1983), three major theoretical explanations:

> psychoanalytic themes [that] focus on stress, anxiety and anger instilled during child rearing . . . social learning theories [that] consider the abuse to be an out-growth of learned patterns of aggressive communication to which both husband

and wife contribute . . . sociopolitical theories [that] hold the patriarchal power
plays of men oppressing women to be at the heart of wife abuse.

For writers such as Brownmiller (1975) and Dworkin (1979), men's
violence, in the forms of rape and pornography respectively, lies at the
very heart of patriarchy and its reproduction. While such arguments,
whether couched in sociological or social terms, are the subject of
great debate, radical feminist ideas of this kind represent the most
profound and solid challenge to men and men's power/violence. They go
far beyond the insights of psychoanalytic and learning theory. Individual
acts of men's violence, including assaults, rape, incest, murder and so on,
are thus considered and understood as gender class actions over women.
Not only do these three major kinds of theoretical explanation suggest
several different levels of explanation of men's violence, but they also vary
in their position *vis à vis* patriarchy: they may be critical of patriarchy, or
directly or indirectly supportive of patriarchy. Furthermore, while different kinds of explanations are distinct, they are not always mutually
exclusive.

Other authors have made more precise differentiations. Lees and Lloyd
(1994) also distinguish a number of further explanations of men's violence
to known women: psychological explanations; social learning theory;
stress, inequality and subculture; the violent society; men's liberation and
sex role strain; multicausal explanations; and the patriarchal society.
Among more structural explanations of sexual violence, the emphasis may
be placed on patriarchal capitalism (Messerschmidt, 1986), patriarchal
social relations and the role of patriarchal institutions in supporting
violence (Kelly and Radford, 1987).

This range of theoretical approaches has recently led to an interest in the
intersection of violence and the social production and reproduction of
masculinities. This is spelt out by Messerschmidt (1993) in his argument
that crime, including violence, is available as a resource for the making of
gender, and specifically a strategy for the making of masculinity, or at least
particular forms of masculinity. It is also detailed in another way by
Miedzian (1992), focusing particularly on the link between masculinity and
violence in dominant ways of rearing boys and sons. Her approach is not
just a simple model of socialization but rather an attempt to see the
construction of masculinity within broader society as intimately interconnected with violence. There are also hints at this attempt to speak
simultaneously of masculinity/violence in Stanko's (1994) analysis of the
power of violence in negotiating masculinities. While this may be clearest
in considering men's violence to each other, such an analysis needs to be
extended to men's reproduction of violence/masculinity in relation to
women.

Within this context, let us consider the sociopolitical critiques and the
psychological theories, and then their interrelationship, a little more
closely. According to anti-patriarchal critiques, men's violence is a general
means of maintaining and reinforcing power that is available to men.

Carlson (1979, cited in Gondolf, 1985: 36), in her discussion of violence to women, says:

> Part of [the] tradition [of the family home] has the husband and father as absolute ruler. Out of generosity he may give some of his power away. He may help with the dishes or help with the kids. But it is understood he doesn't have to do it; it is 'helping', it is a gift. His work is to maintain his version of a proper family. His wife and children must be trained to his standards of decorum. If he feels the need to use physical force to maintain the version, he has had considerable social support.

In this context, men's violence to known women is in large part a development of dominant–submissive power relations that exist in 'normal' family life. Men may resort to violence when men's power and privilege are challenged, and other strategies have failed. Such violent actions may be available as part of men's repertoire at all times, but are most used at times of particular threat, such as the physical and emotional demands of babies and young children, or the resistance to authority of teenagers, or simply women's response and resistance to the situation. Furthermore, men's violence to known women may develop in association with feelings of threat when women do not do what men expect, in terms of child care, housework, paid work, sexuality, and so on. Repeated 'justifications' for violence to women were given by men in the course of this research. Frustration and anger at possible or potential loss of power in one sphere may also be acted upon in another sphere or relationship, where there may be less resistance.

This structural perspective on the 'normality' of men's violence within dominant masculinities and men's domestic power within patriarchy is not necessarily at odds with psychoanalytic accounts of men's violence. The fact that there are violent men is not the product of psychological traits – all men can be violent. However, it is certain men who do violence to known women and it is possible that these men, like other men, can be assessed and understood psychodynamically. This still leaves the question of the place of violence, both in general and to known women, within the psychodynamics of men who are not currently physically violent, and within what is seen as 'normal masculinity'.

That said, psychoanalytic theories, both feminist and non-feminist, have connected men's 'overmothering' (and 'underfathering') as infants and boys with the development of excessive dependence on their mothers and, subsequently, other women. One argument is that a process of 'more emphatic' individuation of boys takes place, initially from the mother and later from others. This entails the defensive establishment of ego boundaries as an overlay on fundamental emotional insecurity (for example, Chodorow, 1978). In turn, these defences may develop to become forms of compensatory hypermasculinity, forms of violence when women cannot or do not satisfy men's dependency needs, and misogyny itself. Although such accounts are couched largely in terms of the connections between the initial mother–son relationship, these arguments may be extended to men's subsequent violence to known women. For example, men's over-dependence as boys on their sisters might be transferred to hostility to wives and other known women. More simply, and this is where socio-political and psychoanalytic explanations can meet, men may lash out when threatened in terms of material power and/or rigid ego boundaries.

Similarly, psychological studies of the violence-prone person do not necessarily mean a negation of broader social, political and structural questions. For example, Toch's (1982) study, *Violent Men*, conducted through interviews with offenders, prison inmates and police, details *situations* that promote violence in terms of 'self-preserving strategies'; that is, reputation-defending, norm-enforcing, self-image compensating, self-defending, pressure-removing strategies; and *people* 'who see themselves (and their own needs) as being the only fact of social relevance', and thus including bullying, exploitation, self-indulging, catharting. Such situational and personal orientations may focus on the individual, but are quite amenable to linking with social, political and structural formations, in this case of men to known women.

Furthermore, while certain types of psychoanalytic thinking, such as strict Freudianism, can be antipathetic to sociopolitical critiques of patriarchy, psychoanalysis is not, of itself, for or against patriarchy. Indeed, feminist and anti-patriarchal psychoanalytic thinking has emphasized the way in which patriarchy is reproduced at the psychodynamic as well as the social level. The practical and political implications of seeing men's violence as psychological, social and political in character are considerable for state, agency and welfare intervention.

In addition to the theoretical positions outlined above, it is necessary and important to address the issue of men's sexual abuse of women specifically in terms of men's violence. The relation of physical and sexual abuse is clearly complex. While some actual cases of men's physical abuse may not appear to be sexual in nature, and some actual cases of men's sexual abuse may not appear to be violent in nature, in reality the connections are numerous. Whereas physical abuse is not necessary sexual abuse, sexual abuse, other than psychological sexual abuse, is also physical abuse. Men's sexual abuse is both part of the broad practice of physical abuse, and a special and specific practice, with its own extra complications of power. Thus, all of the above 'general' arguments on the explanation of men's violence can be applied to men's sexual abuse, but there are also some additional ways in which the explanation of men's sexual abuse may be seen in terms of men's violence.

First, sexual abuse may involve or occur in association with explicit physical violence, that may appear to some people as non-sexual in nature. Secondly, physical abuse itself, which may appear to some people as non-sexual in nature, may be sexual in the eyes and minds of the man/men. Indeed, one major problem is the way in which violence has often taken on sexual meaning for men. Dominance, including violence, has become eroticized for most men and some women (MacKinnon, 1983; also see

MacLeod and Saraga, 1988). I refer here not just to what is usually labelled 'sexual violence' but to the more general association of violence and sexuality for men. Indeed, Kelly (1988: 59) has argued for the use of the general term 'sexual violence' 'to cover all forms of abuse, coercion and force that women experience from men'. According to Dworkin (1981), sexual intercourse may be understood as the cumulative reduction and annihilation of women – the practice of men wishing to kill women (see also Cameron and Fraser, 1987).

Thirdly, sexual abuse is itself violence. This is most obviously so in rape; it applies both in the use of overt force – assault, slapping, beating, pushing and bodily invasion – and in the more subtle use of caress within an enpowered (that is, acting within power relations) and abusive relationship. Caress can be just as much a form of violence as more overt force; it can be a means of manipulation; an unwanted intrusion; a sign of power; an additional encroachment on and domination of parts of the body, that are, in this society at least, associated with personal/sexual privacy and extra-personal/sexual power.

Although there are occasionally some fine lines between ambiguities around different forms of touch – comfort, caress, cuddle, hugging – one usually knows when they are or could be selflessly loving, taking advantage of or exerting power in touch. Such culturally specific 'knowledge' of particular men is likely, however, to neglect the full weight of power relations between men, women and young people, especially in the family. For this reason it is unlikely, and probably impossible, for men to touch in a completely non-dominant, and thus potentially non-abusing, way, unless the whole relationship itself is without dominance. To put this another way, men living and acting within dominating, hierarchical relationships may touch with what is felt to be 'selflessness' and 'love' yet at the same time their touch may be (received as) an exertion of power, even as abuse.

This brings us on to the significance of the ideology of family 'love' within the complex relationship of men's sexual abuse and men's violence. 'Within the family . . . rape is possible and other violence is not uncommon' (Hearn, 1987: 91). In this arena, men's power, men's violence and men's sexuality are all in intimate connection. This process of power involves the mystification of love, the assumption of 'desire' for others as 'primordial' (MacKinnon, 1982), as well as feelings of reciprocity and mutuality.

These theories and the debate around them are vital, as they inform practical agency interventions, the development of policy, the work of professionals and, significantly, the views of those involved, both as violators and violated. Theories of violence can be taken on by both men and women to explain away, excuse or even cope with men's violence. This can be a very problematic process as there are numerous complex interplays between social scientific, agency, professional and individual actor's theories and explanations of men's violence. Men who have been violent and have had considerable contact with agencies often take on agency and professional explanations. This is especially easy if those theories are focused on the individual and provide individualistic explanations. More structural explanations are more difficult to respond to and have farther reaching implications for agencies and agency staff. Accordingly, psychological and psychoanalytic explanations of violence were often favoured by men who had had extensive psychiatric involvement. Learning theory explanations were found sometimes coupled with psychological accounts for men who had long prison sentences. More structural explanations were given by a few men in men's programmes. But here, where the emphasis is on the possibility of personal change, a composite account of psychological and more social explanations was more usual.

Men's Violence and Social Theory

Finally, it may be useful to broaden the analysis still further. Research on violence also raises many questions for social theory and specifically how the social is theorized. These include the reformulation of historical and cultural definitions of meaning, individual action, organizations and social structure; the place of experience in the creation of knowledge; the rethinking of power and the deconstruction of 'the self'. One example of such questions concerns the way in which violence is generally not understood in social theorizing as a characteristic form of interpersonal or structural relation. The most usual model of interpersonal or structured relations is of the 'rational individual', with a 'unified self', who conducts 'his' affairs in a liberal and reasonably tolerant way. This model informs much study of families, groups, organizations and so on. In this situation, violence is portrayed as relatively isolated exceptions to normal life. Violence often does not even figure prominently in debates in social theory on power. In such formulations, violence is not understood as integral or embedded or imminent in social relations, and social relations are not understood as characterized by violence, actual or potential. Thus, when a man is violent to a woman 'he loves' or 'is married to' or 'has a sexual relationship with', the violence is portrayed as aberrant.

These features are paralleled almost exactly in men's accounts of their own violence and men's social theory. Violence is generally presumed to occur as 'incidents'; it is literally 'incidental'; violence is incidentalized. It is understood as occurring as exceptions within non-violent, ordinary normal life. This is comparable to national, international, inter-ethnic violence on a mass scale that may occur after many years of living 'peacefully' as 'good neighbours', as in the former Yugoslavia and elsewhere. Such challenges are bringing violence into the centre of social theory.

Something similar can be said about gendered relations and power. Within the social sciences, particularly sociology, it is now legitimate to bring gender into the subdisciplines and topic areas of sociology, but this is often predicated on the assumption that social cohesion between women and men is basic and therefore existing theoretical frameworks can continue to be used. Work that challenges this cohesion is marginalized, or simply not taken up in a larger way (for example, O'Brien, 1981; MacKinnon, 1982; Delphy and Leonard, 1992). When violence is understood as fundamental to gender, and power is recognized as adhering to all social relationships, then a different kind of social theory is required: one that simultaneously deals with differences, conflict, and forms of violent contact.

Note

1. This section draws on the ESRC Research Project No. L206 25 2003, 'Violence, Abuse and the Stress-coping Process, Project no. 2' (April 1991 – March 1993).

References

Atkins, S. and Hoggett, B. (1984) *Women and the Law*, Oxford: Blackwell.

Bagarozzi, D. and Giddings, C.W. (1983) 'Conjugal violence: a critical review of current research and clinical practices', *The American Journal of Family Therapy*, 11: 3–15.

Beneke, T. (1982) *Men on Rape*, New York: St Martins.

Binney, V., Harkell, G. and Nixon, J. (1981) *Leaving Violent Men*, London: Women's Aid Federation.

Bourlet, A. (1990) *Police Intervention in Marital Violence*, Milton Keynes: Open University Press.

Boyle, C. (1980) 'Violence against wives', *Northern Ireland Law Quarterly*, 35: 50.

The British Women's Studies Group (1979) *Half the Story: an Introduction to Women's Studies*, London: Virago.

Brophy, J. and Smart, C. (1982) 'From disregard to disrepute: the position of women in family law', in E. Whitelegg, M. Arnot, E. Bartels, V. Beechey, L. Birke, S. Himmelweit, D. Leonard, S. Ruehl and M.A. Speakmann (eds), *The Changing Experience of Women*, Milton Keynes: Open University Press, pp. 207–25.

Brownmiller, S. (1975) *Against our Will: Men, Women and Rape*, New York: Simon and Schuster.

Cameron, D. and Fraser, E. (1987) *The Lust to Kill*, Cambridge: Polity Press.

Carlson, M. (1979) 'What's behind wife beating?', in E. Shapiro and B. Shapiro (eds), *The Women Say/the Men Say: the Women's Liberation Movement and Men's Consciousness*, New York: Dell.

Chodorow, N. (1978) *The Reproduction of Mothering*, Berkeley, CA: University of California Press.

Cobbe, F.P. (1878) 'Wife torture in England', *The Contemporary Review*, April: 55–87.

Cobbe, F.P. (1894) *Life of Frances Power Cobbe by Herself*, London: Bentley, vol. 2.

Collier, R. (1995) *Masculinity, Law and the Family*, London: Routledge.

Coote, A. and Campbell, B. (1982) *Sweet Freedom: the Struggle for Women's Liberation*, London: Picador.

Delphy, C. and Leonard, D. (1992) *Familiar Exploitation*, Cambridge: Polity Press.

Dworkin, A. (1979) *Pornography: Men Possessing Women*, New York: G.P. Putnam's.

Freeman, M.D.A. (1987) *Dealing with Domestic Violence*, Bicester: CCH.

Gelles, R. (1983) 'An exchange/social control theory', in D. Finkelhor, R. Gelles, G. Hotaling and M. Straus (eds), *The Dark Side of Families*, Beverly Hills, CA: Sage, pp. 151–65.

Gondolf, E. W. (1985) *Men who Batter*, Holmes Beach, FL: Learning Publications.

Hanmer, J. (1990) 'Men, power and the exploitation of women', in J. Hearn and D.H.J. Morgan (eds), *Men, Masculinities and Social Theory*, London: Unwin Hyman, pp. 21–42.

Hanmer, J. (forthcoming) *'I Will Survive': a Research and Policy Report on Women's Experiences of Violence from Known Men*, Violence, Abuse and Gender Relations Research Unit, University of Bradford, Research Paper no.5.

Hanmer, J. and Saunders, S. (1984) *Well Founded Fear: a Community Study of Violence to Women*, London: Hutchinson.

Hearn, J. (1987) *The Gender of Oppression: Men, Masculinity and the Critique of Marxism*, Brighton: Wheatsheaf; New York: St Martins.

Hearn, J. (1988) 'Child abuse: violences and sexualities to young people', *Sociology*, 22 (4): 531–44.

Hearn, J. (1990) 'Child abuse and men's violence', in Violence against Children Study Group (ed.), *Taking Child Abuse Seriously*, London: Unwin Hyman, pp. 63–85.

Hearn, J. (1992) *Men in the Public Eye: The Construction and Deconstruction of Public Men and Public Patriarchies*, London and New York: Routledge.

Hearn, J. (1994a) 'Men's heterosexual violence to women, the presence and absence of "sex" in men's accounts of violence to known women', Conference Paper, British Association, University of Central Lancashire; mimeo, University of Bradford.

Hearn, J. (1994b) 'The organization(s) of violence: men, gender relations, organizations and violences', *Human Relations*, 47 (6): 1–24.

Hearn, J. (1995) *"It Just Happened': a Research and Policy Report on Men's Violence to Known Women*, Violence, Abuse and Gender Relations Research Unit, University of Bradford, Research Paper no.6.

Hearn, J. (1996) *The Violences of Men*, London: Sage.

Home Office (1989) *Report of Her Majesty's Chief Inspector of Constabulary for 1988*, London: HMSO.

James, J.S. (1986) *Stroud's Judicial Dictionary of Words and Phrases*, 5th edn, vol. 1, London: Sweet & Maxwell.

Jukes, A. (1993) *Why Men Hate Women*, London: Free Association Press.

Kaufman, M. (1987) 'The construction of masculinity and the triad of men's violence', in M. Kaufman (ed.), *Beyond Patriarchy: Essays by Men on Pleasure, Power, and Change*, Toronto: Oxford University Press, pp. 3–29.

Kelly, L. (1988) *Surviving Sexual Violence*, Cambridge: Polity Press.

Kelly, L. and Radford, J. (1987) 'The problem of men: feminist perspectives on sexual violence', in P. Scraton (ed.), *Law, Order and the Authoritarian State*, Milton Keynes: Open University Press, pp. 237–53.

Kimmel, M. (ed.) (1990) *Men Confront Pornography*, New York: Crown.

Lees, J. and Lloyd, T. (1994) *Working with Men who Batter their Partners*, London: Working with Men/The B Team.

McCann, K. (1985) 'Battered women and the law', in C. Smart and J. Brophy (eds), *Women-in-Law*, London: Routledge and Kegan Paul, pp. 71–96.

MacKinnon, C. (1982) 'Feminism, marxism, method and the state: an agenda for theory', *Signs*, 7 (3): 515–44.

MacKinnon, C. (1983) 'Feminism, marxism, method and the state; towards feminist jurisprudence', *Signs*, 8 (4): 635–58.

MacLeod, M. and Saraga, E. (1988) 'Challenging the orthodoxy: towards a feminist theory and practice', *Feminist Review*, 28, spring: 16–55.

Messerschmidt, J.W. (1986) *Capitalism, Patriarchy and Crime: Toward a Socialist Feminist Criminology*, Totowa, NJ: Rowman and Littlefield.

Messerschmidt, J.W. (1993) *Masculinities and Crime*, Totowa, NJ: Rowman and Littlefield.

Miedzian, M. (1992) *Boys Will Be Boys*, London: Virago.

O'Brien, M. (1981) *The Politics of Reproduction*, London: Routledge and Kegan Paul.

Pankhurst, C. (1913) *The Hidden Scourge and How to End It*, London: E. Pankhurst.

Scully, D. (1990) *Understanding Sexual Violence: a Study of Convicted Rapists*, London: Harper Collins.

Select Committee on Violence in Marriage (1975) *Report, together with the Proceedings of the Committee. Volume 2: Report, Minutes of the Committee and Appendices*, London: HMSO.

Stanko, E.A. (1994) 'Challenging the problem of men's individual violence', in T. Newburn and E.A. Stanko (eds), *Just Boys Doing Business? Men, Masculinities and Crime*, London: Routledge, pp. 32–45.

Toch, H. (1982) *Violent Men: an Inquiry into the Psychology of Violence*, Harmondsworth: Penguin.

Wooden, W.S. and Parker, J. (1982) *Men Behind Bars: Sexual Exploitation in Prison*, New York: Plenum.

Wyre, R. (1987) *Working with Sex Abuse*, Oxford: Perry.

PART II

GENDERED ORGANIZATIONS

3

The Organization(s) of Violence: Men, Gender Relations, Organizations and Violences

Jeff Hearn

This chapter is concerned not just with the relationship of gender and organizations, but more specifically with the relationship of gender, sexuality, violence and organizations. In particular, it considers the case for an analytical perspective on organizations through the lens of violence. While gender and sexuality have been relatively neglected issues in organizational analysis (Hearn and Parkin, 1983), violence has been even further marginalized from the mainstream or 'malestream' (O'Brien, 1981) as an important issue or focus in the study of organizations. Throughout, special attention will be paid to men's power as a major element in the structuring of sexuality, violence and organizations.

The chapter is in three main parts. The first charts the movement of organizational analysis from agendered and implicitly gendered approaches to studies of gender and sexuality and towards a perspective on organizations based on violence. The second section outlines this violence-based perspective and some of the key questions it highlights for organizational analysis. The third illustrates some of these through a case study of organizational responses to violence.

Towards a Violence-based Perspective on Organizations

Organizations and Human Relations

This first section charts how organizational analysis has shifted in recent years from apparent gender absence to a concern with issues of gender and sexuality; and how this shift provides the basis for the development of a further gendered approach to organizations, namely one that emphasizes violence and responses to violence in and around organizations. This section thus attempts to move analysis and debate toward a violence-based perspective on organizations.

The early modern development of organizational analysis is typically presented as if it were agendered, as if it were gender-neutral. Yet the analyses of, say, Classical Theory and scientific management were over-whelmingly by men, about men, for men. These prescriptions could also be interpreted as an attempt by male managers to control growing numbers of women or migrant workers in particular commercial and state sectors in the early twentieth century. Additionally, Classical Theory and related theories carry implicit, and sometimes explicit, conceptualizations of gender and sexuality (Hearn and Parkin, 1987: 17–21).

Much subsequent organization theory, and human relations theory *par excellence*, can be read as a series of limited and usually implicit attempts to engage with gender and sexuality within organizations. Indeed, while the idea of 'human relations' would seem to suggest the need for full attention to gender and sexuality, in historical practice 'human relations' have often been conceptualized in ways that either deny or obscure gender and sexuality, or have constructed them in agendered, asexual terms. This is both a theoretical issue and a very practical managerial issue, as, for example, the human relations theory of Elton Mayo and his colleagues and successors has been used to legitimate increased managerial surveillance and control of workers, and particularly women's emotional and even sexual lives. This gendered, 'sexuated'[1] reinterpretation of human relations theory is described in '*Sex' at 'Work*' (Hearn and Parkin, 1987). Import-antly, human relations theory also contributed to the establishment of the system as the prime paradigm for the analysis of organizations. In one sense, the system reduces social divisions, including gender and sexuality, to systemic language; in another, systems thinking often reproduces gendered dualities between goal attainment and system maintenance. Systemic theorizing can thus be used both to obscure gender, sexuality and violence and to justify and perpetuate the 'maintenance' roles of women in lower paid and less powerful organizational positions.

In Britain, the Tavistock School, with its own particular version of 'human relations', has been very influential in the development of organiz-ational analysis, systems thinking and the conceptualization of gender and sexuality. While the extent to which it is a specific and identifiable 'school' at all may be contentious (Miller, 1992), the emphasis that it brought to the fore was primarily the extension of psychoanalytic insights from individual to group and organizational dynamics through the development of problem-focused consultancy and intervention. There are many ways in which this approach is necessarily gendered and sexuated. Assumptions about gender and sexuality are fundamental to psychoanalytic theorizing, not just a contingent addition. This is most obviously so in the emphasis upon infant sexuality and the establishment of gender identity.[2] The

Tavistock's work has also addressed the unconscious preoccupations of members of groups and organizations, including unconscious sexual preoccupations, for example, in Bion's (1948–51) analysis of pairing in groups manifesting underlying sexual dynamics; Jaques' (1955) and Menzies' (1960, 1970) studies of defences against paranoid and depressive anxiety; and Bowlby's (1953) attention to the interrelation of institutional dynamics and personal well-being.

Furthermore, the Tavistock's work on organizational analysis can also be seen as centrally concerned with violence. At the most general level, it has attended to the destructive aspects of individual and group dynamics, the death-instinct and 'the violence and intensity of feeling' (Menzies, 1970: 7). More particularly, there was the practical work with the survivors of violence, with prisoners of war, and with psychological casualties of war. In addition, action research on high anxiety institutions can be understood as partly about people's experiences of violation in organizations. For example, Jaques' and Menzies' analysis of deeply stressing and distressing tasks and events lead them to focus on collective defence mechanisms, most often through the use and reinforcement of the organization, its rules, procedures and formalities. Thus, the organizational mode coexists with the severely distressing *and* its avoidance. The Tavistock Programme has contributed significantly to 'the government of subjectivity and social life' (Miller and Rose, 1988), including the place of violation and defences against it within organizations. Even so, it has been left to subsequent, particularly feminist, work to bring issues of gender, sexuality and indeed violence to centre stage in organizational analysis.

Organizations, Gender and Sexuality

Throughout most of the developments of the major traditions of organiz-ational analysis described above, gender and gendering have been implicit. Even by the late 1970s, the field of organization theory was uneven and disparate in its treatment of gender and sexuality, comprising a mixture of social systems theory, studies of the 'sexual' (i.e. gender) division of labour, studies of women entering management, as well as a wide range of specialist studies in labour relations, social psychology, groups dynamics, and so on (Hearn and Parkin, 1983).

In the mid-1990s, the study of women, men, gender and organizations is now paradoxically both well established and marginalized in organization studies. Currently, there is such a wealth of relevant empirical and theoretical work that it would seem difficult to ignore these issues and connections. Yet, at the same time, this continues to be done, particularly by men within organization studies. Meanwhile, the study of women, men, gender and organizations has been extended to the study of women, men, sexuality and organizations, so that the interrelationship of gender and sexuality is increasingly recognized as an important theme in gendered analyses of organizational life. This paradox continues to pervade this chapter; on the one hand, sexuality and violence can be more easily acknowledged as significant in organizations; on the other, fundamentally reorientating the field to recognize these issues as central remains difficult and is indeed resisted.

A strong empirical focus on sexuality and organizations has developed in at least three main ways. First, the study of sexuality in organizations developed initially from surveys of political interventions in and *naming* of sexual harassment. Early journalistic reports were followed by general social analyses (Farley, 1978), detailed examinations of legal cases (MacKinnon, 1979), and broad social surveys (Gutek, 1985), all establishing the pervasiveness and frequency of sexual harassment by men. Secondly, there has been a much smaller development of empirical studies of heterosexual relationships and sexual liaisons in organizations. Thirdly, another important strand of empirical studies has related to lesbian and gay men's experiences in organizations, particularly, though not only, experiences of discrimination and violation. As with sexual harassment surveys, these have often initially been developed as part of campaigns or other political interventions (Taylor, 1986).

These specific empirical studies have been followed by more general reviews of the place of sexuality within organizations (Hearn and Parkin, 1987; Hearn et al., 1989; Pringle, 1989). Above all, these more general surveys have emphasized the interconnection of sexuality and power in organizations, and the pervasiveness of the power of men, particularly heterosexual men (Cockburn, 1991; Collinson, 1992). They have also shown how sexual processes and organizational processes are intimately connected, in both the general structuring of organizations and in the detail of everyday interaction.

From Gender to Sexuality to Violence

The recognition of the importance of gender and sexuality in organizations has provided much of the groundwork for analysing organizations through the perspective of violence. In this, feminist theory and practice on gender, sexuality and violence, both in and outside organizations, has been central.

In referring to violence, I mean that which violates or causes violation, and is usually performed by a violator upon the violated. There are at least three possible standpoints from which to define violence further:

1   The point of view of those directly involved, either as the violator or the violated.
2   The point of view of other social actors involved in dealing with violence; for example, lawmakers or enforcers, social workers.
3   The point of view of the analyst, who may or may not be involved in such intervention.

These three perspectives are clearly not distinct or separate; indeed, someone may occupy all locations simultaneously. Furthermore, all three are mediated through representations and perceptions, often very different for violators and violated, men and women.

Thus, violence is not one thing. It includes *force and/or violation*: force *by* the violator; violation *of* the violated. It may be physical, sexual, emotional, verbal, cognitive, visual, representational. Indeed, these discriminations may in practice break down as, for example, in the understanding of all forms of violence from men to women as sexual violence (Kelly, 1987). Violence may also comprise the creation of the conditions of violence, potential violence, threat and/or neglect. Sometimes the mere presence of someone is violating, and thus becomes violence. Violence can be dramatic or subtle, occasional or continuous.

The dominant forms of violence in organizations, as elsewhere, are by men to women, children or other men. These include verbal and emotional attacks, assaults, use of weapons and other objects, destruction of property, rape, murder. While men's collective, institutional, and indeed interpersonal domination of violence is immense, it is important to recognize women's and indeed children's violence, both to each other and to others.

A developing focus on organizations through violence is not just because of the recognition of sexual harassment as a form of (sexual) violence but because feminist work more generally, particularly that on sexuality, has increasingly acknowledged the underlying importance of violence. Forms of sexuality, especially men's (hetero)sexuality, that are not usually constructed as sexual harassment or sexual violence, may only be understandable in terms of their relationship to or reconstruction as sexual violence. For example, MacKinnon (1983) and Dworkin (1979) have explored the ways in which hierarchy and dominance have become subject to eroticization, for many men at least (Litewka, 1977; Coveney et al., 1984; Buchbinder, 1987; Kelly, 1988). An emphasis on violence as a fundamental part of the gendered analysis of society has followed from feminist theory and practice in general (MacKinnon, 1982). To put this another way, domination by men is clearly associated with violence. For men to respond positively to feminism, to be pro-feminist, necessitates direct attention to men's power. Men's violence is one major element in the perpetuation of that power, and is thus a necessary object of analysis and intervention in pro-feminist theory and practice.

Furthermore, a variety of other work has prompted the development of a violence-based perspective on organizations. This includes work on violence by organizations, such as the military; work on violence in organizations, such as bullying; and work on organizational responses to violence, both by state organizations and feminist and other campaign organizations against, usually men's, violence. In all these ways, organizations have come to be seen as sites or structures of violence. Organizations may be understood as constellations of violent, potentially violent or threatened as violent actions, behaviours, intentions and experiences.

In simple terms, the critical edge of organizational analysis has moved from *agendered* approaches, to approaches that *incorporate* gender and sexuality in implicit ways, to approaches that recognize *social divisions* of which gender would be one example, then onto the *more explicit recognition* of first gender and gender relations, then sexuality and relations of sexuality, and now violence and relations of violence. This kind of 'progression' is, as we shall see, not a narrowing of focus in organizational analysis but a theoretical repositioning. Assumptions that agendered approaches are broader than gendered approaches, and that gender relations are broader than sexuality or indeed violence, carry with them assumptions of a hierarchical view of reality that places concepts before experience.

The Violence Perspective

While it is accepted that organizations are centrally concerned with power, domination and control (Morgan, 1986), it may seem strange at first to talk of organizations and violence together. And yet, many concepts in organizational analysis, such as 'power', 'domination', 'control', even 'authority', can be used as euphemisms for violence. This is most obviously so in analysing organizations where there is legitimized use of violence, as in the police force, the military, prisons and other state custodial organizations (Scraton et al., 1991).

In this section, I present a framework for organizational analysis through the lens of violence. This is developed for several reasons: as a framework for theoretical development, as a general research agenda, and as a guide to the empirical analysis of particular organizations. This is not, of course, to suggest that all organizations and all organizational life can be reduced to violence. Rather, it is to argue that the question 'What is happening in organizations?' can be answered more fully by bringing violence into the picture. Putting 'violence' and 'organizations' together throws both concepts into doubt and opens up new research questions.

This perspective is developed through two frames of reference:

1   Organizations and organizing as violence, including the context and formation of organizations.
2   The general orientation of organizations to violence, and their consequent structure, function and operation; and organizational process (Figure 3.1).

These differentiations may apply to both different types of organizations and different social relations of violence within a given organization.

The Context and Formation of Organizations

What has the context and formation of organizations got to do with violence? Organizations are typically formed *in the context of* the structural relations of domination, control and violence. The formation of organizations may also contribute to the reproduction of those structural relations, and may only be understandable in that context, whatever immediate

Figure 3.1   *Types of organizational orientation to violence*

practical relations of violence are operative. This is most apparent in the historical formation of the state, and the historical development of the political and economic systems of slavery, feudalism, capitalism, imperialism, communism, and so on. The formation of states and political and economic systems frequently involve, and have involved, violence. States, especially nation-states, have been established in competition with others, primarily by men to maintain rule, albeit historically temporary rule, over women. States retain the ability to use force through military and paramilitary organizations. The streets, the land, and indeed the buildings in a given area of land, usually belong to the state if that need arises, as in wartime. Capitalism and capitalist organizations may not be actively violent at a given point in time. Yet the system of capitalism depends upon the obtaining of property both in the past and in other parts of the world. Thus, for example, food or minerals may be 'peacefully' consumed in the First World following organized/organizational violence in, say, South America. For these reasons, organizations need to be understood in the context of histories and theories of patriarchy, and especially public patriarchy (Walby, 1990; Hearn, 1992), of patriarchal relations of violence, of the patriarchal state (Burstyn, 1983; MacKinnon, 1989; Connell, 1990), and of patriarchal capitalism and other economic systems (Mies, 1986; Waring, 1988). A central feature of such patriarchal systems is not only men's domination over women, but also some men's rule over other men through organizational hierarchies, organized by age, class, race, or other social divisions (Hearn, 1992).

Specific organizations may be formed through or by specific processes or acts of violence. For example, a prisoner of war camp is only understandable by the violence of the war that precedes its formation. Alternatively, organizations may be formed by non-violence, for example, a pacifist organization, or by some combination of processes involving violence, non-violence, and intermediate, ambiguous actions, for example, a psychiatric institution. The conditions of formation of an organization may well have a lasting effect on organizational processes not only in formal structures, but in continuing resentment, guilt and anxiety. Furthermore, particular organizations exist in relation to other organizations (Evan, 1976). Thus, to understand fully the place of violence in a given organization, it is necessary to consider its relation to other organizations with their own agendas of violence.

However, what is perhaps more interesting is the extent to which the basic activity of organizing, of forming and maintaining organizations, can be said to involve violence. Organizations depend for their continuation upon obedience not just to authority, but to authority that is at least to some degree unaccountable and unjustifiable. Thus, a useful avenue for theoretical and empirical development in organizational analysis would be the examination of the extent to which particular organizations, and examples of organizing, make explicit the forms and sources of authority in use, and how these authorities are gendered. For, in most cases, the unaccountable and unjustifiable authority of organizations is men's, and it is that which is violating. In terms of how this works in particular organizations, there may be several paradoxes. For example, organizations which rely most explicitly on violence for authority may need only periodically to justify such general authority through violence, and yet routinely not need to justify that particular authority through the very force of the violence. On the other hand, organizations which rely on non-violence for authority may routinely need to justify such particular authority, and yet periodically may not need to justify the general authority through the very absence of explicit violence. Indeed, in some organizational settings a norm of 'non-violence' may mean that social exchanges employing heavy persuasion and other techniques of authority are experienced as violating by those with less power. This may help to explain why, although coercive power may tend to be associated with alienative involvement with organizational members (Etzioni, 1961), in some correctional institutions, social deprivation and anti-staff culture may be *negatively* correlated (Cline, 1968).

Organizational Orientations to Violence

Organizations have an *explicit* or an *implicit* relation or orientation to violence (see Figure 3.1). Explicit relations include:

(a)   the legitimated use of violence by organizations (e.g. the state, sport, schools);

(b)   organizations created to respond to violence (e.g. criminal justice system, anti-violence/peace organizations);
(c)   organizations explicitly responding to violence in other ways.

Implicit relations include:

(d)   the illegitimated use of violence by managers/controllers/owners (e.g. capitalist, counter-state);
(e)   organizations where other violence is used (e.g. resistance);
(f)   organizations where violence is not an overt issue.

These distinctions may apply to particular organizations or to particular parts or aspects of a given organization. Thus it is quite possible, indeed more than likely, that there will be more than one orientation to violence within a given organization. Within each type of organization or organizational aspect, different structures, functions, operations and processes are likely to occur (Table 3.1).

I will now briefly consider each of the six types of organizational orientation to violence.

Organizations using Legitimated Violence   In organizations where violence is legitimated, an important question is how this is articulated and framed within the goals and objectives of the organization. The main literature here derives from studies of the military and the police (Harries-Jenkins and van Doorn, 1976). Such organizations are simultaneously engaged in the doing of violence, the maintenance of the potential for violence, and the justification of violence. It is useful to consider such legitimated use of violence within a broad social framework, and particularly men's use of violence (Morgan, 1987). The dominant way of enacting these is through the reproduction of hierarchy, often strict hierarchy. Even in such organizations, there are great variations in the extent to which overt violence is part of the organizational routine. For example, a martial arts organization may be routinely involved with controlled violence within the rules of that activity, while the dominant goals may be the making of profit. On the other hand, military organizations may not necessarily routinely engage in violence. The organizational forms of routine social processes or social activities as overtly or physically violent may be relatively rare, outside sport, pornography, criminal, sado-masochistic, and genocidal organizations. In the case of sport, the routine organizational activity may often be characterized as ritualized violence. In addition, in some organizations a major element of their organizational activity involves the watching of violence. This would include, for example, professional boxing promotions and pornography cinemas (see Kimmel, 1990, for a comparison of boxing and pornography).

A problematic issue that particularly concerns military, paramilitary and similar organizations is the difficulty of maintaining the potential for violence to others outside the organization while minimizing, or at least

Table 3.1 *Context, structure and process of organizations*

Types of organizational orientation to violence	Examples	Structure, function and operation	Process
Organizations using legitimated violence	State (police, military prisons) Sport Schools	Presence of violence in goals Hierarchical structure	Production of violation, pain and damage Legitimation Control of violence to members of organizations
Organizations created to respond to violence	State (criminal justice system) Anti-violence/peace organizations	Hierarchical Non-hierarchical	Reduction of violence to routine/work Relation of means and ends
Organizations explicitly responding to violence in other ways	Full range of organizations	Variety of forms	Misunderstandings and ambiguities Avoidance of violence
Organizations using illegitimated (or ambiguous) violence	Capitalist/imperialist/ multinational Counter-state (e.g. paramilitary, organized crime, private armies) Closed institutions	Variety of forms of managers', owners', controllers' power	Production of violation, pain and damage Interaction with specific managerial, professional and other ideologies Control of violence to members of organization Secrecy
Organizations where other violence is used	Full range of organizations (e.g. resistance to domination, harassment)	Variety of forms	Production of violation, pain and damage Legitimation Relation of means and ends
Organizations where violence is not an overt issue	All except examples above	Variety of forms	Obscuring of violence

reducing, violence to each other (and the self) within the organization. This classic dilemma for armies is partly the subject of Dixon's (1976) analysis of 'the psychology of military incompetence', in which he argues that the primary anxiety is redirected by and controlled through organizational devices, such as rules and procedures. However, the most important element of organizational process in such organizations is that they produce and reproduce violation, pain and damage. Accordingly, people with such experiences may remain in the organization, may be expelled from it, or may even be killed.

Organizations Created to Respond to Violence   In organizations created to respond to violence, 'violence' becomes both an element in the achievement of goals, and an element in the routine performance of work. This is most clearly seen in psychiatric institutions, criminal justice agencies, the Probation Service and anti-violence/peace organizations. In some cases, violence may be transformed into a file, a case. Such definitions may be overlain by professional ideologies that are either tolerant, even accepting, of violence, or are unambiguously opposed to violence.

In such organizational situations, responses to violence are often part of the organization–client relation. Accordingly, this is likely to involve engaging with the pain and damage from violence, past or present. The place of the violated is undervalued and undervoiced in most organizational contexts. There may even be a sense in which organizational process is (usually) antithetic to the recognition of the full experience of pain from violence. On the other hand, organizing around pain and damage can produce very powerful organizational processes, not least from the movement from violation to anger to action. Such organizational dynamics and contradictions may be especially important in organizations of survivors of violence. Organizations responding to violence, past or present, may develop ambiguous social processes between destructive violating experiences and 'de-violenced' structures and modes of being.

Organizations Explicitly Responding to Violence in Other Ways   Explicit responses to violence, and indeed threatened and potential violence, are also found in many other organizations, in the form of policies and procedures on violence and sexual violence, for example, sexual harassment and 'campus rape'. This is becoming increasingly common in British welfare agencies, sometimes prompted by physical violence and threats from clients to workers. A summary of organizational policies on violence among trade unions, local authorities, and other organizations is provided by Joeman et al. (1989) (see also Poyner and Warne, 1986, 1988; NALGWC, 1991). It is also becoming an increasingly important issue in commercial organizations, particularly in terms of the safety and security of staff. There are a number of organizational considerations which may highlight these questions, including workers working alone or in small groups, the handling of money or other valuable goods, the entry of women into organizations and occupations that have been 'men's domains', work in high-risk areas of cities, and other organizational activity that is unpopular or perceived as hostile by others.

Organizations using Illegitimated (or Ambiguous) Violence   In this situation, violence may not be part of the official goals of an organization but may be officially sanctioned or may be an ambiguous phenomenon, as in some uses of corporal punishment and other violence in schools. Elsewhere, violence may become part of the unofficial goals or at least taken-for-granted practices of the organization. This could be argued to have been the case in the Pindown episode (Levy and Kahan, 1991), where violent regimes became institutionalized, even though violence was not part of official organizational aims or practices. In such situations, violence may express and reproduce hierarchies. In some organizations, for example, prisons, violence between peers (inmates) may be used as a form of control by managers, staff or others in authority.

Organizations where Other Violence is Used   Violence may also occur in a number of other ways in organizations. These include the use of violence to resist authority, hierarchy, or even presence in the organization at all. Thus the organizational relationship between the violator and the violated is a crucial issue in understanding how violence relates to organizational dynamics. Such relationships might include violence between workers and managers, between organizational peers, between clients and professionals (Phillips et al., 1989).

An important and intensely practical issue is how organizational members maintain organizational relations when violence does occur in or around organizations. This is especially important when violence is relevant to the task of the organization. This is one of the challenges examined by Baron (1987) in *Asylum to Anarchy*. Following a violent incident in a therapeutic community, in which a patient is badly injured and two staff are punched in the face, the staff move on to discuss the violence as an instance of differing perspectives on the ideology of the organization. This includes differences in how staff respond to violence, and differences in how staff re-interpret, through psychodynamic or other frameworks, the position of other staff. In particular, a key area for attention is the interrelation of administrative and therapeutic concerns. To collapse them into one 'system' of authority and control opens up the way for totalitarianism (whether by totally administrative or totally therapeutic modes); a partial solution is the creation of separate modes by time, place or personnel.

Organizations where Violence is not an Overt Issue   In some, indeed many organizations, violence does not appear as an overt issue at all. This may be because violence does not occur; or because talking about violence is not part of the dominant discourse(s) of that organization; or even because violence does occur, and is experienced as such, but it is in the interests of the violators not to recognize this as an overt issue.

Interrelation of Forms of Violence

These aspects of the relationship of organizations and violence are all interrelated. For example, violence by organizations, violence in organizations, and organizational responses to violence may all overlap with each other; they are conceptually distinct but in practice they may be simultaneous.

Organizational responses to violence may be part of the goals of an organization, including, for example, the extent to which violence and restraint are used. Furthermore, all these aspects of the relationship of organizations and violence are, or at least may be, contested. This is most easily seen in debates around talking about violence, for talking about violence may be a means for further violation by the violator of the violated. In these and other ways, organizations are also engaged in the process of constructing and defining violence. This process of organizational/cultural construction applies to all three aspects – violence by organizations, violence in organizations, and organizational responses to violence. All three aspects are in part cultural constructions, and contribute to the cultural construction of violence. Such cultural constructions of violence contribute to the reproduction of masculinities and femininities in organizations and elsewhere. For example, masculinity may be defined through the perform-ance of violence, the potential for violence, the emulation of others' violence, the denial of violence, or even opposition to violence.

The interrelations of coercion, violence, abuse and confinement are particularly important areas for study within total institutions. Such organizations are frequently, perhaps characteristically, bound in a pro-found paradox whereby they are separated off from the rest of society for specific purposes and yet that separation creates the conditions for other purposes to be pursued there. This may mean that societal or official purposes of violence may be subverted, or offical purposes of non-violence may be subverted so that violence is enacted. These issues are especially significant where residents of an organization are not there voluntarily.

Organizational Responses to Violence: a Case Study

In order to illustrate some elements of the violence perspective outlined above, I shall focus in this last section on a case study of 'organizational responses' to men's violence to known women, arising from recent empirical research. This combines elements of the first five organizational types described above. In this research, the issue of the relationship of organizations and violence has figured in at least six main ways:

1 in gaining the general cooperation of agencies;
2 in gaining research access to men;
3 in the interviews and accounts by individual men;
4 in follow-up interviews with agency personnel, where permission is given by individual men;
5 in the general policy response of agencies to violence;
6 in the agency's routine conduct.

Seventy-five men were interviewed, and 130 follow-up contacts were completed, of which 69 were interviews. Organizations involved include the police, the Crown Prosecution Service, the Probation Service, Social

Services, HM Prison Service, housing agencies, programmes for men who have been or who may become violent, solicitors, doctors, psychiatric and other welfare agencies.

In considering this case study, it is first necessary to locate the whole analysis within the context of men's general domination of women. It is also necessary to understand organizations not as isolated but in relation to each other. The various agencies involved operate within their own networks of inter-organizational relations, with their own separations and connections. There are in effect arrays of organizations that deal with violence, even though they are rarely considered together either in policy or analytical terms. This might appear surprising; after all, organizational responses to men's violence to women might be understood in relation to or in association with the 'criminal justice system' or 'the law' more generally. This, however, would be something of an illusion. In practice, the arrays of organizations are diffuse, with many different organizations dealing with the issue in many different ways and with very different forms of problem definition, explanation, and record-keeping. The complexity of these arrays is increased by the dominant construction of men's violence to women as a private matter, albeit through public discourses. Such constructions are being challenged and are changing, not least through changing police policy which recognizes violence in the home or from known others as being as serious as violence in the street or from strangers. They are also being challenged through the development of inter-agency work in relation to women, who leave men after having experienced violence, and the men themselves.

One way of making sense of this pattern of organizational relations is in terms of their differential locations in relation to the state – within the state, on the periphery of the state, outside the state. In this sense, the state is a rather diverse set of organizations, a multi-organization. As Rose (1987: 71) puts it: 'The state is not a unified and internally coherent entity which is the locus of all social power, but a complex set of agencies which are involved to different extents in projects for the regulation of social economic life whose origins, inspirations and power often come from elsewhere.' This seems to be a relatively accurate assessment of the interrrelations of organizational responses to violence. Significantly, these state organizations, professions and other organizations are themselves gendered. Professional interventions around men's violence to women are structured in terms of gender. Usually this involves men's domination of management; men's numerical domination of the criminal justice agencies, especially the police, Crown Prosecution Service and prisons, as well as women's greater presence in social work, therapeutic, counselling, and medical organizations, especially at the lower and sometimes the middle levels in the hierarchies. Most, perhaps all, of the organizations are dominated by men. Possible exceptions include some small voluntary organizations and general practitioners, though even here such small-scale organizations are themselves located within broader spheres of organizational power, dominated by men (Cohen, 1979). The organization(s) of violence thus represent a web of men's management of violence, structured through an impressive and overlapping collection of professional cultures, dominated by men (cf. Hearn, 1990: 67). In the case of 'domestic violence' there is the added complication that this has itself become a possible specialization for women within organizational hierarchies which remain in the hands of men. Indeed, the very term and definition of 'domestic violence' can divert attention from the specific problem of men's violence to known women.

Organizational responses to violence involve a complex pattern and network of agencies. It is the interaction *between* individuals and agencies and then *between* agencies that is important in any particular case. This involves organizations with different relationships to violence. They include organizations with legitimated use of violence (police, prisons); organizations created to respond to violence (Probation Service, Crown Prosecution Service, courts, solicitors, men's programmes); and other organizations that are involved in responding but have not been created for that purpose (social services, housing, doctors). These different agencies involve both different orientations to violence, and different professional and occupational ideologies.

While the police and prisons define and relate to violence in the first instance in quasi-legal terms, this is supplemented by their legitimated use of violence and their own hierarchical structure. An important issue then becomes how that use of violence is controlled within and outside the hierarchy. Police officers may thus operate in ways that both maintain rules and hierarchy and seek to maximize discretion. Among officers interviewed, one of their common complaints was the lack of discretion in the context of an arrest policy towards men who have been violent to known women. Some of the men interviewed spoke of police condoning their violence ('I would've done the same myself'); others saw arrest as less dramatic, even routine ('They just took me in'); others still complained of violence from the police ('gave me a good going over').

Inevitably, professional ideologies are particularly important, whether it is the use of humanistic client-orientated therapeutic ways of working or the use of more directive approaches. Other background assumptions include the extent to which anger, stress, aggression and violence are understood to coexist or correlate with each other. Dankwort (1988) also points to the ways in which organizational and techno-bureaucratic forces tend to subordinate more radical practice and dilute ideological positions inconsistent with the prevailing political climate (Etzioni, 1974; Chevalier, 1981). According to this 'logic', the interests of management go before innovation, and women-centred work, practice and politics thus become incorporated within dominant professional and managerial ideologies (Sullivan, 1982; Davis, 1987).

Then there is the question of the differential significance of violence in different agencies in terms of its goals, tasks, definitions and presence or absence of policies on violence, as part of the formal operation of organizations. A crucial question is the extent to which violence is seen as a central, explicit part of the organization's work and to what extent that task (though not necessarily the violence) is seen as non-problematic. This is most clearly the case with the police, the Crown Prosecution Service, the Probation Service, the prison service and specialist counselling groups. In other organizations – for example, housing agencies, social services, and general counselling – the relation to violence is less clear. Particularly interesting are housing agencies, as violence may be highly relevant to housing need but not necessarily the dominant operative definition for housing clients. Furthermore, some housing agencies are engaged in attempting to house men who have been violent; others take the opposite view.

In each agency concerned, violence is defined in a characteristic way by the managers, workers and other staff. These definitions reproduce the agency's function and structure, as well as particular professional and occupational ideologies. This appears to be clearest in the case of the Crown Prosecution Service, where there are explicit guidelines on prosecution in terms of (a) evidential sufficiency criteria, and (b) public interest criteria. These provide a rational-legal framework for organizational responses to violence. The Code for Crown Prosecutors mentions 'likely penalty', 'staleness', 'youth', 'old age and infirmity', 'mental disorders', 'sexual offences', 'change in the complainant's attitudes', and 'peripheral dependants'. However, these still involve the use of judgement and discretion. This can include 'the presence of slight or minor injuries', 'weak evidence', 'plausible explanation by defendant', 'how realistic is the prospect of conviction', 'great provocation', 'age', 'previous convictions', 'seriousness', and 'complainant's wishes', as suggested by staff interviewed.

Thus, organizational responses to violence characteristically involve negotiation within a zone of uncertainty – about what constitutes violence, about why and how violence occurred, about what to do about violence. This is not to say that each agency is unified, far from it; rather that disunity, tensions and even conflict in definitions can be characteristic in agencies. This is perhaps clearest in the Probation Service where there is considerable variation in the extent to which the problem of men's violence to known women is treated as a priority at work. In addition, probation straddles the traditions of law and the traditions of social work, so that different officers may be able to find a different relation to work depending on their team locations, specialty, and personal style. One way in which the tension between the legal and social work traditions in probation is mediated is through explaining violence by drink. This both confirms the man's culpability (in legal discourse) and creates a space for him being different at other times (in social work discourse) (Philp, 1979).

Such differentiations of violence and the client interrelate with other distinctions around whether organizational personnel are concerned with only men known or potential clients who are now known; with only men who are sought or those who are not sought too; and whether violence is seen as separate from or an integral part of the man's/client's masculinity. (These questions have been central in the construction of research access to men who have been violent to women via agencies and agency personnel. While in some cases men have been referred in 'batches', by virtue of their definition through violence in other cases, each man has been seen as individual and not pre-defined through violence.) This links with another relevant contrast: namely, that in those agencies, most obviously the specialist counselling groups which define the violence as the prime problem, the violence is also seen as part of 'the whole person'. Yet at the same time, such groups are founded on the assumption that it is possible for men to change. They thus embody a paradox between a broader view of the relationship of violence and masculinity, and yet a commitment to the change of that broad connection.

Finally, there is the place of violence within organizational processes – in managerial and work cultures, in the ordinary enactment of authority, in normalized harassment, in dealing with the violence of others, in talking about violences, as well as the process of keeping records around violence. Violence becomes 'reduced' to the material task and the culture of the organization – it can be processed, reconstructed, ignored, joked about, like any other cultural organizational currency. In one sense, 'violence' is like any other work object – to be worked on and made 'social'. However, to have a work process around violence may well cause extra complications for those concerned. For those who are responding to violence there are likely to be not just pain and distress but also strategies of avoidance, such as its 'conversion' to work. There may also be forms of resistance to violence, its recognition, and its direct opposition.

An example of this is how work process may relate to the reproduction of masculinities and men's power. At several points in this research I have been told 'horror stories' by male workers; these have either been about particular horrific cases of men's violence to women or men's threat to male professionals. These stories seem to have several meanings: they may simultaneously convey a sense of both voyeurism and bravado. They may confirm a certain kind of masculinity ('I can take it'), while at the same time admitting an emotional response to violence. Past events are objectified and externalized, and simultaneously the worker is saying something for his benefit, dealing with the feelings that persist. This kind of talk can, of course, easily slip into a verbally or even physically violent work culture, as when clients are characterized as 'full of shit'. Such issues of men-to-men talk have been examined elsewhere in factories (Cockburn, 1983) and in sport (Curry, 1991). In the context of the male professional workers, such as probation officers, solicitors and social workers, encountered in this research, there is often a profound ambiguity between a routine 'straight' masculinity (set within a conventional homosexual subtext) and a less obviously heterosexual, more ambiguous sexuality, that is saying 'I'm not like that.'

In the face of all this, the resort to proceduralism is perhaps not surprising. The processing of violence thus interrelates with other diverse organizational processes, including the construction of rules around how violence is handled in the organization. To make sense of this case study, it is necessary to consider the interrelation of organizations and violence in a broad context. Men's violence to women outside the organizations in question becomes 'reduced' to an element of the organizational structure, function, operation and process. The way this happens and continues to happen involves interrelations between the men's violence to women, men's explanations of that violence, professional–client relations within a work culture, formal organizational goals and talks, and violence in the organization more generally. Through these kinds of interconnections, we are not only concerned with the links between client relations and team/ group work cultures (Blau and Scott, 1963), but the links between client relations and patriarchalism/anti-patriarchalism in organizations.

Indeed, of particular interest is the way in which the accounts given by individual men and the accounts of staff in agencies that deal with them often mirror each other. For example, men in contact with the Probation Service may see their violence to women as secondary to other crime and may talk at length of their violence to men; probation officers may often not focus on violence to women as the main issue in their work with the men. In contrast, men in counselling groups and men's programmes accept that violence to women is the central problem and may develop relatively sophisticated explanations thereof; workers in these programmes similarly see violence as central and develop complex understandings of it that relate both general questions of power and control, and the individualities of particular men. Working on and responding to violence involves not just dealing directly with violence but also constructing accounts and explanations of violence. Importantly, definitions and explanations of violence by agencies and agency staff are themselves often dominated by men. The way that men who have been violent provide definitions of, and excuses and justifications for, their violence is often mirrored in the accounts of staff in agencies that deal with men that are also dominated by men (Hanmer and Hearn, 1993). While both individual men and agency men may avoid the topic of violence, both may also reproduce it by treating it as a separate and separable activity (Jukes, 1993): this separation of 'violence' from men's power and control in general is part of the problem.

Thus, while the place of violence within the structure, function and operation of organizational responses to violence is very significant in providing the broad contours of organizational life, it does not address the complexities of violence within the organizational process. Nor does it fully convey how organizational life is lived and experienced by organizational members in relation to violence.

Conclusion

This chapter has approached organizational analysis through a focus on violence. In many ways this perspective continues some of the tradition of the Tavistock School, exemplified by Jaques' (1976) analysis of the psychological dynamics of bureaucracy. He argued that if accountability and authority were not clearly specified, delegitimated power will develop, so that '[i]f the situation becomes widespread it is a potential source of energy for social violence' (1976: 68). While this does seem an overly deterministic (and prescriptive) formulation, it does highlight the way in which (social) violence can be intrinsically embedded in organizational processes. Whereas Jaques sees accountability, authority and organizational rules as necessary to control and deflect 'social violences', I see such organizational structures and processes as a means of managing, masking and obscuring the pervasiveness of violence.

This suggests a need for more conceptual thinking on the relationship of organizations and violence, including the extent to which organizations can be understood as violence. By this I do not mean that organizations are simply violent by virtue of their use of violence, both within and beyond themselves; rather, I am thinking of the extent to which organizations depend for their continuation upon obedience to unaccountable or un-justifiable authority (see Lessnoff, 1986). For these and other reasons, organizations and violence may correlate; organizations may be forms of violence, may use violence, may house violence, may respond to violence, and may be characterized by organizational processes around violence. This perspective on what might be called 'organization violence' (cf. 'organization sexuality'; Hearn and Parkin, 1987) is an open-ended approach that could reformulate organizational analysis towards a more fully gendered view of power in organizations. In organizations that are responding to violence, particular attention may need to be directed to the reconstruction of violence as work and work routine, and the unanticipated consequences of such ways of working, such as the mirroring of accounts of violence by those who have been violent 'in the first place'.

On the other hand, the violence perspective may also be limited in directing attention away from other organizational perspectives, such as that emphasizing mutual cooperation. Moreover, the perspective outlined in this chapter leaves as open questions the extent to which organizations are distinct from other areas of social life in terms of violence; and the extent to which violence, in its non-physical or less directly physical senses, is distinct from power in organizations (see Chapters 4, 5 and 6).

Acknowledgements

This chapter was first published in *Human Relations*, 47 (6), June 1994, pp. 731–54. It arises from the ESRC Research Project No. L206 25 2003,

'Violence, Abuse and the Stress-coping Process, Project no. 2' (April 1991–March 1993) which has examined men's violence to known women. Project no. 1 was a linked, but separate, project on women's experiences of violence from known men, and was directed by Jalna Hanmer.

I am grateful to Jalna Hanmer, Mary Maynard, David Morgan and other members of the Research Unit on Violence, Abuse and Gender Relations, University of Bradford, for discussion on these issues; to David Collinson, Elizabeth Harlow and Wendy Parkin for related discussions; to Celia Davies, Jean Neumann and anonymous reviewers of *Human Relations* for detailed comments on the text, and to Linda Arbuckle for typing the script. Parts of this chapter were presented to the Gender Research Seminar at UMIST, January 1992. I am grateful to participants for their very helpful comments.

Notes

1. By 'sexualed' I mean how a particular interpretation is given sexual meaning or meaning in terms of sexuality. I use this as distinct from 'sexual', which means pertaining to sexuality, or 'sexualized', which carries the connotation of having been given heightened sexual meaning, that is becoming sexual 'in' meaning.

2. The relationship of psychoanalysis, gender, sexuality, and feminism and pro-feminism is a vast arena of debate, which space prohibits exploring here (for example, Sayers, 1986). Relevant issues include the patriarchal bases of psychoanalytic theorizing, especially in its initial development; the use of psychoanalysis to reinforce sexual/gender stereotyping; and the complex interplay of pleasure and danger, risk and fears about sexuality within psychoanalysis.

3. Of these, 60 made up the main sample.

References

Baron, C. (1987) *Asylum to Anarchy*, London: Free Association.

Bion, W. (1948–51) 'Experiences in groups I–VII', Human Relations: 1 (3): 314–20; 1 (4): 487–96; 2 (1): 13–22; 2 (4): 295–304; 3 (1): 3–14; 3 (4): 395–402; 4 (3): 221–8.

Blau, P. and Scott, W.R. (1963) *Formal Organisations*, Boston and London: Routledge and Kegan Paul.

Bowlby, J. (1953) *Child Care and the Growth of Love*, Harmondsworth: Penguin.

Buchbinder, H. (1987) 'Male heterosexuality: the socialised penis revisited', in H. Buchbinder, V. Burstyn, D. Forbes and M. Steadman (eds), *The Politics of Heterosexuality*, Toronto: Garamond, pp. 63–82.

Burstyn, V. (1983) 'Masculine dominance and the state', in R. Miliband and J. Savile (eds), *The Socialist Register*, London: Merlin, pp. 45–89.

Chevalier, J. (1981) *L'Institution*, Paris: PUF.

Cline, H.F. (1968) 'The determinants of normative patterns in correctional institutions', *Scandinavian Studies in Criminology*, 2, London: Tavistock.

Cockburn, C. (1983) *Brothers, Male Dominance and Technological Change*, London: Pluto.

Cockburn, C. (1991) *In the Way of Women: Men's Resistance to Sex Equality in Organizations*, Basingstoke: Macmillan.

Cohen, G. (1979) 'Symbiotic relations: male decision-makers and female support groups in Britain and the United States', *Women's Studies International Quarterly*, 2 (4): 391–406.

Collinson, D.L. (1992) *Managing the Shopfloor: Subjectivity, Masculinity and Workplace Culture*, Berlin: de Gruyter.

Connell, R.W. (1990) 'Gender, the state and sexual politics: theory and appraisal', *Theory and Society*, 19: 507–44.

Coveney, L., Jackson, M., Jeffreys, S., Kay, L. and Mahoney, P. (1984) *Sexuality and the Social Control of Women*, London: Hutchinson.

Curry, T.J. (1991) 'Fraternal bonding in the locker room: a pro-feminist analysis of talk about competition and women', *Sociology of Sport Journal*, 8: 119–35.

Dankwort, J. (1988) 'Batterers' programs and issues of accountability: a critical evaluation from Quebec', unpublished paper, Montreal, Canada.

Davis, L.V. (1987) 'Battered women: the transformation of a social problem', *Social Work*, July-August: 306–11.

Dixon, N. (1976) *On the Psychology of Military Incompetence*, London: Jonathan Cape.

Dworkin, A. (1979) *Pornography: Men Possessing Women*, New York: G.P. Putnam's.

Etzioni, A. (1961) *A Comparative Analysis of Complex Organisations*, Glencoe, Ill.: Free Press.

Etzioni, A. (1974) *Modern Organizations*, New York: Prentice-Hall.

Evan, W. (ed.) (1976) *Inter-organization Relations*, Harmondsworth: Penguin.

Farley, L. (1978) *Sexual Shakedown: the Sexual Harassment of Women on the Job*, London: Melbourn House.

Gutek, B. (1985) *Sex and the Workplace: Impact of Sexual Behaviour and Harassment on Women, Men and Organizations*, San Francisco: Jossey-Bass.

Hanmer, J. and Hearn, J. (1993) 'Gendered research and researching gender: women, men and violence', British Sociological Association Conference, University of Essex, April.

Harries-Jenkins, G. and van Doorn, J. (eds) (1976) *The Military and the Problem of Legitimacy*, London and Beverly Hills, CA: Sage.

Hearn, J. (1990) 'Child abuse and men's violence', in Violence against Children Study Group (ed.), *Taking Child Abuse Seriously*, London: Unwin Hyman, pp. 62–85.

Hearn, J. (1992) *Men in the Public Eye: the Construction and Deconstruction of Public Men and Public Patriarchies*, London and New York: Routledge.

Hearn, J. and Parkin, P.W. (1983) 'Gender and organisations: a selective review and a critique of a neglected area', *Organisation Studies*, 4: 219–42.

Hearn, J. and Parkin, W. (1987) *'Sex' at 'Work': the Power and Paradox of Organisation Sexuality*, Brighton: Wheatsheaf; New York: St Martin's. Revised edn (1995) London and New York: Prentice-Hall; New York: St Martin's.

Hearn, J., Sheppard, D., Tancred-Sheriff, P. and Burrell, G. (eds) (1989) *The Sexuality of Organization*, London and Newbury Park, CA: Sage.

Jaques, E. (1955) 'Social systems as a defence against persecutory and depressive anxiety', in M. Klein, P. Heimann and R.E. Money-Kyrle (eds), *New Directions in Psychoanalysis*, London: Tavistock, pp. 478–98.

Jaques, E. (1976) *A General Theory of Bureaucracy*, London: Heinemann.

Joeman, L.M., Phillips, C.M. and Stockdale, J.E. (1989) *The Risks in Going to Work: Bibliography*, London: The Suzy Lamplugh Trust.

Jukes, A. (1993) *Why Men Hate Women*, London: Free Association.

Kelly, L. (1987) 'The continuum of sexual violence', in J. Hanmer and M. Maynard (eds), *Women, Violence and Social Control*, London: Macmillan, pp. 46–60.

Kelly, L. (1988) *Surviving Sexual Violence*, Cambridge: Polity Press.

Kimmel, M.S. (1990) 'Insult or injury: sex, pornography and sexism', in M.S. Kimmel (ed.), *Men Confront Pornography*, New York: Crown, pp. 305–19.

Lessnoff, M. (1986) *Social Contract*, London: Macmillan.

Levy, A. and Kahan, B. (1991) *The Pindown Experience and the Protection of Children: the Report of the Staffordshire Child Care Inquiry 1990*, Stafford: Staffordshire County Council.

Litewka, J. (1977) 'The socialized penis', in J. Snodgrass (ed.), *A Book of Readings for Men against Sexism*, Albion, CA: Times Change, pp. 16–35.

MacKinnon, C.A. (1979) *Sexual Harassment of Working Women*, New Haven, Conn.: Yale University Press.

MacKinnon, C.A. (1982) 'Feminism, Marxism, method and the state: an agenda for theory', *Signs*, 7 (3): 515–44.

MacKinnon, C.A. (1983) 'Feminism, Marxism, method and the state: toward feminist jurisprudence', *Signs*, 8 (4): 635–58.

MacKinnon, C.A. (1989) *Toward a Feminist Theory of the State*, Harvard, Mass. and London: Harvard University Press.

Menzies, I.E.P. (1960) 'A case study in the functioning of social systems as a defense against anxiety: a report of a study of the nursing service of a general hospital', *Human Relations*, 13 (2): 95–121.

Menzies, I.E.P. (1970) *The Functioning of Social Systems as a Defence against Anxiety*, London: Centre for Applied Social Research, The Tavistock Institute of Human Relations.

Mies, M. (1986) *Patriarchy and Accumulation in a World Scale*, London: Zed.

Miller, P. (1992) 'The Tavistock mission: a review essay', *Human Relations*, 45: 411–26.

Miller, P. and Rose, N. (1988) 'The Tavistock programme: the government of subjectivity and social life', *Sociology*, 22: 171–92.

Morgan, D.H.J. (1987) 'Masculinity and violence', in J. Hanmer and M. Maynard (eds), *Women, Violence and Social Control*, London: Macmillan, pp. 180–92.

Morgan, G. (1986) *Images of Organisation*, Newbury Park, CA: Sage.

National Association of Local Government Women's Committees (1991) *Responding with Authority: Local Authority Initiatives to Counter Violence against Women*, Manchester: NALGWC.

O'Brien, M. (1981) *The Politics of Reproduction*, London: Routledge and Kegan Paul.

Phillips, C.M., Stockdale, J.E. and Joeman, L.M. (1989) *The Risks in Going to Work: Full Report*, London: The Suzy Lamplugh Trust.

Philp, M. (1979) 'Notes on the form of knowledge in social work', *Sociological Review*, 27 (1): 83–111.

Poyner, B. and Warne, C. (1986) *Violence to Staff: a Basis for Assessment and Prevention*, London: Tavistock Institute of Human Relations/Health and Safety Executive.

Poyner, B. and Warne, C. (1988) *Preventing Violence to Staff*, London: Tavistock Institute of Human Relations/Health and Safety Executive.

Pringle, R. (1989) *Secretaries Talk: Sexuality, Power and Work*, London: Verso.

Rose, N. (1987) 'Beyond the public/private division: law, power and the family', *Journal of Law and Society*, 14 (1): 61–76.

Sayers, J. (1986) *Sexual Contradictions: Psychology, Psychoanalysis and Feminism*, London: Tavistock.

Scraton, P., Sim, J. and Skidmore, P. (1991) *Prisons under Protest*, Milton Keynes: Open University Press.

Sullivan, G. (1982) 'Cooptation of alternative services: the battered women's movement as a case study', *Catalyst*, 14: 39–55.

Taylor, N. (ed.) (1986) *All in a Day's Work: a Report on Anti-Lesbian Discrimination in Employment and Unemployment in London*, London: Lesbian Employment Rights.

Walby, S. (1990) *Theorising Patriarchy*, Oxford: Blackwell.

Waring, M. (1988) *Counting for Nothing*, Wellington, NZ: Allen and Unwin.

4

Gender, Violence and Social Work Organizations

Elizabeth Harlow

Violence may not readily spring to mind when one thinks of social work organizations. This chapter attempts to consider some of the ways in which social work organizations are concerned with violence on a day-to-day basis. While the most overt kinds of violence between organizational members and their clients are acknowledged, it is to the more covert and taken-for-granted forms of violence occurring within the organization that most attention is given. The main focus will be on men's violence against women. The definition of violence is taken from feminist and anti-sexist writers and connected with some of the experiences of women in social work organizations. It is acknowledged that this is a huge topic and that it is impossible to explore all the aspects fully in this chapter. However, the aim is to stimulate further thought and discussion in this area.

Clients and Workers

Social work organizations offer services to a variety of people including those who have experienced violence, for example, abused children or women fleeing violence. Work is carried out with those who are attempting to change particular violent behaviours, for example, men on anger management courses or therapeutic programmes for men who are the perpetrators of child sexual abuse. Certain forms of violence may be viewed as legitimate as a means of preventing individuals from behaving violently towards themselves or others; for example, compulsory detention within a psychiatric hospital. In a similar but slightly different way, 'legitimate' violence may be used as a means of maintaining formal authority; for example, disciplinary procedures within a residential home for children and young people. Such procedures may go beyond the bounds of acceptability and become illegitimate violence as in the case of the 'Pindown scandal' (Levy and Kahan, 1991). In this instance, instead of a social work organization preventing violence or dealing with its effects, the social work organization was responsible for it. Another example might be the case of Frank Beck (Kirkwood, 1993) who violated both staff and young people for whom he was responsible when he was officer-in-charge in Leicestershire children's homes.

Social workers may also be subjected to violence from their clients. This may be in the form of subtle sexual threat (Wise and Stanley, 1990), physical attack or murder. Between 1984 and 1986 three social workers were murdered by clients (Rojek et al., 1988). All of the victims were women. In general, violence against social workers has become more fully recognized as a conscious issue in recent years (Parton and Small, 1989).

Social work organizations relate to violence through the course of their work with clients in at least six ways:

1 attempting to prevent violence;
2 ameliorating the consequences of violence;
3 employing societally legitimate forms of violence as a means of control;
4 administering societally and organizationally illegitimate violence;
5 individual social workers perpetrating the abuse of clients;
6 organizational members themselves being subjected to violence from social work clients.

Almost all of these examples are concerned with overt forms of violence. But violence need not always be overt and it need not only be in connection with social work clients. Overt violence does occur between staff members of social work organizations, as exposed by the Frank Beck case (Kirkwood, 1993). Covert violence, however, can also be said to occur as part of daily routine practice and indeed may be fundamental to the very nature and structure of, not only social work organizations, but all organizations to a greater or lesser extent. It is with these internal structures and practices that this chapter is concerned. It may be appropriate at this stage to define the term 'violence' as it is used in this chapter.

Violence

The common-sense definition of violence would probably emphasize physical force but violence can be construed in different ways. According to constructions of violence used by (among others) feminist and anti-sexist writers there exists a range of oppressive phenomena which might constitute violence. For example, structures of organizations might be considered to be violent.

> Violences should be understood as any action or structure that diminishes another human being; and in accepting this definition we must see that the basic structures of our society are often violent in concept. We must recognise the violence built into many of our institutions such as schools and places of work in that they are competitive, hierarchical, non-democratic and at times unjust. (Pinthus, 1982: 2, quoted in Ramazanoglu, 1987: 64)

Using this definition, it is possible to explore the forms of violence that are perpetrated by the very structure of social work organizations.

This is not the only way that violence might be seen. Using the definition employed by Hearn (1994; see also Chapter 3), violence might also be seen as that which violates or causes violation. It can take varying forms including physical, sexual, emotional, verbal, cognitive, visual and representational forms. 'Violence may also comprise the creation of the conditions of violence, potential violence, threat and/or neglect. Sometimes the mere presence of someone is violating and thus violence. Violence can be dramatic or subtle, occasional or continuous' (Hearn, 1994: 6) (also see pp. 43, this volume). If violence is considered in these ways it may be possible to identify a whole range of practices carried out within social work organizations which are violating and diminishing. Such practices may often be taken for granted and their connection with gender not made. It is to these connections that we will now turn.

Making the Connections

Violence might be relevant to gender and social work organizations in the following ways:

1 Social work organizations, like most organizations, are part of the public realm. They are spaces which are seen as belonging to men (Hearn, 1992). Despite the concerns of social work organizations and the preponderance of women employed within them, this is no less the case.
2 Organizations are usually structured along the lines of gender. This can also apply to social work organizations.
3 Organizations are sites where gendered violence occurs on a routine basis, for example:
   (a) It is usually men who violate women, children and other men, although it is important to recognize that women and children can also be violent.
   (b) Violence may not only be considered as specific dramatic isolated acts but as a part of the continuous, routine process of gender relations which result in the subordination of women.
   (c) The subordination of one gender to another is in itself a violence.
   (d) The construction of 'gender', the gender categories of man and woman (Findlay, 1987–8), and the characteristics which are attributed to each of these categories, and the gendered subjectivities which result are in part dependent upon this subordination.

Each of these main categories will be considered in relation to social work organizations.

The Public Space of Men and the Private Place of Women

In terms of their construction, organizations are public places which, according to gender differentiation, makes them appropriate spaces for men while women are constructed as being predominantly concerned with the private sphere of the domestic. Organizations are perceived as being based on task-focused scientific rationality. Task orientation and rationality are characteristics which are predominantly attributed to men. Women, constructed as irrational, intuitive, emotional and caring are therefore viewed as more suited to homemaking. Despite the current predominance of women as social workers and the fundamental contribution women have made to the development of social work (Berg, 1978; Younghusband, 1981; Gordon, 1989), there has, throughout history, been at least ambivalence and at worst hostility to women's public presence in social work organizations. In order to explore this argument, account will be taken of the historical development of social work and social work organizations.

Last century's charity organizations were the forerunners of today's social work organizations. Walton (1975) and Berg (1978) both argue that it was very difficult for married middle-class women to participate in the early charity work or other public work as their public participation was considered unseemly and was therefore resisted by their husbands. For many women involvement in the first social work organizations also involved them in personal struggle. Once social work became more organized the picture did not change. In fact, the opposite may be said to be the case. Gordon (1989: 65) suggests that once the charity field became established women were no longer welcome: 'the movement they themselves had created now expelled them, as the charity field became professionalised. 'Scientific' charity wanted no sentimental, muddle headed ladies dispensing alms, but tough minded men engaged in long range vision and strategies.'

The transition of social work from charity to profession (or semi-profession) extended over a period of years and depended on a number of factors, one of them being the increased complexity of social work organizations (Younghusband, 1981). Women continued to play an important part even though they were subject to marriage bars (for example, in the Probation Service) and were paid less for doing the same work as men (Walton, 1975). Social work became comprehensively established in Britain after the Second World War with the development of the welfare state. Ironically, this extended opportunity for women to pursue careers in social work and participate publicly in social work organizations coincided with a vigorous restatement that a woman's place was in the home (Wilson, 1977). Women were expected to leave the way clear for men to resume full-time employment once they had left the armed forces. In addition, there were concerns about the break-up of the family during wartime and women were encouraged to invest their energies in rebuilding the home and family as a haven of love and warmth. There was the growing belief that responsible adulthood depended on good mothering, hence women should devote themselves to the needs of their children in order to prevent problems later (Mitchell, 1979). Therefore, at the time when the profession was becoming more established and job opportunities became available, women were encouraged to invest their energies into being the lynchpin of the nuclear family, caring for their husband and raising their children. In order to encourage the participation of men in social work, which would resolve the labour shortage but also improve the image of social work at the time when the status of profession was being sought, salaries were increased and career structures were incorporated. The drive was successful and more men entered social work, although they took up posts which were seen to require male attributes, for example in the Probation Service. Although the current situation may be much altered, the number of women entering the Probation Service during the 1960s declined (Walton, 1975).

This very brief consideration of aspects of the historical development of the social work profession gives some indication of the way women, despite their crucial contribution, have been positioned as having little right to participate in certain ways in social work organizations. Today, the expectation that children are the primary responsibility of their mother and therefore that a woman's place is in the domestic sphere remains to a large extent, and continues to have an impact on women's participation in paid employment and organizational life.

> The way women do or do not fit into the schema of paid employment and organizational life is seen primarily as a correlate of their marital status and, more important still, whether they do or do not have children. This is what women are to most men (and to most women): people who have domestic ties. Even if the woman in question is celibate or childless she is seen and represented as one of the maternal sex. (Cockburn, 1991: 76)

Such beliefs about women are 'violent' in that they are potentially restrictive and curtailing, and may lead to real material consequences. Women either stay at home or undertake a double burden of work at home and in the organization. But women do clearly still participate in social work and social work organizations. They are not, however, distributed evenly throughout the organizations and for Cockburn this is linked to their perceived location within the domestic sphere. The argument could also be made that women are only welcome within organizations as long as they undertake tasks unattractive to men and in keeping with the general construction of femininity. This takes us to the exploration of the gendered structure of social work organizations.

The Gendered Structure of Social Work Organizations

Although it has been suggested that all organizations, including all social work organizations, are structured along the lines of gender, for the purposes of this chapter particular exploration will be made of Social Services departments (SSDs). For some time now there has been a recognition that SSDs are segregated along gender lines (Howe, 1986; Hallett, 1989; Grimwood and Popplestone, 1993). Attention has been drawn to the fact that women are concentrated in specific areas of work which are closely associated with domestic tasks (Howe, 1986). As a result women are segregated within the organization both vertically and horizontally. Horizontally, women are to be found in areas of work that are more directly concerned with the caring rather than the controlling aspects of social work, for example, work with elderly people and hospital social work. Vertically, more women are concentrated in the 'hands on' area of direct service provision, for example, as domiciliary workers, care assistants and social workers, with very few women becoming senior managers despite their overwhelming predominance as employees within the organization. In 1990 there were 364,785 employees of SSDs in England and Wales. Of these, 86.5 per cent were women and 13.5 per cent were men. The largest group of employees were women in part-time employment (SSI/Department of Health, 1991: 5). In the same year, 82 per cent of senior managers of SSDs in England and Wales were men, and 18 per cent women (SSI/Department of Health, 1991: 6).

The proportion of men and women as Directors of SSDs in England has not significantly changed over a recent 19-year period. In 1971, 90 per cent of directors were men, while in 1990 men were 89 per cent of the total. Horizontal segregation may be connected to vertical segregation, in that the concentration of women in particular areas of work may count against them in terms of achieving success along the vertical axis. Clearly this structural hierarchy of SSDs is not to the advantage of women and may in fact constitute the kind of violence that is referred to by Pinthus (1982) and Ramazanoglu (1987). Structural inequality means that women are more likely to suffer from low pay and unlikely to enjoy the organizational perks enjoyed by those in senior management. It is less likely that they will be in a position to participate in decision-making and are thus more likely to be seen as marginal to the organization in general. According to Cockburn (1991), men in organizations are resistant to equal opportunities policies which might begin to address some of these structural injustices. While the structure itself may be diminishing, to women the practices within the organization might also be thought to be so. Continuing with this broad definition of violence, it is to these practices that I will now turn.

Men, Women and Violent Practices within Social Services Departments

There are a multitude of ways in which men can, on a daily basis, within social work organizations undermine women or make them feel excluded and marginalized. Even a small group of men, who are numerically in the minority, can demonstrate their preference for one another, their 'homo-sociability' (Lipman-Blumen, 1976), in a loud and excluding manner. This can revolve around such things as sport appreciation, sporting activities or trips to the pub. This in itself may not seem problematic but it occurs within the context that the organization itself is already appropriated by men in terms of the public/private difference and men have formal control via the hierarchy. These behaviours can then become imbued with specific meaning. The situation can be worse for those women who have moved up the management ladder and find themselves numerically in a minority. They may be excluded from any social life or informal networking that goes on because of homosociability and the form it takes. One woman in a senior management position said that she joined her male colleagues in the pub one evening. The conversation revolved around building patios and other DIY from which she felt excluded. By the time the conversation turned to work she felt so isolated and ignored that she was unable to contribute. She did not join their company again. Even when women are knowledgeable on the subject under discussion their contributions may not be heard if they do not fit with the dominant perceptions of women (SSI/Department of Health, n.d.).

These experiences of women managers in SSDs are backed up by research which indicates that men dominate conversations where the topic is seen as a man's topic (James and Drakich, 1993). This may have serious consequences for women in management as management itself is frequently identified as a subject for men. Whether at work or socializing with male colleagues women may feel excluded and ignored. This is in itself diminishing and may therefore be considered violent. In addition, however, the exclusions from social and possibly influential networks can also lead to the inhibition of career opportunities.

A range of other practices by men in mixed groups can lead to the silencing and diminishing of women. Interruptions, sarcasm and put-downs are all practices which regularly occur (Ramazanoglu, 1987). Some studies on gender and conversational interruption conclude that men interrupt more than women but, more significantly, that they are likely to interrupt women more than men. The current research in this area is, however, rather inconclusive (James and Clarke, 1993). While such practices may be conscious they may also be unconsciously and routinely employed by men when in mixed gender groups with the result that women are inhibited. Moyer and Tuttle (1993) suggest the following list of practices carried out by men when in the company of women:

- 'hogging the show'
- being a continual problem-solver
- speaking in 'capital letters'
- defensiveness
- task and content focus, to the exclusion of nurturing
- put-downs and one-up meetings
- negativism
- transfer of the focus of discussion
- holding on to the formal powerful positions
- intransigence and dogmatism

- listening only to oneself
- avoiding feelings
- condescension and paternalism
- using sexuality to manipulate women
- seeking attention and support from women while competing with men
- running the show
- protectively storing key group information for one's own use
- speaking for others

Women managers also acknowledged that men often attributed their contributions to another man even when that man had not spoken (SSI/Department of Health, n.d.). This can be particularly frustrating in formal meetings where men may take the credit for the efforts of women.

I have attempted to describe the ways in which women can feel excluded, isolated and diminished within SSDs. Sexual harassment can also contribute to these feelings. Although sexual harassment is often quite narrowly defined, Wise and Stanley (1990: 16) make the case for a broader definition,

> sexual harassment is not of the 'sledgehammer' variety, of obscenities and physical assaults. Rather it is ambiguously expressed behaviour by men which, by virtue of its ambiguities, often renders women complicit within it before they realize what its intent is; and it happens so many times that its effect can be described as a 'dripping tap' to which one becomes accustomed as the ordinary condition of everyday life.

According to Wise and Stanley, these ambiguous behaviours might consist of 'compliments', 'flattery', 'jokes', persistent slighting remarks about women's minds, behaviours and bodies, and men's demands for time and attention. Wise and Stanley suggest that because organizations are meant to be scientific and rational, and therefore places for men only, sex is expected to be absent. They point out the contradiction here for gay men but argue that it is the assumption of heterosexuality that is dominant. Sex is seen as being introduced into the organization by women. For two reasons women might be deemed to be available for the attentions of men: (a) because men are believed to be driven by forceful sexual drives which are triggered by women, and (b) men hold more power than women, sexual harassment having more to do with power than sex. As a result, many of the behaviours men exhibit towards women which may seem ambiguous, may, according to Wise and Stanley (1990), be a part of this power/sex context.

A wide range of practices carried out by men on a daily basis may contribute to the structural location and the general diminishing of women. This is not to suggest that all men behave in this way all of the time or that women never consciously or unconsciously diminish others. Rather it is an attempt to explore some of the more covert and taken-for-granted ways in which women can be subjected to violence from men within social work organizations.

Discussion

Three particular ways in which gendered violence might occur in social work organizations have been identified and separately considered. In practice they are not separately occurring phenomena. Each occurs simultaneously, effects the other and contributes to the whole, a part of which is the way in which men and women are constructed and positioned in relation to one another. This construction/relational position is not static and it may be that 'violence' is one particular means for men to maintain the status quo. This highlights a weakness of the above argument in that the ways women struggle against their position is not acknowledged. Also men are always construed as powerful and women vulnerable to their abuse. This is an over-simplification. In addition, there are differences between men and between women. For example, some women do not wish to have paid employment, while others who do work for a wage only do so through necessity. Some women enjoy and value the areas of work in which they are involved, for example, hands on work with clients and may not feel a constraint in any way and may find opportunities for autonomy which are less likely in other organizational positions. This does not justify, however, the low status that is attributed to such work.

The violence that women themselves initiate should also be examined to give a full and accurate picture of violence within social work organizations. For example, black women may experience violence at the hands of white women. Finally, this broad concept of violence itself may be problematic. Those who have experienced the horrors of serious physical assault may object to a use of the term which waters down its impact. However, when considering men's daily routine attitudes and behaviours towards women, it may be the constant potential threat of physical violence that is the unspoken component which gives them force.

Conclusion

This chapter has recognized the way in which the construction of organizations in general, and social work organizations in particular, can be unwelcoming to women. This, together with the domestic responsibilities of women, contributes towards their structural location within organizations. All of this diminishes women in the sense of contributing towards a narrow definition of 'woman' and hence a curtailment of options and potential. Some of the routine practices of men towards women within social work organizations might also be described as 'violating' and may contribute towards the general position of women within social work organizations.

There are limitations to this argument, however, and consideration of these matters is only at an early stage. There is no suggestion that the forms of violence perpetuated by men against women in social work are the only forms of violence that occur. Consideration could and should be given to violence perpetrated against other groups who experience injustice and oppression. In addition, attention could be given to the part women play in the complex dynamics of organizational violence. If taken seriously, social work organizations, and indeed social work educators, have to look more closely at their practice. These related issues may usefully form the focus of future debates.

Acknowledgements

Many thanks to Brid Featherstone and Jeff Hearn who made suggestions helpful in the completion of this chapter.

References

Berg, B.J. (1978) *The Remembered Gate: Origins of American Feminism, the Woman and the City*, New York: Oxford University Press.

Cockburn, C. (1991) *In the Way of Women: Men's Resistance to Sex Equality in Organizations*, Basingstoke: Macmillan.

Findlay, C. (1987–8) 'Child abuse: the Dutch response', *Practice*, 1: 374–81.

Gordon, L. (1989) *Heroes of their own Lives: the Politics and History of Family Violence, Boston 1880–1960*, London: Virago.

Grimwood, C. and Popplestone, R. (1993) *Women, Management and Care*, Basingstoke: BASW/Macmillan.

Hallett, C. (1989) 'The gendered world of the social services department', in C. Hallett (ed.), *Women and Social Services Departments*, London: Harvester Wheatsheaf.

Hearn, J. (1992) *Men in the Public Eye: the Construction and Deconstruction of Public Men and Public Patriarchies*, London: Routledge.

Hearn, J. (1994) 'The organization(s) of violence: men, gender relations, organizations and violences', *Human Relations*, 47 (6): 731–54.

Howe, D. (1986) 'The segregation of women and their work in the personal social services', *Critical Social Policy*, 15: 21–35.

James, D. and Clarke, S. (1993) 'Women, men, and interruptions: a critical review', in D. Tannen (ed.), *Gender and Conversational Interaction*, Oxford: Oxford University Press.

James, D. and Drakich, J. (1993) 'Understanding gender differences in amount of talk: a critical review of research', in D. Tannen (ed.), *Gender and Conversational Interaction*, Oxford: Oxford University Press.

Kirkwood, A. (1993) *The Leicestershire Inquiry 1992*, Leicestershire: Leicestershire County Council.

Levy, A. and Kahan, B. (1991) *The Pindown Experience and the Protection of Children: the Report of the Staffordshire Child Inquiry 1990*, Stafford: Staffordshire County Council.

Lipman-Blumen, J. (1976) 'Towards a homosocial theory of sex-roles: an explanation of the sex segregation of social institutions', in A. Blaxall and B. Reagan (eds), *Women and the Workplace*, Chicago: University of Chicago.

Mitchell, J. (1979) *Psychoanalysis and Feminism*, 2nd edn, Harmondsworth: Pelican.

Moyer, B. and Tuttle, A. (eds) (1993) 'Overcoming masculine oppression in mixed groups', in *Off their Backs . . . and on their Own Two Feet*, Philadelphia: New Society Publishers.

Parton, N. and Small, N. (1989) 'Violence, social work and the emergence of dangerousness', in M. Langan and P. Lee (eds), *Radical Social Work Today*, London: Unwin Hyman.

Pinthus, E. (1982) 'Peace education', Quaker Peace and Service, reprinted from *Friends Quarterly*, Winter, London: Friends House.

Ramazanoglu, C. (1987) 'Sex and violence in academic life or you can keep a good woman down', in J. Hanmer and M. Maynard (eds), *Women, Violence and Social Control*, London: Macmillan.

Rojek, C., Peacock, G. and Collins, S. (1988) *Social Work and Received Ideas*, London: Routledge.

SSI/Department of Health (n.d.) *Women as Managers.*

SSI/Department of Health (1991) *Women in the Social Services: a Neglected Resource*, London: HMSO.

Walton, R.G. (1975) *Women in Social Work*, London: Routledge and Kegan Paul.

Wilson, E. (1977) *Women and the Welfare State*, London: Tavistock Publications.

Wise, S. and Stanley, L. (1990) 'Sexual harassment, sexual conduct and gender in social work settings', in P. Carter, T. Jeffs and M.K. Smith (eds), *Social Work and Social Welfare Yearbook 2*, Buckingham: Open University Press.

Younghusband, E. (1981) *The Newest Profession: a Short History of Social Work*, Community Care/IPC Business Press.

5

Gender and Power in Organizations

Wendy Hollway

This chapter is in contrast to the others because it takes as its central theme *power* and its relation to gender, rather than *violence* and its relation to gender. There is another difference in emphasis: whereas most of the chapters are looking at the clients of social services, or social workers' relations with clients, this chapter looks at the gendered power relations *within* an employment organization. A Social Services department is, in this sense, typical, since it is a largish bureaucratic organization, structured in a hierarchy. However, the fieldwork on this chapter comes from the Tanzanian civil service.[1]

Having outlined the differences in my subject matter, how can I justify its relevance? My purpose in talking about gendered power relations in a relatively non-violent setting (that is, in a setting where inequality and discrimination are usually reproduced without the use of what would be called 'violence', in common-sense terms) is to provide a perspective on power which identifies its multiplicity and the resulting contradictions and examines the differing potential for change in specific circumstances.

When is the exercise of power violent? Answers backed by theory have ranged from 'only rarely' to 'always'. Feminist analyses have emphasized the continuity between everyday patriarchal power and male violence, for example in rape and in domestic violence, and this has been a useful antidote to the wider tendency to see violence as something pathological and different from normal everyday gender relations. However, if no conceptual distinctions can be made between violence and power in patriarchal relations, there is a danger that mild and extreme forms of oppression are insufficiently distinguished. Moreover, it suggests a politics in which the exercise of power is eschewed for fear of being oppressive or for fear that being a 'villain' is worse than being a 'victim' of power.

Much depends on the way that power is defined, and in the next section I shall sketch different possible approaches and their effects. I shall then take the example of the 'glass ceiling', first to classify the approaches of the relevant literature and then to illustrate the concept of gendered power relations in an employment organization.

Power

Recent movements in social science theory, influenced considerably by Foucault, have revolved around challenges to notions of power traditionally conceptualized as 'an entity [which] may be ceded from one person to another and may be acquired by virtue of one's position within a social hierarchy or through sheer brute force'(Radtke and Stam, 1994: 2). In the traditional conception, power is a possession of individuals, albeit one that can be lost and gained. Force, violence or other necessarily negative power is not a defining characteristic; for example, Giddens defines power as 'the capability to secure outcomes where the realisation of these outcomes depends on the agency of others' (1979: 92). The benefits, or otherwise, of these outcomes, and to whom, is a question which can only be addressed in specific instances.

Violence is often seen as (and indeed used as) the inevitable backstop: 'if we/they don't get our/their way, we/they could be violent.' Definitions which rest on power as an individual possession, especially when applied to gender, support the traditional and common version which sees male power as resting on the possibility or threat of violence, propped up by patriarchal ideology, sex-role socialization, financial, legal and status inequalities, leading to women's subordination. When power is understood as a possession, the corollary is usually to juxtapose the powerful with the powerless. A now frequent criticism of the use of such a model of power within feminism – even if implicit or unintentional – is that it tends to construe women as victims[2] and hence to lose sight of women's own power (and, at the extreme, of women's own capacity for violence). Foucault explored an alternative approach in which power is seen as 'never in anybody's hands': 'individuals . . . are always in the position of simultaneously undergoing and exercising this power. They are not only its inert or consenting target; they are always also the elements of its articulation. In other words, individuals are the vehicles of power, not its points of application' (quoted in Radtke and Stam, 1994: 4).

Foucault's historical examples concentrated on the macro-level where the burgeoning of new 'technologies of power' in Europe from the eighteenth century demonstrated, according to Foucault, the multiplicity and productivity of power. My focus, in contrast, is on power in micro-social relations, in this case in the management hierarchies of bureaucratic organizations. However, from Foucault's and similar approaches, now commonly labelled post-modern views of power, I borrow three premises. First, power is productive and its effects are not necessarily negative. Secondly, it is multiple, not monolithic and in its multiplicity different expressions of power can contradict each other and offer openings for change. Thirdly, women, as well as men, exercise power as well as undergoing the effects of others' exercise of power, and women's actions may therefore serve to challenge gender discrimination or to reproduce it.

The charge is often mounted against post-modern views of power that, by fragmenting and multiplying power, different powers become seen as relative and the dominant and oppressive nature of patriarchal power cannot be recognized. I believe that it is still possible to understand the systematic character of women's subordination within the dominant patriarchal social forms. To say that women, too, have power is not to claim that it is equal or symmetrical to men's. However, it does encourage research to look at the specific ways in which power circulates in different social relations. The case of women managers is an example of women who are not powerless. Or, put another way, the organizational power created by a bureaucratic hierarchy and invested in specific posts circulates through women in their managerial social relations, though not in the gender-neutral way implied in the ideal type of rational, impersonal bureaucracy.

The 'Glass Ceiling'

The popularity of this metaphor for the obstacles which women face in reaching senior positions in the hierarchies of employment organizations is, I think, because it captures their invisibility. Typically, neither the women nor the men working in such hierarchies understand the nature of those obstacles. For this reason, the 'glass ceiling' is an interesting test case of the gendered workings of power. To understand how it works, it is important to see how it is possible for some women to breach it, as well as to understand the obstacles which mean that such a small number of women do so.

In the UK, equal opportunities policies and practices have provided one of the main channels through which workplace discrimination has been recognized and resisted. Because of the links to legislation and personnel practice, equal opportunities has concentrated on the formal organization; that is, those aspects of practice which are intended to be governed by explicit structures, rules and procedures. The expectation often is that, given time, a typical basket of interventions will result in equal numbers of women at senior levels. Such a basket usually includes the following (but, in my discussion, I shall only consider the interventions that relate specifically to women):

- recruitment and selection
- promotions
- personal harassment
- child-care facilities
- carer's leave
- flexible working
- physical access
- training
- monitoring

These are in the basket because there are things which the formal organization – specifically through personnel policy and practice – can do about them. Cockburn (1991) describes these as a relatively 'short agenda' of equal opportunities because they do not address the wider and deeper issues of gendered power relations or the structuring of work and domestic labour. However, even these interventions work in different ways and thus have different effects on the goal of equal treatment for discriminated-against groups. The provision of *physical access* for disabled people is a question of resourcing changes to infrastructure. Its absence denies access to the organization's services and to its employment opportunities. *Selection, promotion and training*, all informed by *monitoring*, have often been seen as crucial, because a set of technical procedures can be generated whereby the bureaucratic administration can achieve a reach into actual practice without affecting the basic structuring of work organization. For example, a precise job specification, against whose criteria all applicants can be judged, and those judgements recorded, is now the central tenet of equal opportunities selection practice in British organizations with an equal opportunities policy. Similarly, *promotion* panels should judge all candidates 'objectively' against a common set of job-related criteria. The problem with this model is that it attempts to regulate decision and judgement according to notions of bureaucratic rationality which conceive of power only as something which is exercised through formal channels, and can therefore be subverted. For example, it is not uncommon for gendered power relations actually to modify formal structures, for example, when a woman is appointed to a key position and finds that certain responsibilities formerly associated with the post are exercised by others (men), in a new structural configuration.

Child-care facilities, carer's leave and *flexible working* are aspects of practice which can also be influenced by formal changes in structures, rules and procedures. However, they are frequently regarded as more difficult to introduce because they challenge the traditional structure of work (which historically has been dominated by men). Moreover, for their success, they depend on the interface between the work organization and the domestic sphere: for example, will men as well as women take parental leave and choose part-time work in order to fit in child and family care? If not, if the wider gendered division of labour between the spheres of paid employment and the domestic sphere is not disturbed, will flexible working provisions only serve to reproduce women's subordinate status in the labour market? The personnel department can work bureaucratically to do what is seen to be in the interests of effective (and preferably fair) management of the workforce, but major changes in the structures of work which disadvantage women are outside its remit; in particular, the gendered division of domestic labour.

Personal harassment is usually the only equal opportunities issue on which the formal organization has attempted to regulate informal social relations in the workplace, through, for example, codes of practice and grievance procedures. Sexual harassment, more than any other sex discrimination issue, has begun to make visible gendered power relations in the workplace. It is also the issue which demonstrates those relations in their most blatant form, a form which sometimes borders on violence. However, because the kind of sexual relations which are characteristic of sexual harassment are so deeply inscribed into the wider culture of gender relations, it is also an area which requires the regulation of everyday, informal social relations and therefore largely eludes personnel policy.

In summary, equal opportunities is a product of bureaucratic principles which, with the partial exception of sexual harassment, focus on the formal organization. In contrast, the literature on the 'glass ceiling', and more broadly the women in management literature, has emphasized other aspects of power relations in organizations which discriminate against women, almost all of them informal: for example, women's absence from informal male networks and venues and the differential availability of mentors to men and women who are seeking promotion. This is a literature which emphasizes visibility to those higher up the hierarchy, know-who as well as know-how, as crucial in the informal power relations which influence career and promotion. It understands employment organizations (in practice it deals only with managerial relations) as places where power circulates inevitably through the micro-social relations of individuals who call on all modes of power at their disposal, every minute of the day, to be effective and advance themselves. However, this literature has unfortunately left out an analysis of the systematic nature of gendered power relations, and does not make the link to material structures like the gendered divisions of labour inside and outside employment organizations, preferring to believe that women can go through the 'glass ceiling' by acquiring the same resources and capacities as men: for example, assertiveness, mentors and informal networks.

Both the equal opportunities and the women-in-management (WiM) approaches plausibly reflect certain features of organizational discrimination against women. Their differences from each other are striking, forged by their different histories: the equal opportunities approach is predominantly home-grown and public sector, while the WiM approach is an American import and is private sector inspired. On top of these differences, however, the equal opportunities approach treats the *formal* organization, while the WiM approach treats the *informal* organization.

Since power circulates through both formal and informal channels, and since these do not necessarily pull in the same direction, the uneven workings of the formal and informal practices affecting women's access to promotion produce contradictions which are potential sites of change. A strong bureaucracy which has embraced equal opportunities can be effective on issues which are part of the short agenda and create contradictions in the dominant gendered power relations which can provide potential locations for women's advancement.

Contradiction

Elsewhere (Hollway, 1994), I have examined in more detail the effects on Tanzanian women civil servants of the breakdown of the working of the formal bureaucratic procedures in relation to unequal access to training, appraisals, developmental work experiences and promotion decisions. My conclusion was: 'that a formal bureaucracy which is based on principles of gender equality is undermined in practice by the gendered power relations of the organization and its wider cultural context. Bureaucratic organiz-ation usually provides a site of contradiction between the two' (Hollway, 1994: 253). One way of summarizing this contradiction is as follows:

> Women exercise managerial authority despite – or in the midst of – one basic contradiction. On the one hand, they occupy a defined place in the hierarchy which prescribes lines of authority and responsibility over subordinates and accountability to bosses. On the other hand, gender difference systematically prescribes power relations in which men expect to have authority over women. (Hollway, 1991: 3)

In what follows, I use three examples to explore this contradiction. They derive from interviews with three different women managers in the Tanzanian Civil Service:

> They work alright for me, so long as I give them work and everything is in order. But in my view, men, deep down, they're not so happy that their bosses are women.

> My subordinates cooperate very well with me and they respect me as their boss and because they know my abilities. As you grow older, they respect your age. I am fortunate because my decisions are accepted by both seniors and juniors.

> I am working with a male officer who is anti-women. I once went for special duties in the region and left written handing-over notes on what was supposed to be covered while I was out. When I came back, everything was untouched. When I enquired, he said that he did not touch anything because he will not take instructions from a woman.

These are responses which represent varying degrees of success in exercising managerial authority over subordinates who include men. Why does the third one fail and the second apparently succeed with ease? The first example illustrates the central contradiction: the woman manager is aware of a tension resulting from the conventions of patriarchal relations, but her formal position, given by the hierarchical structure of the organization, and backed up by such features as her qualifications and professional experience, and probably personal credibility, means that her managerial authority is not obstructed. In the second example, one could be forgiven for thinking that the formal bureaucracy has reduced gendered power relations to an irrelevance, so much so that this informant, her authority enhanced with increasing years, does not even think to dis-tinguish between subordinates according to sex.

The woman in the third example fails to secure the intended outcomes despite the fact that the power to instruct another officer is conferred on her as legitimate authority attached to whoever occupies her formal position in the hierarchy. Despite the illegitimacy (in formal organizational terms) of his refusal, the man resists. Where does he derive the power from which to do so?

Gendered power relations have deep historical roots in the patriarchal family and the history of the organization of work reveals how profoundly those gendered power relations have been inscribed in employment organizations (Hollway, 1996). This power manifests both in the structuring of work – for example, the horizontal and vertical segregation of women and men – and also at the level of the psyche, such that his masculinity may be threatened if a man accedes to a woman's authority, even when the formal hierarchy requires that structure of command. This man presumably derives legitimacy for his refusal to take orders from a woman from the wider patriarchal culture, from which the organization is not exempt. To the extent that this is the case, other men will commonly identify with him, and therefore be likely to support his actions, thus reproducing men's and women's positions in the patriarchal family culture inside the organization.

However, this patriarchal family culture tends to come into conflict with the organization's attempts to formalize management practice. Hence the central contradiction for women managers' exercising of authority is often between the power conferred by the formal and the informal organization. The former is in principle gender neutral, but still dependent on the cooperation or compliance of senior male employees in particular. The latter is saturated with patriarchal principles and practices. However, the picture is more complex than an opposition between two powers, one working for women and one working against.

Given the existence of a clash of powers pulling in different directions, there will be different consequences, depending on the wider constellation of powers. One outcome, quite possible in a public sector organization in the UK (such as a Social Services department) may be that, for example, equal opportunities promotion practices take root firmly to become an accepted part of bureaucratic principles. Alternatively, where bureaucratic principles are widely ignored in practice, decision-making may evade formalization and move to locations where it is held in a net of informal social relations. As one Tanzanian woman said 'They [the men] meet in the club and next morning, his file moves.'

In the Tanzanian case, without equal opportunities legislation or a history of equal opportunities practices, women would be unwise to depend on the fair working of bureaucratic principles if they seek advancement. They may, however, use whatever informal social powers are available to them as women. For example, one woman experienced her marital status as advantageous in several ways:

> The fact that I was married to the regional Party boss was important. I was promoted as a result of my husband's position. Then when we moved to Dar es Salaam, my husband was no longer a regional Party boss . . . but with the

contacts previously made I was promoted. My boss was a man. He was capable of listening to me. I took initiative on a lot of things and I always got his approval. He was also my husband's friend.

In many cultures, a woman's social status is dependent on her being married (and having children) and the wives of elite, powerful men derive enormous power as wives (the 'first lady' syndrome). In the above case, the woman achieved a cooperative professional relationship, as a result of which her managerial authority and career prospects were enhanced. However, her power is dependent upon being 'owned' by one man and upon the primacy of two men's relationship in which she is an object of exchange. A different man expressed it as follows: 'it is difficult to work genuinely with a woman for fear that people might have the wrong ideas. But the women I work with, I know their husbands and they [the husbands] have a great trust in me.' A further contradiction is evident here, one located within the multiplicity of powers characteristic of informal social relations. Women who draw on such resources as marital and family status gain individual power and advantage. They are precisely the ones who, in the Tanzanian context, are most likely to break through the 'glass ceiling'. However, dependence on such resources reproduces women's structural positions within patriarchal relations.

The same relations of ownership may advantage a woman at the same time as they entail minor or major sacrifices or compromises. For example, one woman, who had achieved a great deal of independence, still had to be careful of her husband: 'I never give him cause for alarm. I'm very particular before I travel . . . I never give him surprises. So I try as much as possible to respect him as head of the household.' Another chose to sacrifice one way of networking professionally in order to protect her marriage: 'Such clubs are good [for networking], but I am not a member. When I tried to join the club, my husband became suspicious.'

These are not examples which can be understood simply at the level of individual husband's jealousies (although there are significant individual differences). Women's freedom of movement is not only constrained by child care, but by strong traditions about women's proper place being in the private sphere and a husband's authority over that:

> There's limited movement for women in association just for the sake of it. If I want to meet a woman friend, there's no way I can nip out of my house and just meet her, unexpectedly, like my husband can. And I do think that meeting friends in social clubs is very relevant to your career.

Within the social relations in which she is positioned, such constraints may be experienced as a woman's choice: 'In our society, if you're a female officer, you have to think twice before going to the pub. With my husband, it was OK. But we thought it was best for me to keep in.'

In summary, women managers negotiate their power to be effective in their jobs within a complex set of conditions, both social and psychological, which offer them greater or lesser access to multiple powers, which may be pulling in diverse directions. All three women are subject to the systematic gendered power which has produced women's traditional subordination to male authority, but because of their multiple positions, through which different powers circulate, individual women are more or less likely to transcend the effects of a dominant constellation of powers which would rob them of their capacity to exercise managerial authority and their power to obtain promotion.

The sources of power available to Tanzanian women include other dimensions of social difference (for example, age, education, class, marital or family status), which interact with gender, as well as the formal powers attached to their positions in the employing organization. Paradoxically, some of the powers they may choose to exercise, such as the patronage of a powerful husband or brother, reproduce the traditional position of women as objects of exchange in a patriarchal economy, and in so doing reproduce a set of constraints on their independent status.

Notes

1. In Tanzania, there is nothing equivalent to the British equal opportunities legislation, but there is a tradition of socialist legislation and, more recently, following the end of the International Decade for Women in 1985, pressure from aid agencies to increase the number of women in positions of leadership.

2. The recent importation of certain American feminists for high-profile British media comment has revolved around their representation of British feminists as 'women [who] could have everything if they would only stop seeing themselves as victims' (Coward, 1994, commenting on *The Sunday Times* coverage).

References

Cockburn, C. (1991) *In the Way of Women: Men's Resistance to Sex Equality in Organizations*, London: Macmillan.

Coward, R. (1994) *Everywoman*, March: 12.

Giddens, A. (1979) *Central Problems in Social Theory*, London: Macmillan.

Hollway,W. (1991) 'Advantages and disadvantages for women managing', *The Journal for Women in Organisations and Management*, 1: 2–7.

Hollway,W. (1994) 'Separation, integration and difference: contradictions in a gender regime', in L. Radtke and H. Stam (eds), *Power/Gender*, London: Sage.

Hollway,W. (1996) 'Masculinities and managements in the transition from factory hands to sentimental workers', in D. Collinson and J. Hearn (eds), *The Men of Management*, London: Sage.

Radtke, L. and Stam, H. (eds) (1994) *Power/Gender*, London: Sage.

6

Women, Mental Health and Community Care: an Abusive Combination?

Barbara Fawcett

Mental health and community care are broad areas which affect all of us in many diverse ways. With regard to mental health, there is considerable disagreement about what constitutes mental health for women. Similarly, when considering mental distress, it can be argued that the distinguishing features relate to individual and sociocultural perceptions and manifestations, to social norms and accepted responses, rather than to phenomena which can be objectively defined. 'Community care' is also a ubiquitous term. It applies to all of us in that we are all affected by 'community', however interpreted and we all in various ways and to varying extents, in private and public spheres, give and receive 'care'. The pertinent question which this chapter poses and seeks to address is: how exploitative, oppressive and, indeed, abusive can such combinations be for women?

A major difficulty in exploring such contested and multifaceted areas is deciding where to start and on which aspects to focus. For the purposes of this chapter, I have decided to adopt a framework which allows an examination of general and specific features and also permits enquiry into the interrelationships which operate. This framework utilizes a notion of the public and the private and the interface between.

Hearn (1992) emphasizes the cross-overs between the public and the private and maintains that neither is impermeable nor unbroachable. He also points to the different meanings that public and private have in different analyses. The recognition that such terms are open to numerous interpretations is of great significance for this exploration. Indeed, notions of public and private are not being used in a definitive way, but to facilitate an exploration of issues relating to women, community care and mental health.

Notions of Community Care

Community care has been regarded by writers such as Fiona Williams (1993) as the interface between public and private. She interprets the interface as an area which is 'double edged' in that it can be viewed as 'the space where women can begin to define and determine their own needs and conditions for existence' and the area where women 'know their place' – 'the outer limits of women's restriction to domestic duties' where limited access can be provided to an independent income and way of life (Williams, 1993: 33). This view highlights the opportunities and constraints posed by both community care as a concept and the interpretations of the NHS and Community Care Act 1990 by local authorities and health authorities. It also alludes to tensions and contradictions. These become even more apparent when reviewing perspectives of community care.

Community care is defined in the White Paper 'Caring for People' (Department of Health, 1989), which informs the 1990 Act, as 'providing the services and support which people who are affected by problems of ageing, mental illness, mental handicap or physical or sensory disabilities need to be able to live as independently as possible in their own homes or in "homely" settings in the community' (Department of Health, 1989: 3: 1.1). Community care, so defined, has been predominantly seen as care by women in their private capacities as family carers and in their public capacities as paid carers within health and social services organizations. It is useful to examine care in relation to these two broad domains in more detail.

Private Caring

With regard to private caring relationships, the view that 'care' is exclusively the preserve and domain of women has been overturned by the work of researchers such as Green (1988) and Arber and Gilbert (1989). Nevertheless, while such studies emphasize the caring responsibilities undertaken by men, particularly by spouses for their wives, there is also an acknowledgement that women are more likely to be full-time carers and that married women engaged in caring relationships receive far less support than single men or women and married men. Perceptions of family feature strongly in reviews of caring relationships in the private sphere, with interpretations and prescriptions relating to value and belief systems. Many feminist writers have viewed the family as sanctioning, reinforcing and reproducing patterns of patriarchal relations which emphasize women's roles as carers and family servicers. Consequently, collectivist solutions have been promoted for those requiring assistance. Finch and Groves (1983) and, more specifically, Gillian Dalley (1988) have high-lighted the benefits of communal living for those requiring personal assistance. Dalley views communal living as providing opportunities for collective action and mutual support and regards the potential availability of a number of personal assistants as a means of increasing autonomy while at the same time relieving strain on personal relationships. Other feminist writers question assumed divisions of 'carer' and 'cared for', and empha-size that women with impairments also care. Jenny Morris highlights how older women and women with disabilities have been marginalized by much feminist literature on care. She also does not view communal living quite as positively as Gillian Dalley, maintaining that if 'communal living is such a liberating force for women, then perhaps non-disabled women should try it first' (Morris, 1993b: 161).

Opie (1992) similarly critiques those feminist analyses which have viewed caring as singularly exploitative. She draws from qualitative research she conducted into the everyday experiences of 28 family caregivers, caring for elderly confused spouses or relatives at home in 1990. Accordingly, she asserts that caregivers cannot be represented as 'uniformly (monolithically) exploited or alternatively uniformly (monolithically) willing'. Her research indicates that relationships are constantly open to change and that interpretations of the nature of the relationship continually fluctuate. She also found a plethora of factors which affected perceptions such as generational positioning, age, gender, ideology, prior experience of acting as caregiver, the past and current relationship with the elderly person, and the ability to command resources (Opie, 1992).

Hilary Graham (1993) also warns against singular interpretations. She recognizes that dominant patterns of informal care are linked to the nuclear family but emphasizes the importance of acknowledging other caring relationships. She points to lesbian and gay relationships, particularly with reference to AIDS and to domestic service roles and responsibilities. She also highlights the struggles that many black women have wrestling with racism and immigration laws and trying to bring families together (Graham, 1993). Similarly, critiques of the family have been tempered by writers such as Bhavnani and Coulson (1986) with regard to black women. They emphasize that, although inequalities exist within black households, they are also clearly sites of support for women confronting racism on a daily basis.

Public Caring

The NHS and the public sector are major employers of women generally and black women in particular, yet women are concentrated into the lower echelons (Mama, 1989) and predominate in caring roles (Department of Employment, 1991). Mama (1989) also emphasizes that not only are many women in limited and constraining jobs which relate to stereotypical assumptions about what women do, but that many women are also involved in implementing policies and practices which overall serve to disadvantage women. In particular, Mama targets welfare services and highlights, as do many others (for example, Rojek et al., 1988; Williams, 1992), the ways in which welfare services have never actually been related to citizen's rights but have functioned as privileges delivered differentially to different groups by custodians of public resources. Accordingly, access to welfare provision has related to the notion of the family prevailing at the time of Beveridge and still, despite evidence to the contrary, dogmatically adhered to today. Such notions have both institutionalized and individualized value judgements related to practices seen as acceptable and have also discriminated between deserving and undeserving individuals and groups. Such value judgements, Mama maintains, have invariably been racist.

In reviewing these contradictions and asking why women appear to participate directly and indirectly in their own oppression, Mama offers a range of explanations. She refers to women needing to safeguard their jobs to sustain their families, subscription to the prevailing overt and covert ethos of organizations, sometimes resulting in private anxiety, and the insidious and multifarious nature of the areas requiring challenging.

Indeed, organizational responses to gender and sexuality are critically important areas to consider. With regard to women in professional and managerial capacities, Deborah Sheppard (1989), commenting on interviews carried out with 34 women and 16 men in managerial and professional organizations in Canada, highlighted the important part played by the management of sexuality and gender in the 'construction and enactment of organizational power'. In her survey nearly all those interviewed saw gender as a factor at work and the focus was primarily on femaleness being a problem for women. Male organizational behaviour was seen as the norm and women saw themselves with varying degrees of consciousness as having to manage themselves, their behaviour, dress, emotions, relationships with peers and superiors in ways compatible with the organizational ethos or 'malestream', in order to achieve and maintain credibility. In terms of sexuality, the prevailing view was of having to blend in, to manage sexuality by a process of desexualization which meant adherence to a virtual uniform which displayed the required amount of heterosexual femininity overlaid by a business-like status enforcing polish. Sheppard acknowledges that such strategies can enable some women to reap traditional male rewards such as power, status and wealth, yet highlights that all women continue to remain vulnerable despite their achievements in that their sexuality can always be used against them as a method of control through humiliation or discomfort. Similar processes can occur with regard to all those perceived to be different by virtue of race, disability, sexual orientation and other categories usually referred to by a process of 'commatization' (O'Brien, 1984).

Sheppard's work highlights some of the difficulties and contradictions women face in challenging oppressive practices which simultaneously they may also be involved in perpetuating. In a review of public care it is also useful to examine the responses of organizations with a 'caring' remit, such as Social Services departments, to employees with caring responsibilities. A survey I carried out (Fawcett, 1994) of 60 Social Services departments in England, randomly selected, showed that only a small minority had considered this area in any detail. These departments were considering introducing supportive procedures to clarify the position of those with private caring responsibilities. However, for the majority, the taking of annual leave or applying for compassionate leave were the only options. The granting of compassionate leave appeared highly discretionary and was usually subject to a fixed upper limit of approximately 10 days per annum. This response can perhaps be taken to be indicative of the organizational separation of public and private caring spheres.

Women and Mental Health: Public Illness, Private Distress

It can be argued that mental illness and mental distress relate more to perspective and interpretation than to differentiating features. In Britain, as in many Western societies, we have systems which function to administer to those who decide that they need professional help and those seen to be in need of assistance with regard to their own health or safety or where they are seen to threaten that of others. In Britain, again as in many other Western countries, the medical model is the approach which predominates in terms of language, interpretation, classification and response. Indeed, individuals believing themselves to have mental health problems are invariably advised to contact their GPs as their first port of call. Subsequent referrals to medically trained psychiatrists tend to depend on severity and the GP's interpretation of the problem. Barnes and Maple (1992), in a review of research findings, suggest that GPs define more women as suffering from mental health difficulties than men and that more women are referred on for specialist psychiatric help. However, linked to this, as Barnes and Maple (1992) point out, is the consideration that women are generally more likely to identify problems as emotional and consult GPs about their health than men. Research carried out into the operation of the 1983 Mental Health Act (Barnes et al., 1990) and the study carried out by Michael Sheppard (1991) have also shown more women than men being referred for assessment for compulsory admission. For married people in particular, the rate of both referral and admission is higher for married women than for men. As Barnes et al. (1990) maintain 'more women than men were in situations which would not normally be regarded as indicative of risk' (Barnes et al., 1990: 139).

The reasons posited for the above are many and various. Broverman et al.'s (1970) famous study, highlights how definitions of mental health which view a typically healthy adult in terms of stereotypical and idealized male characteristics, puts women in what is essentially a 'no win' situation. If a woman conforms to the stereotypical, idealized view of womanhood, she is found not to be mentally healthy; if she deviates, she is found to be not only mentally unhealthy but a potential threat to the established order. Both views cite women generally as being in need of care and control. Theories of development which fail to acknowledge women's tendency for interdependence on others, stressing instead independence and separation as being mature adult qualities, have also been viewed as contributing towards women being perceived as having more mental health problems than men. The consequences of this have been emphasized by Kaplan and Surrey (1986) and Barnes and Maple (1992) among others. Other writers have variously emphasized how 'malestream' perceptions and 'malestream' dominance in the medical and indeed in the public sphere have served to condition or pressure women into accepting roles which may not be conducive to their mental health. This has in turn suppressed the voices of women urging alternative interpretations and responses (Oakley, 1981; Eichenbaum and Orbach, 1983; Ussher, 1991; Barnes and Maple, 1992; Gorman, 1992). Busfield (1989: 360), in a review of prevailing perspectives, stresses the importance of 'examining both the complex ways in which sexism may affect constructs and judgements within the mental health field and the complex ways in which social relations generate mental sickness'.

It can perhaps be asserted at this point, that the defining of a psychiatric condition, however problematic the process for women, serves to make public, private mental distress. A further interesting observation is that, while definitions of mental health tend to view women as being in need of care and control, community care policies and legislation place emphasis on women as caregivers and stress their responsibilities for the care and control of others. Mental health and community care systems also appear to fail to give attention to the context, complexities, contradictions and interrelated factors relevant to women's lives.

Overall, an important thread which can be drawn from the discussion so far, relates to the contributions made by differing and contradictory perspectives. The complexity of any investigation becomes clear, as does the danger of regarding any one of these perspectives as definitive and pertaining to 'the truth'. The interpretations reviewed also emphasize that we cannot view either community care or mental health issues as being separate from us, as being 'over there'. Public and private aspects of both affect all of us on an ongoing basis. Furthermore, general perspectives drawn from broad areas are important in that they focus attention and facilitate studies which locate individuals in social, cultural and historical contexts. However, there are obvious dangers in reducing complex areas to broad brush statements and then applying them to all women, regarding women as a unitary group. Concentration on commonalities is important, but the processes involved in making links and the basis on which such links are made, can mark the divide between the empowering and the abusive. For example, emphasis on links between women and depressive illnesses depend for their significance on how the links are made. Are the links made by women and professionals in ways which locate debilitating aspects in a holistic context which is regarded as fluid and subject to change or in a manner which focuses on the classification 'depression' and relates, interprets and fixes positions in relation to this?

The Public and Private: Categorization Processes and Experiences

The discussion now turns to these issues because categorization as a process can be seen to permeate legislative, professional and individual interpretations of community care and mental health. Experience can conversely be viewed as a means of countering and opposing such categorizing processes. Undoubtedly, 'categorization' and 'experience' are terms with many meanings, which can be seen as acting and interacting at the interface between public and private spheres. In a further review of the original question posed, how exploitative, oppressive and abusive can combinations such as mental health and community care be for women? A review of how these terms are used becomes pertinent. Connell (1985) in 'Theorising gender' coins the term 'categoricalism' to refer to a general acceptance of fixed gender categories, and Hester Eisenstein (1984, quoted in Connell, 1985) emphasizes the 'false universalism' of categorical thought. Overall categories can be very broad as in the categories 'men' and 'women' and reasonably broad as in the categories or sub-categories 'black women', 'disabled women', 'lesbian women' and other 'commatizations'. Categories can be projected from without, defined by others for others or be self-chosen.

Processes of Projected Categorization

The processes involved in categorizing from without or projected categorization, tend to fix, typify, impose uniformity and define individuals or groups on the basis of simplistic defining features or labels. Such features can relate to being female, mentally ill, black, disabled or old. As Finkelstein (1993) asserts, these points of definition can also be taken on board and internalized by those being categorized. Connell (1985) maintains that generalizing from categories such as 'men' and 'women' has been expressed in shifts of language, for example, 'malestream language' and 'malestream thought'. He states that what happens in such associations is the coupling of a social fact or process with a biological fact. The result, he maintains, is to collapse together a heterogeneous group. Accordingly, such universalist associations take the heat off, for example, individual men who maintain particularly oppressive positions towards women. The blame is placed on all men who are categorized and singly defined as oppressive, and individual men or groupings cannot by implication be held to account.

Connell's analysis is a useful critique of the application of universalist perspectives. However, generalizing from categories can, provided universalist claims to validity are not made, be seen as a useful way of referring to perceived prevailing norms, such as 'malestream' organizational practices. Such generalizations can then serve to trigger off further analyses and enquiry which can be located in context, utilizing plural rather than unitary notions of, for example, women and taking account of the complexities involved.

It can be asserted that 'categoricalism' and categorizing processes play a large part in assumptions and operating procedures and practices in the arenas of mental health and community care. In Social Services departments such processes can be found in the creation of client groups and in associated responses related to assessment, service provision and resource allocation. The NHS and Community Care Act 1990, and accompanying circulars and guidance, emphasize a 'needs led' service for those whose requirements are complex, yet the indications are that the systems of care management envisaged as providing a 'needs led' service remain differentially constituted according to client group. The grouping of individuals in relation to simple defining features (age, mental illness, disability etc.) tends to be justified on the grounds of administrative necessity and resource allocation. However, the implications for individuals are often overlooked. These include the use of prefixes such as 'the' which differentiate, separate and reduce in status individuals so categorized from others. Service user involvement also, interpreted by many agencies as referring to consultative rather than empowering processes (see Croft and Beresford, 1990; Beresford and Croft, 1993), can also degenerate into individuals being co-opted onto committees to represent all others placed in the same category in a 'Godfather' (GLACHC, 1992) approach. In this context, the processes of categorization can be viewed as a form of group labelling and an administratively convenient way of packaging individuals and determining responses. Similarly, it appears that systems of care management which favour an administrative approach not only fail to address, but actively promote, systems which relate to categories rather than individuals (Biggs, 1991; Challis et al., 1993; Morris, 1993b).

Categorization, as a process, can be applied to all of us. However, there is a tendency for this process to be applied disproportionately to those who differ from accepted 'norms'. What constitutes accepted norms is a much debated question. To adopt a categorical perspective, accepted norms can be viewed as categories or more pertinently as absent categories which reflect white, middle-class, heterosexual 'malestream' power. According to Foucault (1981b), accepted norms reflect the operation of dominant discourses, such discourses achieving or maintaining dominance by means of institutional sanction.

In the arena of mental health, assignment to the category 'mentally ill' can all too quickly lead to a diagnostic label defining an individual or group, with all other factors or features rendered invisible. It is also possible in relation to psychiatry to read classification for category. The processes involved remain similar, although with regard to classification there is also recourse to 'scientific authenticity' and 'objectivity'. It is claimed that diagnostic classification systems, such as the DSM111, minimize individual value judgements based on prevailing norms and negate bias related to gender, sexuality or racism. Other commentators dismiss these claims (for example, Fernando, 1991; Ussher, 1991; Madigan, 1992) and point to a general refusal within psychiatry to address issues of bias and to question the much asserted validity of diagnostic criteria. However, once classified, either individually or as part of a group, the labelling process is a factor to be taken into account. Accordingly, once a label has been acquired, all subsequent actions are interpreted in the light of that label. Autonomous action and challenge as a result become increasingly difficult.

A current example of this process relates to the association of people classified as suffering from schizophrenia with violence and dangerousness, both in the media and in the public imagination. Those diagnosed as having this condition become 'schizophrenics' and, although there is no evidence that random attacks by schizophrenics are increasing, merely to refer to an individual so categorized is to paint a picture of a homicidal maniac. This then affects professional and service responses with the emphasis being on control, containment, medication and the registration and supervision of those seen to pose a significant risk to themselves or others. Such responses can rule out the possibility of an interactive dialogue about self-assessed needs, professionally assessed needs and available resources. As empha-sized above, they can also result in the allocation of such resources as are made available in ways which respond to the category not the individual.

The above exploration is intended to raise issues, to highlight areas of contradiction, to emphasize the implications of categorizing processes and to further open up accepted practices for review and challenge. At this point it is useful to review some current initiatives. A challenge to the making public of private distress can be seen in the calls made by a community-based mental health group in Wolverhampton for mental health services for young Asian women to be informal, supportive and accessible. Current services are viewed as too clinical and restrictive in terms of choice. The focus on assessment and labelling is regarded as having a devastating effect on a young woman's family and upon employ-ment prospects. Accordingly, a holistic approach which is culturally sensitive and based on a social rather than a medical model is advocated (Marchant, 1994: 18). Similarly, drawing from the death of Jonathan Zito by Christopher Clunis in December 1992 (reported on by the Ritchie Inquiry, Department of Health, 1994), the mental health organization Mind is campaigning for rights to community care. This is about challeng-ing the ways in which community care policies are being implemented and managed and resources allocated. The focus is on ways of proceeding which are 'bottom up' rather than 'top down'. This re-orientation is of great significance. Nevertheless, the ways in which collective views are applied, remains of prime importance. If 'bottom up' views are generalized and applied to service users in a uniform, rigid and non-context specific way, the individuals are yet again being categorized and projected into groups on the basis of simple defining features and responded to accordingly.

Fiona Williams (1992) suggests that as a result of the contradictions evident in the 'supermarket' rhetoric applied to community care imple-mentation, and the emphasis on quality control and assurance and consumer choice, individuals and movements have been given the space to push for their demands. However, it is an opportunity which has to be grasped quickly. Despite the rhetoric, consumers do not have actual choices as it is third parties who negotiate and make decisions on their behalf. Similarly, the NHS and Community Care Act makes it clear that assessments for services are professional assessments not self-assessments. The opportunities for negotiation are left to the discretion of the assessor. Nevertheless, the Act can be read as providing opportunities as well as the all too obvious restraints of which resources are a part.

Self-categorization Processes

With regard to self-categorization, Valerie Jenness (1992) provides a useful overview of recent developments. She reviews self-categorization processes in terms of the development of lesbian identities and criticizes how categories can be typified to become 'unexamined understandings . . . oversimplified opinions and images' (Jenness, 1992: 67). However, she does not view categorization and typification as being necessarily synonymous. With regard to self-categorization, she maintains that initially we interpret our world in terms of social categories and that categories recognized by the community indicate the sorts of people it is possible to be. However, we do not self-categorize on the basis of typified categories but by subjecting categories to a process of detypification. This allows for the redefinition of socially constructed categories in relation to how they relate to perceived experiences and biographical contingencies. The congruence of the imagery with individual lived experiences and how positively the categories are viewed is also important. Jenness (1992) also emphasizes the interrelationship between self-categorization and identity formation and regards both as being continually in process.

Processes of Categorization and Oppression

The discussion so far has focused upon how categorizing processes are used. The links between processes of categorization, projected and self-chosen and processes of oppression now require review.

With regard to projected forms of categorization, Brah (1992) re-emphasizes the consequences of individuals being projected into categories on the basis of 'race' and of projected characteristics and differences between categories being viewed as fixed. Accordingly, categories of difference when viewed in terms of accepted value categories or 'norms' become devalued and can be viewed by recipients as categories of oppression. She also identifies a process whereby individuals challenge and re-value projected fixed differences or defining features, but in turn, fix and naturalize differences between themselves and others, or other groupings. An example of this can relate to how people viewed as mentally ill and classified as suffering from depression can be engaged in challenging their label, but at the same time still negatively view as different others classified as 'manic depressives'.

With regard to self-categorization processes linked to notions of experience and identity, the situation is also fraught with difficulty. The popular feminist slogan of the 1980s that the personal is political emphasizes the linking of the private with the public and clearly politicizes experiences and identity. Writers such as Clara Connolly (1990) and Mary Louise Adams (1989) describe the political fragmentation that ensued when women, as a means of recognizing oppressions and moving away from the dominating perspective of white, middle-class heterosexual women, located them-selves in a hierarchical framework that legitimized through naming oppressions. As Ardill and O'Sullivan (1986: 33) point out, 'just to name yourself as part of a given group is to claim a moral backing for your words and actions.' The consequences of claiming legitimacy by citing validating oppressive categories, then using personal experience as a reliable guide to truth have been highlighted by Adams (1989: 30): 'To get our spot on the balance sheet, we spend more time trying to demonstrate our oppression than we do dismantling it.'

The issues raised here can apply to service user groups engaged in challenging processes of categorization. If individuals categorized as mentally ill, or disabled, attempt to revalue the label by citing individual experiences, then competition for who has the most claim to challenge the label can militate against cooperation and fragment emergent groupings. Also recourse to forms of pluralism can, as Gayatri Chakravorty Spivak asserts, be used by central authorities to neutralize opposition by seeming to accept it. 'The gesture of pluralism on the part of the marginal can only mean capitulation to the centre' (Spivak, quoted in Barrett, 1987: 32). Alternatively, if collective experience is used (that is, experience of being categorized as mentally ill or disabled), then not only can groupings representing different collective experiences (the old, mentally ill etc.) be forced into competition with other groupings, for resources which remain scarce, but disagreements can ensue as to how the collective experience is publicized and politicized and which aspects and specific experiences are promoted.

Possible ways forward out of such conundrums may hinge on interpret-ations of 'experience'. If experience is viewed as essentialist, as uniquely applicable to a specific individual and is utilized on this basis, then problems remain. However, if experience is regarded as a 'constellation of mediated relationships, a site of contradictions to be addressed collectively', with emphasis placed on the 'need to re-emphasise a notion of experience not as an unmediated guide to "truth" but as a practice of making sense, both symbolically and narratively; as a struggle over material conditions and over meaning' (Brah, 1992: 141), then avenues for exploration emerge. Such an interpretation stresses processes such as negotiation, facilitation, strategic planning and pragmatic groupings rather than pro-cesses which emphasize essentialist differences and categories.

Michel Foucault: Contributions to the Discussion

So far, it has been argued that the meanings of 'community care' and 'mental health' are contestable and that a combination of these terms may be more or less exploitative, abusive and oppressive for women depending upon how they are used and the processes of categorization employed. To take the discussion further, it is necessary to explore relations of power, and here in particular the work of Michel Foucault is particularly pertinent.

On first examining Foucault's work, it is perhaps a surprise to note that he conceptualizes power as something which is in the hands of the seemingly powerless and not just in the hands of those with legal, professional or bureaucratic authority. It is this perspective of power which is so useful to us in making sense of the constellations of meaning around community care and mental health and the differing positions of women in relation to these areas.

According to Foucault, power cannot be viewed as a thing which some individuals or groups possess and others do not; rather, it can only be viewed in relational terms and as such is ever present. He also views power as productive, rather than repressive and as operating from the 'bottom up' rather than from the 'top down' (Sawicki, 1991). By this he refers to power operating in a low-profile manner at the micro-level in everyday social practices, rather than requiring a high-profile presence to enforce it. By 'social practices' he is referring to 'places where what is said and what is done, rules imposed and reasons given, the planned and taken for granted meet and interconnect' (Foucault, 1981b: 5). Overall, Foucault is interested in 'how' questions, related to how power manifested in social practices operates, not in 'why' questions, exploring why they operate as they do. As a result, as Nancy Fraser observes, he tends to bracket legitimate and illegitimate concerns and to aim for a value-neutral account of how power operates (Fraser, 1993: 18). Nevertheless, there is much in his writing which is relevant for our current discussion.

Of particular relevance are Foucault's concepts of 'genealogy' and 'eventalization'. With regard to genealogy, Foucault developed what he called a genealogy of modern power. This refers to the process, procedures, apparatuses and practices which serve to produce 'regimes of truth' or discourses. He maintains that what genealogy does 'is to entertain the claims to attention of local, discontinuous, disqualified, illegitimate knowledges against the claims of a unitary body of theory which would filter, hierarchise and order them in the name of some true knowledge and some arbitrary idea of what constitutes a science and its objects' (Foucault, in Gordon, 1980: 83). Foucault, with his 'bottom up' view of power, maintains that the target for his analyses are not institutions, 'theories' or 'ideology', but practices. The power relations which inhere in everyday social practices are, according to Foucault, those that matter. Institutions may by giving certain discourses (regimes pertaining to 'truth' by way of 'regimes of practice') institutional sanction, utilize and reinforce aspects of these power relations, but institutions are, overall, utilizing what is already there. The aim of his studies is to understand the conditions which make certain social practices or 'regimes of practices' (Foucault, 1981b: 5) acceptable at a given moment. He also asserts that 'to analyse "regimes of practices" means to analyse programmes of conduct which have both prescriptive effects regarding what is to be done (effects of "jurisdiction"), and codifying effects regarding what is to be known (effects of "veridiction")' (Foucault, 1981b: 5). This is pertinent in terms of posing challenges to the obvious links between categorization processes and forms of oppression. Questions – such as why certain categorization processes are seen to be acceptable at given moments in time, and what techniques are utilized to render such processes acceptable – need to be asked, reflected upon and acted on.

Foucault tended to see the operation of power within routinized social practices as emanating in a piecemeal, local manner from forms of disciplinary power exercised in disciplinary institutions. Disciplinary institutions such as the monastery, prison, army and catch-all hospitals (such as the General Hospital in Paris in 1656), evolved 'micro-techniques' for regulating and objectifying inmates or subjects. With regard to these, Foucault focused particularly on techniques of visibility and identified two main types which he called 'synoptic' and 'individualizing'. With regard to synoptic visibility, Foucault highlights innovations such as Bentham's Panopticon – designs aimed at unidirectional, maximum surveillance. With regard to individualizing visibility, he emphasizes the uses made of techniques for processing individuals, documenting their lives and reconstituting them as 'cases' with attendant files. Such techniques also include processes whereby experts interpret the psyche of their clients and where dimensions of personal life become targets for the intervention of experts and subject to normalization procedures based on psychiatric discourse (Foucault, in Gordon, 1980: 60–1). For women, operating as professionals or responding as clients, such views are pertinent.

According to Foucault, disciplinary practices are also dividing practices which create the divisions, healthy/ill, sane/mad, legal/delinquent. Such dividing practices may involve the use of authoritative status to divide off segments of the population through incarceration or institutionalization or more subtly utilize a labelling process to identify ourselves or others as different or abnormal. Dividing practices can be used as an effective means of normalization and social control. Foucault (cited in Gordon, 1980: 65) states: 'dividing practices separate and objectify people from social groups for exhibiting difference. The actions of dividing practices are made acceptable by claims of science and the institutional backing given to the operation of scientific discourses. This in turn can be seen to lead to scientific classification and categorisation.' Again, at this point, the links made earlier between categorization and classification processes appear to resonate.

Foucault also saw disciplinary power/knowledge regimes operating in a 'self-amplifying way', utilizing opposing or potentially opposing forces and making the subject watch over herself/himself. Such a system produces 'docile and useful bodies' (Foucault, 1979: 136). However, as Sawicki (1991) points out, disciplinary power increases individual power at the same time as it renders individuals docile. This view can indeed be linked to processes of categorization in the ways in which individuals projected into categories can accept projected definitions and define themselves accordingly.

In terms of the operation of power, Foucault related disciplinary forms of power to 'bio-power'. Bio-power can be viewed as the integration of micro-techniques into global macro-strategies. Sawicki (1991: 24) comments that, in accordance with Foucault's concept of power, disciplinary power was not invented by the dominant class and then extended down into the micro-level of society. It originated outside this class and was appropriated by it once it revealed its utility.

With regard to 'eventalization', Foucault used this term to highlight the importance of showing that things were not as necessary as all that; for example, it was not a matter of course that 'mad' people came to be regarded as mentally ill. Similarly, it was not self-evident that the causes of illness were to be sought through the individual examination of bodies and so on. 'Eventalization' is intrinsically linked to genealogy in that it 'means rediscovering the connections, encounters, supports, blockages, plays of force, strategies and so on which at a given moment establish what subsequently counts as being self-evident, universal and necessary' (Foucault, 1981b: 6). The process of 'eventalization' necessitates an appreciation of the multiple causes and practices which can be related to one event and which in turn explode into a myriad of causes, practices and meanings. An example can be related to the practice of hospitalizing women viewed as mentally ill for assessment and/or treatment. This 'event' can be related to notions of asylum, of segregation, of conformity, of women's mental health, of disease, of medicine and so on. Each in turn warrants a separate, multifaceted analysis.

Foucault's perspective relates to the issues raised in this chapter, in that he challenges notions of categories – of women, or phenomena being viewed, or viewing themselves, in a fixed or unitary way. It also highlights that meanings are continually being contested and that there are always alternatives. His concentration on social practices and the relational operation of power also emphasizes that it is not a question of practices/ knowledge/power being imposed by the 'active strong' on the 'passive weak', but that we all, as women, play a part in the operation of power/ knowledge regimes. Some undoubtedly play a bigger part than others and, as previously mentioned, the more authoritatively sanctioned the position, the more docile the incumbent, and the more resistant to challenge and change. However, Foucault regards his concept of genealogy as a form of resistance. As Sawicki (1991) outlines, it involves giving expression to the voices of those relegated to subordinate positions by the operation of disciplinary power. This includes the marginalized voices of women patients, social services clients and those perceived to be different with regard to the operation of dominant discourses. In this vein it is possible to argue that, by focusing on specific social practices, it is possible for women to explore the complexity of the power relations in operation, the resistance and the struggles which are taking place, as well as the adherence to that defined as 'normal'. Similarly, by locating all women within the range of discursive possibilities, an increased understanding, which is always the basis for action, becomes possible.

Conclusion

To return to the initial question posed – is the combination of mental health and community care an abusive one for women? – an answer must relate to perspectives and relative positions and to how processes of categorization are applied. Undoubtedly, the combination can be viewed as abusive if all are regarded as categories which can be used to apply singular and simplistic definitions of meaning to women as if they constituted a unitary group. Similarly, adherence to processes of self-categorization, if this encompasses reliance on the validity of individual experiences and the collecting of projected oppressions, can also be perceived as abusive. However, as outlined, there are other interpretations of experience which can be usefully used. The review of Foucault's work can also serve to increase our understanding about these processes and to formulate appropriate courses of action. Foucault has been criticized for not prescribing solutions or actively discriminating between what can be perceived as legitimate and illegitimate. However, he pertinently asserts:

> Critique doesn't have to be the premise of a deduction which concludes: this then is what needs to be done. It should be an instrument for those who fight, those who resist and refuse what is. Its use should be in processes of conflict and confrontation, essays in refusal. It doesn't have to lay down the law for the law. It isn't a stage in a programming. It is a challenge directed to what is. (Foucault, 1981b: 13)

This view, although not unproblematic, can usefully be applied to unravelling taken-for-granted assumptions and the fixed notions of meaning that surround women, mental health and community care.

References

Adams, M.L. (1989) 'There's no place like home: on the place of identity in feminist politics', *Feminist Review*, 31: 22–33.

Arber, S. and Gilbert, N. (1989) 'Men: the forgotten carers', *Sociology*, 23 (1): 111–18.

Ardill, S. and O'Sullivan, S.(1986) 'Upsetting an applecart: difference, desire and lesbian sadomasochism', *Feminist Review*, 23: 31–55.

Barnes, M. and Maple, N. (1992) *Women and Mental Health: Challenging the Stereotypes*, Birmingham: Venture Press.

Barnes, M., Bowl, R. and Fisher, M. (1990) *Sectioned: Social Services and the 1983 Mental Health Act*, London: Routledge.

Barrett, M. (1987) 'The concept of difference', *Feminist Review*, 26: 29–41.

Beresford, P. and Croft, S. (1993) *Citizen Involvement: a Practical Guide for Change*, Basingstoke: BASW/Macmillan.

Bhavnani, K. and Coulson, M. (1986) 'Transforming socialist feminism, the challenge of racism', *Feminist Review*, 23: 81–92.

Biggs, S. (1991) 'Community care, case management and the psychodynamic perspective', *Journal of Social Work Practice*, 5 (1): 71–81.

Brah, A. (1992) 'Difference, diversity and differentiation', in J. Donald and A. Rattansi (eds), *'Race', Culture and Difference*, London: Sage/Open University Press.

Broverman, D., Clarkson, F., Rosenkrantz, P., Vogel, S. and Broverman, I. (1970) 'Sex-role stereotype and clinical judgements of mental health', *Journal of Consulting and Clinical Psychiatry*, 34: 1–7.

Busfield, J. (1989) 'Sexism and psychiatry', *Sociology*, 23 (3): 343–63.

Challis, D., Chesterman, J., Darton, R. and Traske, K. (1993) 'Case management in the care of the aged: the provision of care in different settings', in J. Bornat, C. Pereira, D. Pilgrim and F. William (eds), *Community Care: a Reader*, Basingstoke: Macmillan/Open University Press.

Connell, R.W. (1985) 'Theorising gender', *Sociology*, 19 (2): 260–72.

Connolly, C. (1990) 'Splintered sisterhood: antiracism in a young women's project', *Feminist Review*, 36: 52–64.

Croft, S. and Beresford, P. (1990) *From Paternalism to Participation: Involving People in Social Services*, London: Open Services Project/ Joseph Rowntree Foundation.

Dalley, G. (1988) *Ideologies of Caring: Rethinking Community and Collectivism*, London: Macmillan.

Department of Employment (1991) *New Earnings Survey*, London: HMSO.

Department of Health (1989) *Caring for People: Community Care in the Next Decade and Beyond*, London: HMSO.

Department of Health (1994) *The Report of the Inquiry into the Care and Treatment of Christopher Clunis* (The Ritchie Report), London: HMSO.

Eichenbaum, L. and Orbach, S. (1983) *What Do Women Want?*, London: Michael Joseph.

Eisenstein, H. (1984) *Contemporary Feminist Thought*, London: Allen and Unwin.

Fawcett, B. (1994) 'Response of Social Services Departments to employees with caring responsibilities', unpublished, University of Bradford.

Fernando, S. (1991) *Mental Health, Race and Culture*, Basingstoke: Mind/Macmillan.

Finch, J. and Groves, D. (eds) (1983) *A Labour of Love: Women, Work and Caring*, London: Routledge and Kegan Paul.

Finkelstein, V. (1993) 'The commonality of disability', in J. Swain, V. Finkelstein, S. French and M. Oliver (eds), *Disabling Barriers - Enabling Environments*, London: Sage/Open University Press.

Foucault, M. (1979) *Discipline and Punish*, Harmondsworth: Penguin.

Foucault, M. (1981a) *The History of Sexuality*, vol. 1: *An Introduction*, Harmondsworth: Pelican.

Foucault, M. (1981b) 'Questions of method: an interview with Michel Foucault', *Ideology and Consciousness*, 8: 1–14.

Fraser, N. (1993) *Unruly Practices: Power, Discourse and Gender in Contemporary Social Theory*, Cambridge: Polity Press.

Gordon, C. (ed.) (1980) *Michel Foucault. Power/Knowledge: Selected Interviews and Other Writings 1972 – 1977*, Brighton: Harvester Press.

Gorman, J. (1992) *Out of the Shadows*, London: Mind Publications.

Graham, H. (1993) 'Feminist perspectives on caring', in J. Bornat, C. Pereira, D. Pilgrim and F. William (eds), *Community Care: a Reader*, Basingstoke: Macmillan/Open University Press.

Greater London Association of Community Health Councils (GLACHC) (1992), in V. Williamson (ed.), *Users First: the Real Challenge for Community Care*, Brighton, University of Brighton.

Green, H. (1988) *Informal Carers: a Study*, London: HMSO.

Hearn, J. (1992) *Men in the Public Eye: the Construction and Deconstruction of Public Men and Public Patriarchies*, London and New York: Routledge.

Jenness, V. (1992) 'Coming out: lesbian identities and the categorization problem', in K. Plummer (ed.), *Modern Homosexualities*, London: Routledge.

Kaplan, A.G. and Surrey, J.L. (1986) 'The relational self in women: developmental theory and public policy', in L.E. Walker (ed.), *Women and Mental Health Policy*, London: Sage.

Madigan, S.P. (1992) 'The application of Michel Foucault's philosophy in the problem externalising discourse of Michael White', *Journal of Family Therapy*, 13: 265–79.

Mama, A. (1989) 'Violence against black women: gender, race and state responses', *Feminist Review*, 32: 30–48.

Marchant, C. (1994) 'Heart to heart', *Community Care*, 24 February: 918.

Morris, J. (1993a) 'Involving service users', in *Implementing the Community Care Act: the Next Key Tasks*, London: Community Care Publication.

Morris, J. (1993b) *Pride against Prejudice: Transforming Attitudes to Disability*, London: Women's Press.

Oakley, A. (1981) *Subject Women*, London: Martin Robertson.

O'Brien, M. (1984) 'The commatization of women', *Interchange: a Quarterly Review of Education*, 15: 43–60.

Opie, A. (1992) 'Qualitative research, appropriation of the "other" and empowerment', *Feminist Review*, 40/42: 52–69.

Rojek, C., Peacock, G. and Collins, S. (1988) *Social Work and Received Ideas*, London: Routledge.

Sawicki, J. (1991) *Disciplining Foucault: Feminism, Power and the Body*, London: Routledge.

Sheppard, D.L. (1989) 'Organisation, power and sexuality: the self-image of women managers', in J. Hearn, D.L. Sheppard, P. Tancred-Sheriff and G. Burrell (eds), *The Sexuality of Organization*, London: Sage.

Sheppard, M. (1991) 'General practice, social work and mental health sections: the social control of women', *British Journal of Social Work*, 21 (1): 663–84.

Ussher, J. (1991) *Women's Madness: Misogyny or Mental Illness?* Hemel Hempstead: Harvester Wheatsheaf.

Williams, F. (1992) 'Somewhere over the rainbow: universality and diversity in social policy', in N. Manning and R. Page (eds), *Social Policy Review*, London: Social Policy Association.

Williams, F. (1993) 'Women and community', in J. Bornat, C. Pereira, D. Pilgrim and F. William (eds), *Community Care: a Reader*, Milton Keynes: Macmillan/Open University Press.

Wolverhampton Asian Women's Project (1994) *Community Care*, 24 February: 18.

PART III

THE PROBLEM OF MEN'S VIOLENCE

7

Men's Violence to Known Women: Men's Accounts and Men's Policy Developments

Jeff Hearn

The significance of violence for men and of men for violence is immense. In saying this, I am referring centrally to the problem of men as the major *doers* of violence to women, children, each other, and indeed ourselves/themselves. Indeed, in modern Western and many other societies, men are the experts, the specialists, in the doing of violence. There are a multitude of connections and associations between the way violence is perpetuated in society and the ways men socially construct themselves/ourselves and are socially constructed.

Naming Men as Men

For men to address these kinds of question involves a challenge to the way we are.[1] It involves a critique of ourselves, that is, first, personally; secondly, in terms of other men we are in contact with in our personal or public lives; and *also*, thirdly, more generally and socially, towards men as a powerful social category, a powerful social grouping.

So to focus on men, the problem of men, in doing this kind of work, whether it is research work or otherwise, is likely to have different implications for women and for men. It raises a variety of problems of how men are, how men behave, how men should behave, why men have power in society, how that power is structured, what different kinds of men there are, and how these current arrangements can be changed.

To put this rather bluntly, to focus on men, and particularly men's violence to women, unsettles and makes problematic the way men are, not just in the doing of these particular actions of violence, but also more generally. It raises question marks against men's behaviour in general. For example, how is it possible that men can be violent to women, perhaps over many years, and this can be part of a socially accepted way of being a man? How does violence relate to the social construction of different forms of masculinity in school, in sport, in work, in the media and so on?

Men's Violence to Known Women

In this chapter, I want to focus on a particular part of those connections between men and violence, namely, men's violence to known women. I am using the phrase 'men's violence to known women' for very specific reasons, and certainly in preference to the phrase 'domestic violence'.

First, speaking of 'men's violence' makes it clear that it is violence by men that is under examination. Secondly, this is violence to 'known women', as opposed to women who are strangers. There are a number of different dimensions that apply when the violator and violated are known to each other, as against when they are strangers. For example, there is the crucial question of the relationship of the violence to what happens between them before and indeed after the violence. Thirdly, the more usual term 'domestic violence' conflates violence by men and by women, and violence to women, men and children. Fourthly, references to 'the domestic' are often misleading in the sense that such violence does not necessarily take place in the home. It may be on the doorstep, in the street, in the pub or other 'public' places.

Furthermore, in considering men's violence to known women, I am particularly concerned with violence in 'intimate', usually sexual, that is heterosexual relationships. When women point out that women are in most danger from men they are in the closest relationship with, this means that we can see why it is that men are most dangerous to the women with whom they have the closest relationship (Edwards, 1989). This effectively raises the question of the relationship of men's violence to women and men's heterosexuality and heterosexual relations.

Undoing the Norm

For too long, men have been considered the taken-for-granted norm[2] against which women have been judged to be different. Yet despite, and indeed because of, this dominance, the psychological and social construction of men has often not been addressed. Men have been all too visible yet invisible to critical analysis and change. Like other 'superordinate' categories and groups (Goode, 1982) (the rich, white people, physically able, and so on), men have been strangely absent from explicit enquiry – and deconstruction. To look at men in this way changes men from being 'naturally like that' or 'just the way they are' or 'that way because they can't help it' to people who are just as socially constructed and socially variable as women. This has got all sorts of implications for social interventions with men and on the effects of men's actions.

Making sense of men necessitates placing men in a social context. This entails considering men's power relations to women, and the social development of boys and men in that general context. For most men, this includes an acceptance of that basic power relation. To do so is a relatively simple way of affirming a sense, first, of being a boy and then of being a man. Thus a common aspect of men's personal and social being is a taken-for-granted acceptance of that power, just as it is also likely to involve an acceptance of being a boy, then a man. The social and psychological identity called 'man' says and shows power relations. It is *'identical'*. An important aspect of men's (sense of) power is the use or potential use or threat of violence. This remains a major and pressing social problem (Dobash and Dobash, 1992).

Having said that, there are two major qualifications to be made. First, men's violence to known women is frequently a contradictory issue for men, in the sense that it can be understood by some men as *both* legitimate and illegitimate. It can be seen as a legitimate use of power; it can also be seen as a sign of 'weakness', an admission of an inability to control, an embarrassment. Secondly, the exact way in which these connections of violence and power operate, as well as the contradictions just described, varies for different men and different kinds of men, at least partly in relation to age, economic class, locality, race and other social divisions.

The Research

It is partly for these reasons that my own work in recent years has focused on men's violence to known women. This has included research into men's experience of their own violence to women they have known, most usually wives, partners and girlfriends. It has involved in-depth interviews with 60 men who have been violent to women, about their understanding and self-understanding of their violence, what they have done and why they have done it, as well as the nature of reactions from friends, family and social agencies. In addition to these qualitative accounts, interviews have included an extensive questionnaire on personal resources, the nature of violence, the helpfulness of agency responses, the forms of coping responses by men, the form and extent of social support, and the state of personal well-being. The kinds of violence described included verbal violence; throwing things; damaging property and killing pets; direct physical violence; assaults; murder; attempted murder; rape; the use of objects, sticks, knives, on the women; abduction/kidnapping; tying up and leaving for several days, as a form of torture.

Table 7.1 *Numbers of agency permissions and agency follow-up contacts by source of referral*

Source of referral	Number of men giving permissions	Housing	Social services	Probation	Police	CPS	Solicitors	Doctors	Counselling groups	Other	Total	Average number of permissions
Police	14*	–	1(1)	3*(3)*	13(28)	4(4)	8*(3)*	5(3)	–	4(4)	38* (46)*	2.7
Counselling groups	11	1(1)	–	–	3(6)	1(1)	2 (2)	2(2)	10(10)	1(1)	20(23)	1.8
Prison	4	–	1(1)	6 (6)	5(5)	5(5)	3 (2)	1(1)	–	–	21(20)	5.25
Probation	7*	–	–	7*(8)*	4(5)	4(4)	7*(7)*	1(1)	–	–	23* (25)*	3.7
Other welfare agencies	4	1(1)	2(2)	2 (3)	1(2)	2(3)	2 (1)	1(1)	–	3(3)	14(16)	3.5
No agency	2	1(1)	–	–	–	–	–	–	–	1(1)	2(2)	1.0
Total	41*	3(3)	4(4)	17*(19*)	26(46)	16(17)	21*(14*)	10(8)	10(10)	9(9)	116* (130*)	2.8

Figures not in brackets equal number of agency permissions; figures in brackets equal number of agency follow-up contacts.
*One man referred from both the Police and the Probation Service.

Table 7.2 *Comparison of total of agency permissions and contacts**

	Agency permissions given	Agency contacts reported
Police	25	47
Solicitor	21	37
Probation	15	20
Social worker/social services	4	7
Counselling groups	10	–
Therapist/counsellor	–	28
Housing	3	7
DSS	–	6
Doctor/GP	10	29
Hospital/medical health	–	8
Mental health	9	15
Other	–	9
Prison	–	10

Note: *41 men gave agency permissions; 55 men in contact with agencies

Following interviews, men have been asked for their permission to do follow-up interviews with agencies with which they have been involved. This yielded permission from 41 men and a total of 130 follow-up interviews and other follow-ups with agency staff (Table 7.1). These have been with the police, the Probation Service, social services, doctors, psychiatrists, advice workers, lawyers and the Crown Prosecution Service (CPS) solicitors and the group leaders of men's programmes that work against violence. Men also reported their contacts with agencies on the questionnaire. This yielded from 55 men 223 named contacts, 10 repeat contacts with current partner and 24 cases of CPS involvement (making 257 contacts in total, Table 7.2).

Having completed these interviews and other investigations, an obvious question is what has been learnt that may be of interest in trying to understand men and men's violence. Not surprisingly, there is a lot that could be said. There are, for example, important issues around men interviewing men, methodology, safety and ethics (Hearn, 1993); there are also questions of statistical and qualitative analyses of research results (Hearn, 1995a); but here I will focus on the questions of how men talk about violence; what talking about violence to women tells us about men, and on the question of policy and practical intervention against men's violence (Hearn, 1995b). These are all major issues for social workers, health workers, housing workers and, indeed, for the full range of interventions and intervenors, actual and potential, against men's violence to known women.

Men Talking about Men's Violence to Women

When men talk about violence they have committed on women they have known, they are doing several different things at the same time. They are giving a report, a descriptive report, of what they have done. They are also presenting an account to another person that is sayable, and is convincing. This involves resort to confession, justifications, excuses and repudiations. Thirdly, talking about violence to known women conveys much information on men's sense of themselves 'as men', and as different from 'women'. Such accounts are simultaneously a means of saying and showing 'this is a man'. They are treasure troves of how men think, feel, use 'logics' (sometimes very oddly), excuse, justify and reproduce their actions. For example, men's accounts of their violence may be structured around the differences between men's violence to men and men's violence to women; around men's sexual and emotional differences from women; and men's assumed greater size and strength. Furthermore, men's accounts and, indeed, explanations of violence to known women need to be understood at the very least within the context of men's power in relation to women, and may indeed often, though not always, be part of a further form of domination of women. Indeed, talking about violence can itself be a way of affirming and justifying violence, and can indeed be a form of violence itself. The violence of violent acts and behaviours cannot be neatly separated off from the violence of talk and text. This separation is itself a product of a well-established distinction between approaches to social life that are social scientific, even mentalistic, and those that are derived from the humanities, and especially the study of representation; this distinction is itself a form of violence that is probably being gradually eroded.

So how do men talk about their violence to women? Here I shall go through some of the devices that men have used to convey that violence and thus a sense of themselves. Men's affirmation of violence and thus of themselves in talking about violence is apparent in the descriptions and explanations of violence, and sometimes too in the absences and silences.

Denial   A first and most basic way to continue violence is to deny it at all. This may be in total or in part.

Forgetting, Blanking out and not Knowing   The refrain 'I can't remember' is another major way of constructing violence. Sometimes this is further elaborated so that the man has a well-developed theory of *not knowing* how to explain or account for his violence.

Exclusion and Inclusion   A third way of talking about violence is by processes of inclusion and exclusion of particular behaviours. In talking of 'violence', men overwhelmingly refer to physical violence. Although some men do refer to emotional, verbal and psychological violence, even these references are often related to the threat of physical violence or are constructed as if they are physical violence in their reduction to incidents. For men, violence to known women is generally constructed as follows:

1   Physical violence that is more than a push. Holding, restraint, use of weight/bulk blocking, throwing (both things and women) are often excluded.

2 Convictions for physical violence.
3 Physical violence that causes or is likely to cause damage that is visible or considered by the man to be physically lasting.
4 Physical violence that is not seen as specifically sexual. Sexual violence is seen as separate (cf. Kelly, 1988).

Thus, men's violence to women is for men a combination of physical force, legal effects and personal effects. Men separate violence from sex/sexuality. Visual violence, including pornography, is excluded from how men talk about violence to known women. This contrasts with women's definitions of violence as related to women's inability to control the situation (Hanmer and Saunders, 1984). Thereafter the greater the uncertainty, the more terrifying the encounter. Such definitions are not specifically or exclusively related to the law or to actual physical damage at the time.

Minimization   This can refer to the minimization of definition, extent, frequency and effects. One of the most important examples of this is 'nominalization' (Trew, 1979) – the reduction of complex violent actions to a word, a name. Another is the use of a very small word, 'just'. This refers to 'precisely that'; 'only that and nothing else'; 'spontaneous action without preplanning'; and 'justice'. All these meanings may be bound up with that little word.

Removal of the Self and of Intention   Another mode is to remove the self of the man. This can be done literally: 'I'm not a violent person', 'I'm not a wife beater', and other similar phrases have been commonplace, even after detailed descriptions of violence.

An alternative approach is to speak of violence as if it happens (or 'just happens') without the intention of the man; as if it has an independent dynamic of its own. Some men specifically spoke of the *lack* of a connection between their intention and the damage resulting, as with one man who said the woman ducked down and so received a blow in her face which was not intended, rather than on her body, which would have caused less damage; and another man who disclaimed the effects of the woman falling down steps even though that was preceded by his pushing her.

These kinds of cutting of cause and effect may be closely linked to explaining violence as a mutual or reciprocal process, between the woman and the man. This is where it is quite possible to reproduce a modified version of family systems explanations within the man's account. Physical violence can also be constructed as the 'natural' outcome of reciprocal anger and arguments.

Excuses   These involve accepting blame but not responsibility (Lyman and Scott, 1970). They place the responsibility firmly *elsewhere* in time or place or person. The people or things usually responsible are:

- in the past (mothers, sexual abusers, school)
- in drink or drugs (including being violent when 'off' them)
- in the woman's behaviour, including her 'nagging', provocation
- inside the man himself (psychiatric disturbance)

Justifications   These involve the acceptance of responsibility but not the blame. Whereas excuses may tend to locate violence *within the man* so that something done 'outside' of him is said to 'trigger' the violence from inside, justifications tend to have a more *conscious* and yet *interpersonal* focus. Justifications are constructed mainly as a *response* to something else in the present or the recent past, particularly something *not* done bringing forth an internalized response in the form of the man's violence to fill the gap/the lack. This is usually the woman's behaviour, particularly that which is *not* associated by the man with violence, abuse and aggression. Violence is thus a corrective, an additive by the man to the social situation. In this sense, violence, like pornography in particular, is gendered speech. These justifications include:

- not being sexually faithful (actual, assumed or expected)
- not doing housework
- not doing child care
- not maintaining her appearance, for example, through *her* drinking 'too much'
- not restricting herself in terms of movement, autonomy, use of the house, her access to her friends

These justifications hinge around the woman *not* doing certain things rather than her doing things like 'nagging'.

Confessions   Confessions of violence can be with or without remorse. One man said he took responsibility for violence, and that he was violent because he loved her so much. Some of the most explicit statements of violence were made by men in a 'naive' way without remorse. As such, these confessions become normalized as part of a violent way of life; they become taken for granted; they are thus denied and repudiated. Confession delivered without remorse brings us fill circle to denial.

Combinations of Talk   These various ways of talking are not, of course, mutually exclusive; they often overlap and occur within the same account. As men proceed through a 'career' of violence, men tend to increase their repertoire of ways of accounting, even though these may be inconsistent with each other. While these are all ways of individual men talking about violence, they are also forms of social talk. For example, the justifications given are part of the way in which women are talked about generally by men. The general ways in which women are constructed by men are reproduced, referred back to and invoked by the individual man, as, for example, when he sees those constructions *not* being kept to by the woman. Much of this is therefore about what is taken for granted about relations between women and men. Perhaps the most pervasive taken-for-granted feature of these interviews has been heterosexuality. For almost all the men interviewed, heterosexuality was taken for granted (Hearn, 1994).

In all these and no doubt in other ways men talk about their violence, maintain power and a sense of being a man, and 'do' masculinity. Developing an analysis of men necessitates detailed attention to describing, and analysing these taken-for-granted ways of doing and being. This is also necessary and important in order to stop men's violence to women and contribute to social and personal change.

Policy, Practice and Talking

Policy development in relation to men who have been violent to known women is fundamental to reducing and stopping violence. Traditionally, this has not been a major area of concern in most agencies. The policy options that have been developed are quite limited. Incarceration is extremely rare for men who have been violent to known women. Fines, community service and injunctions are also used. However, talk is the main medium of agency intervention with men. Talk is used as the way to show that men have moved away from violence; it is also the means of excusing, justifying, denying violence, as well as a way of continuing and reproducing violence. On the one hand, men talking about violence is a way of focusing on and possibly confronting the problem; on the other, it is a way of avoiding the problem. In particular, men talking about violence can easily become part of a therapeutic discourse, in which the talk is structured in terms of 'an explanation' of the individual man's violence, often through recalled 'bits' of his past, his personality, his inclinations, his activities, his drinking, and so on.

Talk-based approaches can detract from approaches that are based on or are focused on removal of men, punishment, non-verbal interventions and communication, the material conditions that promote men's violence to women, the immediate act of violence itself, explicit state and other publicity against men's violence to women, and preventive education of boys and men. Parallel dangers lie in doing research on men's violence to known women, in the sense that the search for explanations for men's violence through men's talk may assist the justifications for and excusing of that violence. This applies not only in the construction of explanations, justifications and excuses by men, but also in the possibility that giving attention to men's accounts may re-centre men, allow men to be the subjects of discourse.

The relationship of talking, not talking (silence) and violence is particularly complex. Talk can be opposed to violence; talk can be violent/violence, just as violence can be talk; silence can be opposed to violence; silence can be violent/violence, just as violence can be silence. One way of

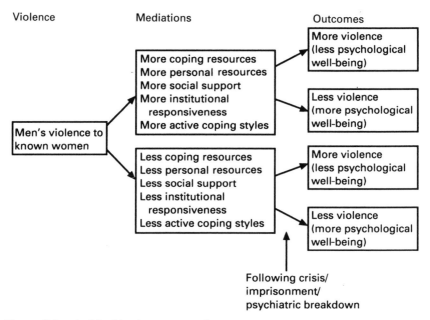

Figure 7.1   *Ambiguities in resources for men*

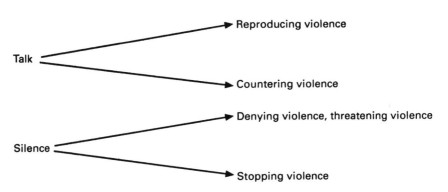

Figure 7.2   *Ambiguities in talk and silence in relation to violence*

thinking about these questions is that both violence and the ability to talk (convincingly) about violence are personal resources for men in relation to women. Personal resources, including violence and talking of violence, can be both a means of continuing and even escalating violence and/or a means of moving away from violence. Thus this ambiguity has to be considered at all times (Figure 7.1). Additionally, just as talk can both reproduce and counter violence, so, too, can silence. Not talking can be a way of denying violence or even threatening violence; or it can be a way of stopping violence, by being quiet, listening, not dominating (Figure 7.2). Thus an important challenge, both theoretical and practical is how to focus on men's violence and men's accounts of violence, without diluting men's responsibility and without placing men at the centres of discourse, as the doers and creators of social reality.

Talking about violence to women may be avoided by many men, but it is a way of coping for some, perhaps increasingly for many men. While many of the men appeared to make few if any responses to their own violence, the more violent the men were, the greater their range of coping responses. This included not only avoiding the problem, but also rethinking the problem and even taking more active steps. For men, the pattern of modes of coping is much more restricted for dealing with violence than for other identified problems. This is most likely to do with the special problems of coping with violence; it could also be that violence is *not* necessarily a problem for men; it does not necessarily cause stress or worry. Indeed, this suggestion is borne out by the fact that for 27 out of 52 men, the prospect or fear of violence *never* made it hard to carry on with their usual activities. In short, violence is not generally a problem for men. It only becomes a problem if the effects of violence produce other effects on men – for example, response or resistance from women, the involvement of the police and so on. On the other hand, it could be suggested that men usually have a rather limited repertoire of useful responses to 'cope with' their own violence. Even so, it is important to see men 'coping' with violence as *not unknowledgeable* or uninformed. Men are not violent cultural dopes, but are knowledgeable actors, able to reflect on their violence, formulate strategies of self-intervention, avoidance and reconstruction, in response to their own actions.

Men's Support for Men

While some of the men were very isolated and lacking in friends to discuss the problem, others did have a large circle of friends, but chose not to use their friends for this purpose. Interventions by other members of the family sometimes reduced the violence, sometimes involved further violence from other men, and sometimes involved the man attacking the others, especially men in the woman's family of origin.

The issue of talk and violence also applies to men's relations *with each other*, as friends, relations, workers and clients and so on. Of particular concern is the need to address the ambiguous nature of men's social support that may both maintain violence and counter violence at the same time. This can apply to both informal social support and institutional support. For some men, the intensity of friends' responses that are both empathetic and avoidant and associated with high levels of violence are particularly serious (DeKeseredy, 1990). This has been confirmed in the in-depth interviews. In addition to direct institutional responses to men's violence in both the criminal justice and welfare systems, there is a strong need to attend to and counter men's passive and active support for each other's violence to known women. This is an important area of practice and policy development in welfare, health, educational, youth and other agency programmes. This can be promoted in a wide variety of ways: within the Personal and Social Development curriculum in schools; in addressing other forms of violence, for example, bullying and pornography in schools; in anti-sexist initiatives; in locating violence in equal opportunity and other policy developments; and in developing non-violent ways of working and behaving in agency programmes.

The general lack of correlative relationships in the area of social support indicates that there is no clear pattern for men. The dominant pattern is that the number of supporters is significantly related to the level of violence, with greater isolation linking with more severe violence. However, isolation may be literal or involve small networks, which may themselves be characterized by empathetic and avoidant responses from friends. A subordinate pattern is that some men who reported high levels of violence also reported large supportive networks. Thus areas for further research are the effects of isolation and friendship patterns of men on violence, and the interplay of the quality and quantity of networks for men. Again, this is an important issue for educational, welfare and health agencies to address.

Men in Agencies

These connections between men apply not only between peers, friends and other male supporters, but also apply between men who have been violent to women and men in agencies as workers, managers and policy-makers. Individual men's accounts and the 'accounts' of agencies may often be comparable, partly through processes of mirroring and partly through similarities in their gendered power relations. Agencies are gendered and present gendered understandings of violence which are directly related to policies and practices. Formal agencies generally operate from men's definitions, which in this context means men's definitions of violence. In the case of state organizations, men's control and definitions, both in general and of violence, are particularly dominant. This applies in both state bureaucracies and the legal system.

Alternative definitions, policies and practices have been developed through women's organizations in relation to violence against women. Such contested definitions and meanings of violence, implicit and explicit, apply not only to agencies and their policy development, but also to academia and social theory. Changing agency definitions involves changing agencies' structures and processes, and their gendering. This necessitates attention to policy, to the internal workings of organizations, to training, and to resource distribution. Changing the internal gendering of agencies is essential in the development of better agency policies against violence.

Focusing on Men's Violence

More generally, it is important to consider that, while men receive a large amount of agency time and agency involvement, few agencies define the violence as their prime concern. At present, the main feature of patterns of agency response is the diversity and spread of those agencies, each with their own agenda, purpose and organization. And yet, while there are many agencies involved with men who have been violent to women, few specialize in, or have men's violence to women, as their main concern. Ones that do include anti-violence counselling groups and men's programmes (these are often run primarily on voluntary effort with some limited support from state agencies and charitable money);[3] and Domestic Violence and Child Protection Special Units, which are part of the organization of the West Yorkshire Police in the area covered by the research, and some other police forces throughout the UK. However, the greater part (about 85 per cent) of their time is spent on child protection work. There is also some limited specialization in some other agencies, for example, the Crown Prosecution Service. This is in contrast with seeing focused work on men's violence solely in terms of the dominant occupational, professional or agency definitions and approaches. Developing focused work on men's violence involves developing expertise in agencies and dealing directly with the problem. It also involves trying to avoid misunderstandings between men and agency staff about the nature and purpose of meetings between them. Some men were very grateful for the support and assistance of their individual probation officers. Yet some of their contacts with probation officers did not focus on violence to known women, though the officers were aware of this (and this indeed had in some cases been the reason for the referral to the research).

One of the most important relevant issues is the low level of contact that the men had had with Social Services and social workers. Only seven of the 60 men had had such contacts. Of the 24 men who said they had committed more than 15 assaults, who had attempted murder or who had murdered, only four reported that they had had contact with Social Services or social workers. This very limited amount of contact contrasted with the much greater level of contacts with doctors or GPs. Of 55 men who had had agency contacts in relation to violence, 29 reported contact with GPs and eight with hospitals in relation to their violence (see Table 7.2).

One of the problems is that in most agencies there are no workers who are specifically directed to work against men's violence to women. There is a need to consider what the development of such an expertise would look like. Would it be appropriate to create (anti-) violence workers who would be able to follow through the inter-agency interventions that are necessary in working against violence? Focusing on men's violence also means taking up the problem of violence in a consistent way throughout agencies. While it may be relatively easy to change policy in word, it is often much less easy to do so in deed. For example, while police arrest policy now treats violence from men to known women, whether in or outside marriage, with equal seriousness as similar violence elsewhere, this is not always reflected in the attitudes of police officers implementing this policy. A common complaint from officers interviewed was the reduction of their discretion in such a policy. Indeed, the police are unusual in that discretion has traditionally increased *down* the hierarchy (Skolnick, 1975; Jefferson and Grimshaw, 1984). In particular, there is a need for a much closer examination of the 'filtering' process at each stage of the criminal justice system, including the discretion that remains between arrest and charging/summonsing, and the partial discretion that exists between charging/summonsing and prosecution, and then conviction processes. Intervening against men's violence to known women in agencies means both effective *policy implementations* and *cultural change* within organizations.

This focusing on the problem does not mean more resources for men. Counselling groups and men's programmes for men who have been violent to known women have received a good deal of attention in recent years. Their possible strength is that they can act as a focus of action against men's violence, not just for individual group members, but also educationally and politically (Gondolf and Russell, 1986; Horley, 1990; Dankwort, 1992–3). Their weakness is that they can divert attention and perhaps resources away from women's initiatives and women's projects. Resourcing of women's projects, such as refuges, has to take priority over the resourcing of new projects for men. Such projects for men also bring more subtle dangers in that the better they are in addressing and making explicit the reasons for men's domination, control and violence, the more dangerous they may be, for some men at least, in that they can educate men in more precise and subtle forms of domination. They can also vary greatly in their political stances towards and style of working on men's violence to women. Thus the development of such projects has to be conducted with care and caution, and in association and accountability with women's projects and women's control. Comparable issues are present in housing associations which set up and provide accommodation for men following violence, without reference to Women's Aid and other similar voluntary sector agencies providing services for women. While some housing projects proscribe violence by their tenants, others aim to provide suitable accommodation for men following violence.

Men's Responsibility

Another issue in agencies that deal with men is that of men's responsibility as workers, officers and managers to attend to this problem. Outside of the men's programmes and to an extent the police and certain other parts of the criminal justice system, this is not identified as a major priority. This is a particularly critical issue throughout the criminal justice system, and in welfare agencies, including social services and medical and psychiatric services. On the one hand, this means not placing oneself outside of the issue of violence; on the other, it means being very clearly against violence.

These issues of the critical connection between violence and different forms of *masculinity*, different ways of *being men*, raise important questions of how men are to behave – as researchers, as workers (be they social workers, police officers), as managers. It is not possible, on the one hand, to work with men against *their* violence and, on the other hand, to behave in violent and abusive ways as men, whether in working with others as colleagues or subordinates. Accordingly, it is particularly important to develop ways of managing that are non-oppressive, non-violent and non-abusive.

Stopping Men's Violence

Finally, responding to and stopping violence means not just trying to 'solve' the problem (indeed, it may be insoluble), whether generally or of an individual man, but changing the conditions that maintain the problem in the first place. This means attention to all aspects of men's support for each other, as friends, family and agency staff, that do not counter violence to women. Passively accepting the problem means, in effect, contributing to its maintenance. It includes both changing men's private and personal practice, and it includes making public campaigns like Edinburgh City Council's 'Zero Tolerance' campaign against men's violence a usual, rather than an unusual, part of public policy. Or how about a state-funded campaign of the car safety-belt type that said simply and directly 'Don't do it, don't think it.' Such campaigns can be created and can be effective when governments and others want them to be. It would do no harm for all agencies in this field to begin by making it part of their public statement of policy that they oppose men's violence to women, in all its forms. This could be a prelude to more focused and consistent work to stop the problem.

Acknowledgements

This chapter draws on the research for 'Violence, Abuse and the Stress-coping Process, Project no. 2', ESRC No. L206 25 2003. I am grateful to Roger Barford, John Davis, Philip Raws and David Riley for conducting interviews with men; Linda Arbuckle for administering the Project; and Jalna Hanmer for collaboration on Project 1. Project 1 is a linked, but separate, project on women's experiences of violence from known men.

Notes

1. The intervention of 'naming men as men' is discussed by Hanmer (1990) and Collinson and Hearn (1994). The dangers of men claiming authority from speaking 'as men' are presented by Stoltenberg (1990).

2. 'Undoing the norm' is a particular example of 'undoing the social' (Game, 1991).

3. Since the conclusion of this research there has been interest in the use of such groups by the Probation Service.

References

Collinson, D. and Hearn, J. (1994) 'Naming men as men: implications for worker, organisations and management', *Gender, Work and Organization*, 1 (1): 2–22.

Dankwort, J. (1992–3) 'Violence against women: varying perceptions and intervention practices with woman abusers', *Intervention* (Quebec), 92: 34–49.

DeKeseredy, W.S. (1990) 'Male peer support and women abuse: the current state of knowledge', *Sociological Focus*, 23: 129–39.

Dobash, R.E. and Dobash, R. (1992) *Women, Violence and Social Change*, London: Routledge.

Edwards, S. (1989) *Policing Domestic Violence*, London: Sage.

Game, A. (1991) *Undoing the Social*, Milton Keynes, Open University Press.

Gondolf, E.W. and Russell, D. (1986) 'The case against anger control treatment programs for batterers', *Response*, 9 (3): 2–5.

Goode, W. (1982) 'Why men resist', in B. Thorne and M. Yalom (eds), *Rethinking the Family: Some Feminist Questions*, White Plains, New York: Longman, pp. 131–50.

Hanmer, J. (1990) 'Men, power and the exploitation of women', in J. Hearn and D.H.J. Morgan (eds), *Men, Masculinities and Social Theory*, London: Unwin Hyman, pp. 21–42.

Hanmer, J. and Saunders, S. (1984) *Well-founded Fear: a Community Study of Violence to Women*, London: Hutchinson.

Hearn, J. (1993) *Researching Men and Researching Men's Violence*, Violence, Abuse and Gender Relations Research Unit, Research Paper no.4, University of Bradford, May.

Hearn, J. (1994) 'Men's heterosexual violence to women: the presence and absence of sex in men's account of violence to known women', British Sociological Association Annual Conference Paper, 'Sexualities in Context', University of Central Lancashire, Mimeo, University of Bradford, March.

Hearn, J. (1995a) *'It Just Happened': a Research and Policy Report on Men's Violence to Known Women*, Violence, Abuse and Gender Relations Research Unit, Research Paper no. 6, University of Bradford.

Hearn, J. (1995b) *Patterns of Agency Contacts with Men who Have Been Violent to Known Women*, Violence, Abuse and Gender Relations Research Unit, Research Paper no.13, University of Bradford.

Horley, S. (1990) 'Responding to male violence against women', *Probation Journal*, December: 166–70.

Jefferson, T. and Grimshaw, R. (1984) *Controlling the Constable: Police Accountability in England and Wales*, London: Frederick Muller/Cobden Trust.

Kelly, L. (1988) *Surviving Sexual Violence*, Cambridge: Polity Press.

Lyman, S. and Scott, M. (1970) *The Sociology of the Absurd*, New York: Appleton-Century-Crofts.

Skolnick, J. (1975) *Justice without Trial*, New York: John Wiley.

Stoltenberg, J. (1990) *Refusing to be a Man*, New York: Meridian.

Trew, T. (1979) 'What the papers say: linguistic variation and ideological difference', in R. Fowler, R. Hodge, G. Kress and T. Trew (eds), *Language and Control*, London: Routledge and Kegan Paul, pp. 117–56.

8

Men's Resistance to Social Workers

Judith Milner

In a summary of current criticisms of feminist analyses of child abuse, Cooper (1993) argues that the feminist argument remains a polemical assertion because it lacks sound and reliable research into the incidence and prevalence of child abuse; restricts intervention strategies by eliminating possible change in fathers from the equation; fails to focus on power imbalances between children and all adults; and, offers little in the way of practical advice to hard-pressed social workers as a result.

Such criticisms have led to a refocusing on the discovery of women's abuse of children, already well documented in cases of physical abuse and neglect (Korbin, 1989; Creighton, 1992) and increasingly in cases of sexual abuse (Elliott, 1993). However, an emphasis on the potential of all women to abuse children, mirroring neatly feminist polemic about all men being potential rapists, misses the point: that the child protection system is but another male system in which women make a considerable contribution yet are rarely in a position to exercise authority and control over fit, adult males (Heidensohn, 1985). The system allows men first to categorize, and then analyse and make decisions about child abuse in a way which processes fathers and mothers, black and white people, middle-class and working-class people differently in order to enable most men to disappear from the system at all stages of the investigative and therapy process by increasing the spotlight on mothers (Milner, 1993a). Effectively, men who abuse children become 'invisible men' as far as family responsibility is concerned (Beagley, 1989; Department of Health, 1994).

Although the effects of race and class need to be considered in any discussion of the abuse of power, I shall none the less focus primarily on gender in this analysis. As male probation officers comment in their discussion of the collusion which occurs in the interactions between male probation officers and their male clients, 'there is more that joins men across class and disability, and even across race and sexual orientation, than divides them' (Cordery and Whitehead, 1992). And, as Statham (1987: 129–49) has pointed out, the way in which social work is currently organized around client groupings is divisive, concentrating on what separates rather than 'the commonalities of class, race and gender. Why else, can we ignore the fact that most clients in the UK are women?'

Nowhere is this divisive separateness more acute than in child protection practice where the categorization of children as victims via the compilation of statistics collated from returns of children on registers separates them from their non-abused siblings and their fathers while tying their abuse to their mothers. This form of categorization provides the bedrock of statistics from which all research/theorizing then emerges and creates a fog of obscuration which enables fathers to remain shadowy figures.

For example, Reder et al. (1993), in their analysis of child death enquiries, find that almost as many women as men were culpable of the death of their child, although careful reading of the reports shows that only a handful were directly responsible. The counting of children at a late stage in child protection procedure operates to over-include mothers via a process which allocates them, first, secondary roles as collusive partners and, secondly, as equal partners in terms of culpability and responsibility. Thus, they figure more substantially in the statistics on the incidence of child abuse than they would if figures were kept on the alleged abuser at the time of the initial referral. Men begin to disappear from the outset. Men also disappear in the conflation of the differing categories of child abuse. Although it is by no means certain that abuse and neglect are manifestations of the same phenomenon (Hallett, 1988), it has been established that mothers are more likely to be processed via neglect categories with brief registration utilized as a means of gaining access to scarce resources (Denman and Thorpe, 1993; Milner, 1993b), although they might well be more fairly processed under the provision for 'children in need' laid down in the Children Act 1989 (s. 17).

An emphasis on mothers, whether from a traditional or a feminist approach, does support Cooper's (1993) criticism that men are left out of the equation. Not only has social work failed to involve fathers in services (Marsh, 1991), but fathers do not see social work services as relevant to them or provided in a way that fits their approach to life (Phillimore, 1981). Bringing them into the equation is therefore decidedly difficult. I wish to explore below some of the strategies used by professionals and their potential male clients which serve to remove the responsibility from male abusers of children. The problems of involving men in social work interventions are described and some strategies social workers could use are suggested.

Primary Processes: Minimization of Male Involvement in Child Abuse

Although feminist analyses have been influential in highlighting concerns about the male abuse of children, particularly with regard to sexual abuse (Finkelhor, 1992), the child protection decision-making process in Britain is largely based on male theorizing, research and management to the extent that Hudson (1992) felt able to complain of men 'hijacking' the child protection system. This means that men are able to minimize men's involvement in child abuse and deflect attention onto women and involve women social workers in this process. Gibbons et al. (1993) in their analysis of 1,888 child protection referrals in eight local authorities found that front-line staff screen out 26 per cent of referrals after checks with other agencies and 50 per cent by investigation, leaving only 24 per cent to be considered at child protection conferences where male voices might be likely to be strongest. So, the first question to be asked is how front-line women social workers are influenced by men's minimization strategies at the initial referral stage?

Men are able to minimize their violent behaviour because social workers' views and attitudes are affected by the differing definitions of fathering and mothering. They do not differ only in terms of gender but in connotations (Graddol and Swann, 1988); fathering at its most basic is no more than a simple biological act yet it has higher status than mothering and is rarely tied solely to the domestic life of the family. For example, in a 'popular' book on fathering, the reader is given the following advice:

> Getting involved means learning to do a variety of everyday things such as feeding, changing nappies, giving a bath etc. Now hold on father, don't get your back up. This doesn't mean you should take over as soon as you get home from work and act as a substitute full-time mother. But, at times, you should include in your day doing these simple things with your baby. It does not take long, especially at first, since new babies spend most of their time sleeping. (Dobson, 1974)

At the same time, mothering is defined as a life-long activity with low status located in the domestic world of the family and with specific qualities demanded of it, most notably nurturance and loving care. Not only are mothers seen as central in providing the correct sort of care which leads to the healthy physical and psychological growth of children (Abbott and Wallace, 1990), but they are also held responsible for managing the emotional tone of the family generally, simply because emotions are assumed to be located within the home (Parkin, 1993). Emotions are marginalized in male discourses in the public so that when they emerge there they are, again, the province of women: 'Women are given caring work on the grounds that they are mothers or may become mothers, or should have been mothers. They are even expected to feel like mothers while they work as teachers, social workers, nurses or help out at play group' (David, 1985: 13). Thus they become enmeshed in what Rich (1977) refers to as 'powerless responsibility', while simultaneously their personal needs go unmet within the context of the family and their needs as carers are largely ignored in society (Nice, 1988). This is most clearly illustrated in relation to child sexual abuse. De Young (1994) shows how the conflict between women's roles as mother and wife in incestuous families is not easily negotiated and that therapeutic efforts fail to address this issue. And:

> it ill behoves mental health professionals to criticise mothers for not behaving or knowing how to respond to indications that their children are being sexually

abused, when the sensitivity of professionals to these events is so newly, so precariously established. The women have very much more to lose. (Glaser and Frosh, 1988: 48)

Thus, the differing definitions of fathering and mothering serve to minimize men's responsibilities, while increasing those of women to such an extent that it could be argued that no theory of fathering exists against which men can be measured (Woodhams, 1994). In child protection practice this is complicated by the use of the term 'parenting' which explicitly means both parents but implicitly means mothering; research into the role of husbands and fathers shows that men are not much involved in family life (Pollock and Sutton, 1985; Brannen and Moss, 1990) and that, where they are more involved, this is not necessarily positive for their families (Lewis and O'Brien, 1987). As social workers cannot clearly identify a role for fathers in this situation, it is not surprising that men are absent from child abuse theory and practice:

> there is a likelihood that women might well be overrepresented in the abuser category because of beliefs about their roles, responsibilities and natures. In this way researchers replicate the views and practices of social workers and other professionals, who carry out much of their work in such cases almost exclusively with women. (Corby, 1993: 65)

And:

> If professionals do not clearly distinguish between non-abusing mothers and perpetrators in their practice, vital opportunities for safeguarding children's welfare may be lost. Treating both parents as a single entity makes it more likely that mothers will feel that maintaining a facade of unity with the abuser is the only way to avoid their children being taken into care. (O'Hara, 1993: 129)

When race and class are significant dimensions, this can have devastating effects as exemplified in the Tyra Henry case where the maternal grandmother (as mother) was expected to cope despite material and psychological disadvantages of enormous proportions. At the same time, male professionals sought to minimize the male abuser's violence. Andrew Neil's well-documented violent behaviour over a wide spectrum of situations, as well as his assault on his first child Tyrone prior to his fatal assault on Tyra, was explained by his probation officer as an assault on a young and difficult baby although there was, in fact, no evidence that Tyrone was a difficult baby. The inquiry report concluded: 'What is in our view beyond doubt is that the paragraph, read as a whole, records an intervention which minimizes the known risk to Tyra from Andrew Neil' (London Borough of Lambeth, 1987: 63).

Psychological theory also promotes differing definitions of fathering and mothering qualities in two ways. First, the very elusiveness of fathering means that men are rarely the subject of research. For example, Brown and Harris' influential study of depression in women (1978) was under-taken because men were unwilling to answer the researchers' question-naires (Harris, 1991). Secondly, any focus on parenting is inevitably translated into mothering in research reports; see, for example, studies of abusing parents in which only mothers were actually studied (Browne and Saqui, 1988; Crittenden, 1988; Stratton and Swaffer, 1988; Petersen et al., 1993). There has been one study of the nature of the father's tie to the infant (Kotelchuk, 1972) but, significantly, it remains an unpublished thesis. Ingleby (1985) suggests that child psychology teaches that mothers carry responsibility for their children's destinies but that, by themselves, they are woefully inadequate.Psychological theorizing thereby bolsters conventional views about the gendered division of labour in the family, minimizing men's widespread violence in the home over a range of situations. Older women are more frequently abused than older men and male carers are more likely to abuse than female ones (McCreadie, 1991; Wilson, 1993); the incidence of violent assaults on female partners across all social classes is substantial (Smith, 1989); and, when accounting for time spent with children, men are more likely to abuse (Parton, 1990; Trotter, 1993).

Social workers unwittingly collude with this effective minimization of fathers' roles and behaviour by concentrating on women who provide a softer target for their efforts. For example, in a case where a child's name was placed on the register because the mother began a relationship with a Schedule 1 offender, the social worker and mother found themselves unable to challenge a situation where the man simply walked out of the house every time the social worker called. The social worker continued to 'work' on the mother's handling of the man's behaviour rather than refer the case back to case conference on the grounds of non-compliance with the care plan (case example brought to in-service training on 'assessment of risk'). Unwillingness to re-evaluate care plans in the light of men's non-compliance (Hallett, 1993) is to fail to process new information – a symptom of 'groupthink' which Janis (1982) identifies as a condition for dangerous decision-making. Effectively, social workers are locked into institutionalized 'groupthink' by the minimization of men's role in the family. New information is not simply disregarded, it is actually suppressed by the way in which fathers' behaviour is framed in theory, convention and practice.

The low status of mothers also means that women's complaints about violence are not accorded the same seriousness as men's referrals in child abuse investigations (Hill, 1978; Dingwall et al., 1983; Packman, 1986): neighbours or female relatives have to make allegations on several occasions before they are responded to effectively (Milner, 1993b); and complaints about spouse violence tend to be reframed as child protection cases by social workers (Maynard, 1985). The lack of credibility on the part of women to complain about violence in the home is bolstered by the constant derogation of women via 'mother-in-law jokes' and sexist language (see, for example, Graddol and Swann, 1988). Thus minimization operates to maintain men's minimal responsibility in the home while asserting his control over it. For example:

The behavioural problems exhibited by Kimberley were said to reflect her [Kimberley's] unacceptance of Mr Hall as her step father . . . he admitted to having 'shaken' and 'smacked' Kimberley, although he sought to minimize any injuries by attributing them to Kimberley having fallen down while playing. (London Borough of Greenwich, 1987: 108)

Secondary Processes which Bolster Minimization of Male Involvement in Child Abuse

Mitigation

While minimization processes serve to render men invisible in the domestic sphere and deflect attention away from widespread male violence, it cannot prevent a small number of men being identified as pathologically dangerous. Secondary processes operate whereby this group of men's behaviour can be minimized via pleas of mitigation. This process again depends upon the differing expectations of fathering and mothering but uses a range of excuses which would not be acceptable if proffered by women. Mitigation has two main themes: intentionality and the ownership of emotional control in the home. Both of these are underpinned by phallocentric notions of men as innately impulsive so that violence is seen as a 'single lapse' which will not demean a man's reputation and respectability with other men.

Intentionality operates at all levels of domestic violence. Higginson's (1990) analysis of 40 case conferences found that dangerous parenting was associated with a perception of deviant behaviour which wilfully transgressed 'community values' yet where such transgressions were interpreted as unintentional the behaviour was excused and justified. It is evident that no one will admit to being intentionally violent so impulsiveness is used to distinguish men's violence from women's. For example, when a man assaults his partner he can inflict serious damage simply because of his superior strength. The obvious implication of this is that men should therefore exercise more self-restraint than women. However, despite the evidence showing that partner violence is usually prolonged and escalates in severity (Smith, 1989), and that partners can and do assess quite precisely how much damage to inflict (MOVE, 1992), this behaviour is usually reframed in court as a one-off, impulsive act.

When a woman assaults her partner, her physical disadvantage means that she usually reaches for a weapon to be effective and this act effectively removes unintentionality as a defence available to her. She is also adjudged to have breached a range of controls which do not apply to men (see Heidensohn's, 1985, study of women and crime for an overview) and as an 'unconventional' woman she receives a harsher outcome (Carlen, 1983; Edwards, 1984; Eaton, 1986; Worrall, 1990). The notion that men do not own emotional control in the home is brought into play in a way which transfers this responsibility to women (Parkin, 1993). Thus a man can plead mitigation over a wide range of 'aggravation' and 'vulnerability'. A standard mitigating plea by men is drunkenness – an excuse not open to women as enquiries show that social workers note their concern when mothers frequent the pub as a moral issue but men's drinking is viewed in terms of traditional behaviour or treatment frameworks (see, for example, DHSS, 1974).

Most frequently though, 'aggravation' takes the form of neglect of emotional management on the part of women. It is not uncommon for social workers to accept that women should do all the emotional work whatever the domestic situation. For example, a student social worker responding to the fears of an elderly, wheelchair-bound woman hospital-ized after her unemployed, unmarried son had beaten her in her own home, found that the son was reluctant to be interviewed at all. When finally confronted with the consequences of his behaviour, he complained that he was embarrassed about pushing his mother in a wheelchair (minimal involvement in domestic duties); that his mother's behaviour aggravated him to this 'one-off' incident; and that he was depressed due to his unemployment (mitigation). Faced with this range of avoidance strategies and working in a setting which did not have a clear policy or procedures for dealing with potentially aggressive clients, the student was deflected onto the elderly mother. She arranged for the woman to have respite care away from her own home; training in handling her son's emotional responses and diffusing his anger; and was requested to be sympathetic to his embarrassment about her wheelchair-bound condition. Thus her manifest fears and needs were all considered subservient to her son's masculine self-esteem and this frail old woman was held totally responsible for managing the emotional tone of the relationship.

This transfer of responsibility away from men has become so in-built that men can escape completely by providing a woman as a scapegoat. One man with convictions for violence regularly beat his partner, including hitting her with a spade, and attacked his 3-month-old son when he was fretful. The mother gave the son a sleeping pill to keep him quiet and safe from assault before reporting matters to the police. Remarkably, the man was not prosecuted while the mother was charged with ill treating her child. Her child was taken into care and she was sentenced to a two-year probation order (*Huddersfield Examiner*, 26 August 1992: 2).

Expressions of remorse

Just as mitigation is used in the legal system to minimize the incidence and severity of violence in the family, so too, expressions of remorse are used to enable reframing of any violent event under official investigation. Expressions of remorse serve to individualize and excuse offenders. The recent case of a young man who assaulted his baby from the age of one week, resulting in 23 fractures, was told by the judge that he no doubt lost his temper on occasion and expressed remorse thus making him a candidate for treatment (anger management course) rather than punishment. This is despite the fact that the Criminal Justice Act 1991 expressly says that remorse is only a mitigating circumstance when accompanied by concern for the victim. The potential usefulness of the anger management course was thereby diminished by the minimizing of the man's behaviour. Expressions of remorse also operate in a more complex manner. As they usually lead to offenders being dealt with under a treatment rather than a punishment framework, they are of obvious use in the processes which minimize the serious and widespread nature of men's violence. There is evidence that police officers conduct interviews in a way which actively encourages expressions of remorse – a form of social constructionism of deviant behaviour which Aronsson (1991) refers to as 'recycling legal evidence'. This is very much a secondary process which comes into operation after minimization and mitigation processes have failed, usually at the point when a lengthy custodial sentence becomes apparent.

However, this means that it operates also as a mechanism whereby potential prisoners are recast as social work clients. Therefore, the inherent praiseworthiness of expressions of remorse are deeply embedded in social work discourses. Expressions of remorse can operate at investigative levels to prevent the intrusion of social work interventions or influence the direction of interventions. For example, when investigating a 'kick mark' bruise on a 6-year-old girl's back (Milner, 1993b), my first contact was with the child's mother who told me that the father was in bed prior to a nightshift duty, although it was late afternoon (men not concerned directly with the domestic life of the family), and she was quite sure that her husband would not do such a thing. Later, when I confronted the father, he said it was an accident caused by the child falling over when shouted at (minimization). When this was not accepted he said that the child was extremely difficult to handle in comparison with the other children (mitigation). When it was clear that I still wished to pursue the matter, he then said that he was very sorry, that it was a 'one-off', that it would not happen again and could he please have some help at school for his daughter's learning difficulties which led to her difficult behaviour in the home (remorse, minimization, mitigation and deflection onto the victim). Faced with multiple avoidance strategies which accorded with my social work values ('subjectifying' the client as Horne, 1990, describes it) and having no strategy for going further, I gratefully seized on the expressions of remorse. I then 'recycled the evidence' and 'screened out' the case before case conference.

There is little doubt that an expression of remorse could not be so easily constructed as an excuse for culpability had it been the mother who had kicked the child. Remorse in this context would have confirmed her as sinner and her subsequent mothering would have been subjected to intense scrutiny. Here, the nurturing role of mothering and psychological theorizing about women's innate moral inferiority would underpin the assessment, even though this theorizing takes some tortuous turns at times to maintain mothers' culpability. For example, a study which compared mothers of children abused by a family member or a teacher with mothers of non-abused children found that the mothers of abused children differed only from the other mothers in that they suffered more from depression and feelings of low self-esteem, and that this was probably a result of the abuse rather than the cause, still managed to conclude: 'While we do not believe it is appropriate to label mothers as "the real abuser" . . . it is possible that a mother may behave in ways that contribute to family dysfunction and increase a child's vulnerability to abuse' (Petersen et al., 1993).

Intimidation

The processes outlined above have the effect of constructing social work strategies for dealing with the victims of men's violence at the expense of developing any strategy for dealing with men other than direct confrontation. Confrontation is an entirely acceptable strategy when used by high-status men in a safe environment such as the treatment of sex offenders in the Gracewell Clinic (Wyre, 1992). Senior (1992), a probation officer, comments that the very words 'confront', 'challenge' and 'enforce' demonstrate the power of the (male) manager to define the tasks, and Dominelli (1992) argues that confrontational work at the Gracewell Clinic encourages male stereotyping of women as women needing men to protect them; men's contempt for women; and the right of stronger men to impose their will on weaker men, thereby maintaining the status quo. Jones (1993: 86) comments that front-line workers, most often women, 'have the difficult task of interviewing the child and disclosing her/his abuse to others within largely male dominated management structures'.

In the home or at case conference, confrontation is a dangerous and ineffective strategy. Violent men simply use intimidation – the ultimate avoidance process. Case conferences are dominated by the male discourses of Social Services managers, police and doctors (see, for example, the case of the 'battering Walshes', in Dingwall et al., 1983: 152–68). Increased parental participation merely permits violent men to re-enter the public sphere where other men will appease and excuse to maintain the reputation of all.

For the social worker who attempts to confront violent men in the home, overt intimidation is a common response. Indeed, identified dangerous men have used intimidation to prevent social workers from actually visiting the home at all even though 'closure' of an active case by fathers has been shown to be a 'danger' point, increasing the risk to children (Reder et al., 1993). For example, despite having killed his first child, George Auckland (DHSS, 1975) subsequently complained about social and health workers' intervention in his family life, resulting in the case being closed, and Nigel Hall (London Borough of Greenwich, 1987) intimidated a variety of professionals. At a neighbourhood centre:

> Mr Hall stood on the threshold of the office, obdurately refusing to go inside. He appeared 'angry and edgy', even aggressive. His speech was loud – 'almost shouting' – and he was abusive of social workers. The message was unmistakably clear . . . The encounter was mercifully short. (1987: 87)

And when he collected a son from school:

> In this way, Miss Rouse met Mr Hall about a dozen times when he would take the opportunity to voice concern about X's reading. She found him somewhat intimidating and felt that she was unsuccessful in persuading him that it was unreasonable to expect X to read a book every night. (1987: 90)

And the health visitor reported:

> Miss Reader told us that she was upset by Mr Hall. She added that the idea of visiting the Carliles was 'the sort of event that you would put off for a day when you were feeling particularly strong and able to cope with it!' (1987: 123)

And Mr Ruddock, although asserting that he would describe Mr Hall's behaviour as assertive rather than angry or intemperate, is contradicted in the report:

> Having ourselves seen and heard Mr Hall, we think that 'assertive' is too mild. We think that many people in Mr Ruddock's position would have found Mr Hall intimidating. (1987: 115)

Men do not need to be as openly aggressive as George Auckland, Nigel Hall or Andrew Neil. For example, one social worker tells of how she was affected by a father who combined reluctant compliance with the care plan with hints of his barely suppressed aggression. Violence was understood by the social worker as the reason for the care plan. She determinedly confronted him with his lack of cooperation but the emotional effort involved meant that she was unable to write up her notes immediately after each visit as was her usual practice (case example given at research seminar, Milner, 1993c). It was as though she was avoiding experiencing a 'second assault' of the sort described by rape victims when they have to retell the details. The main problem here is that social work practice has little to offer social workers in terms of strategy or safety.

Another social worker complained to her team leader on returning from a visit where she was shocked by violence and was told not to visit again alone. However, no plans were made for her to visit accompanied (case example given during in-service training on 'assessment of risk'). As social work practice stresses skills in deflecting and defusing anger (see, for example, Davies', 1988, advice on 'how not to get hit'), so too it values social work independence of action. The promotion of these traditional social work skills has three effects: it places social workers in a similar position to women and children in families in that they become responsible for managing the emotional tone; it hinders the development of skills in confrontation; and it effectively deflects intervention from violent behaviour – the reason why the social worker is involved in the family in the first place. Social work values and techniques which are aimed at subjectifying individuals, actually collide and collude with violence: 'Like mothers with their families social workers are taught, and expect, to put the needs of others above their own or be accused of being "bad" social workers' (Nice, 1988).

Conclusion

The fundamental question in child protection practice is not concerned with whether men or women or both abuse children but why it is that men are not held responsible for such behaviour while women are. The operationalization of the processes outlined above is very much a two-way process. Minimization, mitigation, expressions of remorse and intimidation can only be effective when the responsibility for the behaviour can be deflected onto someone else. While women are held responsible for the provision of a 'secure base' from which men can operate in the public sphere, then the only power they can yield is emotional power. Yet, this is only negative power – the power to stop something happening. It cannot be used to improve the status of women and children who must remain in the domestic sphere, doing a balancing act for the men who leave and return to it at their convenience. This process is mirrored in social work where their skills in 'emotional' work means that social workers step into the vulnerable family members' roles as domestic 'dirty workers' (Blyth and Milner, 1990).

Social workers who attempt to use feminist strategies in their practice are hindered by the constant shifting of responsibility onto women and often find themselves in a paradox of assertion training in which they exhort powerless women to become 'empowered', something which is particularly difficult to achieve if they have been abused as children themselves:

> For women, an internalising response may compound their experience of the interlocking nature of oppression. This would make self assertion very difficult for them as adults. For men, an externalising response, controlling and dominating within the family context, may be a way of managing their own history of oppression in their current circumstances. (Jones, 1993: 80)

Gordon (1989) has identified the most helpful social workers as those who 'understood family violence problems to be simultaneously social/ structural and personal in origin, and therefore offered help in both dimensions' (1989: 298), but this is easier said than done. It also denies the fact that female social workers themselves are placed in similar situations by the very factors operating in the differential processing of mothers and fathers in child protection decision-making. Perhaps one strategy which women could 'borrow' from men is to accept the limitations of their own power and use authority more explicitly. For example, when faced with intimidation early in an investigation, social workers could acknowledge that it is not their role to 'manage' this and go straight to the courts on the grounds on non-cooperation, asking for a child assessment order. Non-compliance is not just passive resistance and men's strategies need to be made more explicit in the judicial arena. Similarly, strategies involving expressions of remorse should not necessarily be 'challenged' by front-line workers but brought to supervision sessions as very real issues requiring guidance and the development of strategies for dealing with them. The Probation Service recognizes the particular difficulties involved in traditional one-to-one supervision in this area of work and, in some areas, has established 'practice fora' as part of management committee structure where staff can bring cases or discuss issues relating to work with sex offenders (Flaxington, 1993).

The Children Act 1989 also gives the courts powers to make an emergency ouster order for the protection of children (see O'Hara, 1993, for an overview) but despite the Law Commission's recommendation that the courts should think in terms of protecting children, the courts have ruled that an order should not be made if it interferes with a man's right of occupation (see Re F, Minors, Parental Home, Ouster, 1993, *The Times*, 1 December 1994). However, use can be made of inherent justice in the High Court if proceedings for a Section 8 order fail (Lyon and de Cruz, 1993). This is an extremely complicated aspect of law, so social workers would need to be aware of the need to take sound legal advice and representation before attempting to obtain an ouster order.

Should these measures fail, then social workers still have recourse to supervision orders. These may seem to be a poor answer when other proceedings have failed but if conditions regarding men's behaviour are added they can be useful. At the very least, specifying conditions would enable the social worker to begin breach proceedings and bring the matter back to the court thereby maintaining an emphasis on the man's behaviour. This will remove pressure from mothers to form an informal alliance with their children against men, one that Smart (1989) sees as fragile in the face of a reassertion of paternal rights. In using the law to highlight men's behaviour, there is more scope for fruitful feminist social work activity which 'has the means to expose how law operates in all its detailed mechanisms. In doing this it can increase resistance to law and may effect a shift in power' (Smart, 1989: 19).

References

Abbott, P. and Wallace, C. (1990) *The Sociology of the Caring Professions*, London: Falmer Press.

Aronsson, K. (1991) 'Social interaction and the recycling of evidence', in M. Coupland, H. Giles and J.M. Weimann (eds), *'Miscommunication' and Problematic Talk*, London: Sage.

Beagley, J.M. (1989) 'Gender issues in child abuse: "she must have known it was happening" ', *Child Abuse Review*, 3 (2): 8–13.

Blyth, E. and Milner, J. (1990) 'The process of inter-agency work', in Violence against Children Study Group (ed.), *Taking Child Abuse Seriously*, London: Unwin Hyman.

Brannen, J. and Moss, P. (1990) *Managing Mothers – Dual Earner Households after Maternity Leave*, London: Unwin Hyman.

Brown, G.W. and Harris, T. (1978) *Social Origins of Depression: a Study of Psychiatric Disorder in Women*, London: Tavistock.

Browne, K.D. and Saqui, J. (1988) 'Mother–infant interaction and attachment in physically abusing families', *Journal of Reproductive and Infant Psychology*, 6 (3): 163–82.

Carlen, P. (1983) *Women's Imprisonment*, London: Routledge and Kegan Paul.

Cooper, D.M. (1993) *Child Abuse Revisited: Children, Society and Social Work*, Milton Keynes: Open University Press.

Corby, B. (1993) *Child Abuse: Towards a Knowledge Base*, Milton Keynes: Open University Press.

Cordery, J. and Whitehead, A. (1992) ' "Boys don't cry": empathy, warmth, collusion and crime', in P. Senior and D. Woodhill (eds), *Gender, Crime and Probation Practice*, Sheffield: Sheffield City Polytechnic, PAVIC Publications.

Creighton, S.J. (1992) *Child Abuse Trends in England and Wales*, London: NSPCC/Longman.

Crittenden, P.M. (1988) 'Distorted patterns of relationship in maltreating families: the role of internal representation models', *Journal of Reproductive and Infant Psychology*, 6 (3): 183–200.

David, M.E. (1985) 'Motherhood and social policy – a matter of education?', *Critical Social Policy*, 4 (3): 28–43.

Davies, W. (1988) 'How not to get hit: violence and the helping professions', in N. Hayes (ed.), *Teaching Psychology to Social Workers*, 7, Leicester: British Psychological Society, pp. 33–7.

De Young, M. (1994) 'Women as mothers and wives in paternally incestuous families: coping with role conflict', *Child Abuse and Neglect*, 18: 73–83.

Denman, G. and Thorpe, D. (1993) 'Participation and patterns of intervention in child protection in Gwent', *A Research Report of the Area Child Protection Committee, Gwent*, Lancaster: Department of Applied Social Science, Lancaster University.

Department of Health (1994) 'Discussion report for ACPC conference: study of working together', Part 8 Reports ACPC Series, Report no. 1.

Department of Health and Social Security (1974) *A Report of the Committee of Inquiry into the Law and Supervision Provided in Relation to Maria Colwell*, London: HMSO.

Department of Health and Social Security (1975) *Report of the Committee of Inquiry into the Provision and Co-ordination of Services to the Family of John George Auckland*, London: HMSO.

Dingwall, R., Eekelaar, J. and Murray, T. (1983) *The Protection of Children: State Intervention and Family Life*, Oxford: Blackwell.

Dobson, F. (1974) *The First Comprehensive Guide for Fathers*, London, W.H. Allen.

Dominelli, L. (1992) 'Masculinity, sex offender and probation practice', in P. Senior and D. Woodhill (eds), *Gender, Crime and Probation Practice*, Sheffield: PAVIC Publications, Sheffield City Polytechnic.

Eaton, M. (1986) *Justice for Women?*, Milton Keynes: Open University Press.

Edwards, S. (1984) *Women on Trial*, Manchester: Manchester University Press.

Elliott, M. (ed.) (1993) *Female Sexual Abuse of Children: the Ultimate Taboo*, London: Longman.

Flaxington, F. (1993) *Working with Sex Offenders*, Greater Manchester Probation Service.

Finkelhor, D. (1992) 'What do we know about child sexual abuse?' Surviving Childhood Adversity, Dublin: Trinity College, 2–5 July.

Gibbons, J., Conroy, S. and Bell, C. (1993) *Operation of Child Protection Registers*, Report to Department of Health, Norwich, Social Work Development Unit, University of East Anglia.

Glaser, D. and Frosh, S. (1988) *Child Sexual Abuse*, Basingstoke: Macmillan Education.

Gordon, L. (1989) *Heroes of their own Lives: the Politics and History of Family Violence, Boston 1880–1960*, London: Virago.

128   *The problem of men's violence*

Graddol, D. and Swann, J. (1988) *Gender Voices*, Oxford: Blackwell.

Hallett, C. (1988) 'Research in child abuse: some observations on the knowledge base', *Journal of Reproductive and Infant Pyschology*, 6 (3): 119–24.

Hallett, C. (1993) 'Working together in child protection', Research Seminar, Centre for Child Care and Child Protection Studies, University of Huddersfield, 18 March.

Harris, T. (1991) 'Getting off the conveyor belt from childhood adversity: what we can learn from naturalistic studies', Surviving Childhood Adversity, Dublin: Trinity College, 2–5 July.

Heidensohn, F. (1985) *Women and Crime*, Basingstoke: Macmillan.

Higginson, S. (1990) 'Distorted evidence', *Community Care*, 17 May: 23–5.

Hill, P. (1978) 'Evaluating inquiries to Nottingham's NAI Register', *Social Work Today*, 9: 19–20.

Horne, M. (1990) 'Is it social work?', in Violence against Children Study Group (ed.), *Taking Child Abuse Seriously*, London: Unwin Hyman.

Hudson, A. (1992) 'The child sexual abuse "industry" and gender relations in social work', in M. Langan and L. Day (eds), *Women, Oppression and Social Work: Issues in Anti-discriminatory Practice*, London: Routledge.

Ingleby, D. (1985) 'Professionals as socializers: the "psy complex" ', in S. Spitzer and A.T. Scull (eds), *Research in Law, Deviance and Social Control*, New York: Jai Press.

Janis, I . (1982) *Groupthink: Psychological Studies of Policy Decisions and Fiascoes*, London: Houghton Mufflin.

Jones, J. (1993) 'Child abuse: developing a framework for understanding power relationships in practice', in H. Ferguson, R. Gilligan and R. Torode (eds), *Surviving Childhood Adversity: Issues for Policy and Practice*, Dublin: Social Studies Press.

Korbin, J. (1989) 'Fatal maltreatment by mothers: a proposed framework', *Child Abuse and Neglect*, 13: 481–9.

Kotelchuk, M. (1972) 'Nature of the child's tie to his father', unpublished PhD Thesis, Harvard University, Massachusetts.

Lewis, C. and O'Brien, M.(eds) (1987) *Reassessing Fatherhood: New Observations on Fathers and the Modern Family*, London: Sage.

London Borough of Greenwich (1987) 'A child in mind: protection of children in a responsible society', *The Report of the Commission of Inquiry into the Circumstances Surrounding the Death of Kimberley Carlile*, London: HMSO.

London Borough of Lambeth (1987) *Whose Child? The Report of the Panel Appointed to Inquire into the Death of Tyra Henry*, London: HMSO.

Lyon, C.M. and de Cruz, P. (1993) *Child Abuse*, Family Law, 2nd edn, Bristol: Jordan and Sons.

McCreadie, C. (1991) *Elder Abuse: an Exploratory Study*, London: Age Concern Institute of Gerontology, Kings College.

Marsh, P. (1991) 'Social work with fathers', in Family Rights Group (ed.), *The Children Act 1989: Working in Partnership with Families, Reader*, London: HMSO.

Maynard, M. (1985) 'The response of social workers to domestic violence', in J. Pahl (ed.), *Private Violence and Public Policy*, London: Routledge and Kegan Paul.

Milner, J. (1993a) 'A disappearing act: the differing career paths of fathers and mothers in child protection investigations', *Critical Social Policy*, 38 (13): 2.

Milner, J. (1993b) 'Avoiding violent men: the gendered nature of child protection policy and practice', in H. Ferguson, R. Gilligan and R. Torode (eds), *Surviving Childhood Adversity: Issues for Policy and Practice*, Dublin: Social Studies Press.

Milner, J. (1993c) 'The gendered nature of child protection interventions', Research Seminar, Centre for Child Care and Protection Studies, University of Huddersfield, 3 June.

MOVE (1992) 'Men (men overcome violence) surviving childhood adversity', Surviving Childhood Adversity, Dublin: Trinity College, 2–5 July.

Nice, V. (1988) 'Them and us: women as carers: clients and social workers', *Practice*, 2 (1): 58–73.

O'Hara, M. (1993) 'Child protection in the context of domestic violence: recognising the links', in H. Ferguson, R. Gilligan and R. Torode (eds), *Surviving Childhood Adversity: Issues for Policy and Practice*, Dublin: Social Studies Press.

Packman, J. (1986) *Who Needs Care?*, Oxford: Blackwell.

Parkin, W. (1993) 'The public and the private: gender, sexuality and emotion', in S. Fineman (ed.), *Emotion in Organisations*, London: Sage.

Parton, C. (1990) 'A feminist perspective on child abuse', in Violence against Children Study Group (ed.), *Taking Child Abuse Seriously*, London: Unwin Hyman.

Petersen, R.F., Basta, S.M. and Dykstra, T.A. (1993) 'Mothers of molested children: some comparisons of personality characteristics', *Child Abuse and Neglect*, 17: 409–18.

Phillimore, P. (1981) *Families Speaking*, London: Family Services Unit.

Pollock, S. and Sutton, J. (1985) 'Fathers' rights, women's losses', *Women's Studies International Forum*, 8 (6): 593–99.

Reder, P., Duncan, S. and Gray, M. (1993) *Beyond Blame: Child Abuse Tragedies Revisited*, London: Routledge.

Rich, A. (1977) *Of Women Born: Motherhood as Institution and Experience*, London: Virago.

Senior, P. (1992) 'Gender-conscious service delivery: implications for staff development', in P. Senior and D.Woodhill (eds), *Gender, Crime and Probation Practice*, Sheffield: PAVIC Publications, Sheffield City Polytechnic.

Smart, C. (1989) *Feminism and the Power of the Law*, London: Routledge.

Smith, L.J.F. (1989) *Domestic Violence: an Overview of the Literature*, Home Office Research Study 107, London: HMSO.

Statham, D. (1987) 'Women, the new right and social work', *Journal of Social Work Practice*, 2 (4): 129–49.

Stratton, P. and Swaffer, R. (1988) 'Maternal causal beliefs for abused and handicapped children', *Journal of Reproductive and Infant Psychology*, 6 (3): 201–16.

Trotter, J. (1993) 'Non abusing fathers – where are they?', Research Seminar, Centre for Child Care and Child Protection Studies, Huddersfield: University of Huddersfield, 21 October.

Wilson, G. (1993) 'Disclosing the truth about "granny bashing" ', *Family Policy Bulletin*, London: Family Policy Studies Centre: 4–5.

Woodhams, R. (1994) Personal communication.

Worrall, A. (1990) *Offending Women*, London: Routledge.

Wyre, R. (1992) 'Gracewell clinic', in W.R. Stainton, D. Hevey, J. Roche and E. Ash (eds), *Child Abuse and Neglect: Facing the Challenge*, 2nd edn, London: Batsford.

9

Working with Men who Sexually Abuse Children: the Experience of the Probation Service

Elizabeth Lancaster

By the end of the 1980s one particular aspect of men's violence – the sexual abuse of children – had become well known. Practitioners in various social work agencies in Britain had become accustomed to the fact that, whatever preventative measures were in place, a growing amount of worker time and agency resources were being taken up in working with people who had been the victims of such offences. The more recent development has been in respect of practice initiatives concentrating on those who perpetrate sexual offences and it is these which form the subject of this chapter.

The aim of such intervention is to protect children by reducing the risk of re-offending in identified individuals. Additionally, information may be gathered about methods and modes of offending which offenders may have in common, and so assist in the protection of children generally. One of the principal agencies involved in working with the perpetrators of sexual abuse is the Probation Service and my intention is to focus on the development of work in this agency with a view to helping to identify some of the issues surrounding social work involvement with the perpetrators of sexual crime. My initial discussion concerns the apparent growth in the incidence of sexual abuse in the 1980s and the effect this has had on the Probation Service; this is followed by a brief history of the techniques used when working with sex offenders; a description of the theoretical developments of the past decade; the reasons why these have developed into an orthodoxy for probation officers; and the organizational context of this.

Some preliminary clarification of subject and setting needs to be made. In the context of work being undertaken within the Probation Service, the primary concern is with men who abuse; abuse by women does happen, but the current state of knowledge indicates that the huge majority of abusers are men and prosecutions are almost exclusively of men. Further to this, my discussion focuses specifically on men who abuse children, as this is the offender group targeted by most of the Probation Service programmes. The research literature reveals differing uses of the terms 'child sexual abuse' and 'sexual abuse', the main variant being in the inclusion or not of non-contact offences, such as indecent exposure. Northamptonshire Probation Service define the term, and the scope of their intervention, thus:

> Child sexual abuse is the involvement of dependant children or adolescents in sexual activities with an adult, or any person older or bigger, in which the child is used as a sexual object, for the gratification of the older person's needs or desires, and to which the child is unable to give consent due to the unequal power in the relationship. (Northamptonshire Probation Service, n. d.)

The majority of attenders involved in a Probation Service sex offender programme will have done something which has been identified and punished as a sexual offence by the criminal justice system, although some programmes do accept 'voluntary' referrals from other agencies. The range of offences committed by such offenders is huge, from single offences of indecent exposure involving unknown victims, to multiple offences of gross indecency, buggery and rape against known children. This variation arises because the programmes are used to provide input as part of a community penalty or as part of an early release plan in respect of offenders who receive a prison sentence.

Inter- and intra-agency initiatives focusing on preventing or reducing re-offending, by working with the source of the abuse – the offender – rather than forever dealing with the aftermath, were isolated phenomena a decade ago, but are now comparatively commonplace, generally employing a groupwork model of intervention. Charitable organizations such as the National Society for the Prevention of Cruelty to Children and National Children's Homes are participating in planning and staffing treatment programmes in conjunction with statutory agencies such as the Probation Service and Social Services. Additional input is made by individuals from voluntary agencies, the psychological services of the National Health Service, or on a freelance basis, acting as consultants who advise the staff group of a project on practice aspects of the work, an input increasingly unlikely to be part of the skills and probably the functions of the standard line manager. Viewing the groupwork initiatives as a whole, the organization most commonly involved is the Probation Service.

Popular knowledge and understanding of the role of the Probation Service are fairly rudimentary. Yet the Probation Service in England and Wales has a specific professional responsibility for working with offenders, and its functions are central to any discussion about society's response to people who offend. In Scotland the functions of the Probation Service are incorporated into the duties of social work departments. It is clear from surveys of probation practice that specialized work with people who have committed sexual offences has been going on for some time; for example, programmes in Avon and Hampshire were established in 1977 and 1978 respectively, and the Nottingham group programme was set up in 1980. However, most probation-run treatment programmes for sex offenders were established in the late 1980s and early 1990s, some 60 being set up between 1986 and 1992 (Barker, 1991: 4).

Such a focus on a small group of offenders is unusual, if not unprecedented, and has required a combination of practitioner interest, management support and Home Office sanction. This was not inevitable, and in some ways is contradictory. The intention, therefore, is to examine why such initiatives have moved from the sidelines to the mainstream of practitioner intervention in the only organization which has statutory responsibility for working with people who have broken the law from the time of their appearance in court, through to post-custody supervision. The point that this could not have happened without management involvement and Home Office approval should not be lost; however, the particular discussion I want to pursue centres on the factors which generated practitioner interest in working with a group of offenders whose behaviour is popularly adjudged to be both abnormal and irredeemable.

Sexual Offending: a Growing Problem?

The broad and familiar context of this discussion is that during the 1980s there was a growing public awareness of the existence of child sexual abuse, aided by such initiatives as ChildLine, the telephone counselling service for children and young people, founded in 1986. A factor contributing to this developing consciousness has been the emergence and growth of 'victimology' as a distinct area of specialism within the broad sweep of criminology generally. 'Victimology' represents the study of victims of criminal behaviour, partly as a means of assessing the amount of crime which is unrecorded and hence invisible in statistical terms, and also as a means of acknowledging the qualitative, and possibly long-term, impact of crime on victims. Victim survey literature in respect of sexual crime suggests a significant degree of under-reporting. The methodology employed in such surveys raises the possibility of biased samples and false responses; furthermore, definitional differences in respect of the term 'sexual abuse' do not allow universal conclusions to be drawn. These caveats notwithstanding, self-reporting studies in respect of child sexual abuse demonstrate prevalence rates of 6–62 per cent for women, and 3–30 per cent for men (Warwick, 1991: 9).

Limited evidence is available from older victim studies which demonstrates that the prevalence of sexual offending is not a new phenomenon (Warwick, 1991: 9). What does appear to be new, however, is a qualitatively different understanding of the impact of sexual abuse, both in the short and long term. Although research studies have made some contribution in this respect, a more profound awareness has been developed via the consciousness-raising impact of feminism. In simple terms, the reassessing and reordering of relationships which form an integral part of feminism have permeated the attitudes and expectations of women generally. While these processes are far from complete, women, individually and collectively, have consequently been encouraged to make public a range of experiences which had hitherto been kept private, or whose impact had been otherwise unacknowledged. Women are becoming able to identify themselves as victims of crime, especially victims of sexual assault and what is colloquially known as 'domestic violence', and are able to describe the qualitative impact of such events. More specifically, the growth of the women's refuge movement and an increase in rape crisis centres have helped provide the emotional and practical support needed by individual 'victims', and the opportunity for adults to undertake counselling retrospectively. I would also argue that changes in the broad climate of awareness is encouraging male victims to come forward in a similar manner. Credit has to be given also to the organizational response of the police in the establishment of specialist domestic violence units, child abuse units and the promotion of training in respect of the interviewing and investigation of alleged offences of rape.

An important qualifying point needs to be made here as there was, and still is, a reluctance on the part of the public to accept that such offending may be part of the behaviour of men who in all other respects are 'normal'. While there is an awareness of the occurrence of sexual abuse, this is related to specific, high-profile cases or to a superficial acknowledgement of the existence of victims of abuse. It is as if the majority of offences were committed in some abstract manner, and did not take place in ordinary families (and some would argue not to ordinary children): the perpetrators are still the 'sex beasts' and the 'dirty old men' of popular imagination and popular reporting, outsiders in some way and beyond the reach of society. Thus, no attempt is made at unravelling processes by which 'those males caught offending are scapegoated and disowned from the very society that provided the conditions in which their psycho-sexual development took place' (Gocke, 1991: 8). It is possible, therefore, for a public distancing from the commission of such offending to take place, and for the simplistic analysis of who offends to be accompanied by an equally simplistic analysis of what the judicial response to such behaviour should be – incarceration, preferably lengthy, and ideally, permanent.

Official statistics bear witness to this superficial public awareness of sexual abuse and form the conventional starting point of a discussion which considers why there has been such a growth in the number of projects working with sex offenders. Between 1980 and 1990 the number of notifiable sexual offences recorded by the police in England and Wales rose from 21,107 to 29,044, an increase of nearly 38 per cent (Home Office, 1991a). Within this total, the number of offences of rape has increased steadily since 1983, the figures for indecent assault on a female beginning to rise in 1985 and for indecent assault on a male in 1986. Taking sexual offending as a whole, the period of most noticeable growth in this decade was between 1985 and 1989, when the total of recorded offences rose from 21,456 to 29,733. However, there was a numerical growth in *all* categories of notifiable offences recorded by the police and these categories remained roughly proportionate to each other throughout the decade;

sexual offending did not increase out of proportion to other recorded offences, and remained at under 1 per cent of the total. Yet what may single sexual offending out is not a greater incidence of these sort of offences, but a greater willingness on the part of the public and victims to report abuse. A casual reading of the statistics might pessimistically conclude that the number of offenders and offences was increasing, a more thoughtful approach might speculate that victims were gaining the confidence to make public their private traumas, and thus focusing attention on a level of offending which had always existed.

An initial outcome was that professional attention was drawn to a subject that had hitherto been a private concern; for example, the period 1983–7 saw an increase of 800 per cent in the registration of children on the child protection registers of Social Services departments as a result of sexual abuse (Home Office, 1989, quoted in Morrison et al., 1994: 26). Yet the response of the Probation Service in this situation cannot be taken for granted and has to be seen in the context of the number of people actually prosecuted for these offences, and additionally in how these offenders were being sentenced, bearing in mind that behaviours which come to the attention of the Social Services, and indeed other child welfare organizations, do not necessarily find their way into police statistics as recorded offences. Additionally, those which are recorded do not necessarily make a full passage through the length of the criminal justice system, due variously to insufficient evidence, difficulty in identifying or apprehending the perpetrator or in proving guilt, in the context of a trial, beyond reasonable doubt.

About three-quarters of all recorded notifiable sexual offences, that is, offences reported to the police, are cleared up, in that an offender is identified. Criminal justice statistics throughout the 1980s indicate that a declining number of offenders were actually sentenced for an indictable sexual offence, while the number cautioned grew, both numerically and as a proportion of the total number of offenders identified. Thus the total sentenced in 1980 was 8,000 with a further 2,800 cautioned; and in 1990, just over 6,500 (plus 3,300 cautioned). The numerical low point of sentencing was 1986, when 5,500 offenders were found guilty, with 2,800 offenders being cautioned (Home Office, 1991a).

The figures do not indicate the number of offences for which a particular individual was sentenced, and it is this which may explain some of the difference between recorded offences and offenders actually sentenced over and above the allowance which has to be made for unidentified offenders. Discrepancies could be further accounted for by the fact that an offender is not necessarily sentenced for offences which took place in the same statistical year, and the obvious point that the identifying of an offender does not always lead to a successful prosecution. An additional factor is that figures for the reporting and disposal of the summary offence of indecent exposure are recorded separately, and, by the end of the decade, accounted for over 1,000 successful prosecutions each year. In conclusion, about 1,000 offenders a year received a probation order or a supervision order, while the total receiving a sentence of immediate imprisonment which might attract some future post-custodial supervision varied between 1,200 and 2,500 a year during this decade. Probation orders on male offenders, including those sentenced for indecent exposure, represented 3 per cent of all orders; the total in respect of children and young persons' supervision orders was 2.5 per cent (Home Office, 1991b: 23, 27).

Effects on the Probation Service

The point arising out of such statistical discussion is that the apparent increase in sexual offending did not translate directly into an increased caseload for probation officers; the sudden growth in the late 1980s of sex offender projects was not a response to numerical pressure. Yet in spite of the small numbers, probation officers and their managers were clearly seeing this group of offenders as problematic, both in terms of the risk such offenders posed, and the disproportionate amount of time in caseload terms such offenders occupied. Thus the various team or divisional registers of 'serious', 'high risk' or 'potentially dangerous' offenders invariably included those who had committed sexual offences, often both in terms of current offences and where sexual offences were listed as previous convictions. This represented an acknowledgement of risk, heightened by a growing professional understanding of the impact of abuse on a victim. Divisional registers did not necessarily generate coherent workplans, and this lack of certainty about what could be done was further exacerbated by the increasing amount of time taken up by such offenders, for example, in attending case conferences. This quantity of input and anxiety about what would happen if things went wrong could simply not be acknowledged by a statistical levelling of 'contact hours' across cases.

Practitioner uncertainty about this group of offenders has to be seen in the context of the general discussions about the nature and purpose of Probation Service intervention at this time. Briefly summarized, conventional descriptions of the theoretical influences on the Probation Service in the late 1970s and early 1980s stress the undercurrent of fatalism associated with the 'nothing works' school of thought. This was the common, though not necessarily uncontentious, interpretation of research on the outcomes of social work with offenders taking place during the 1970s (Blagg and Smith, 1989: 85–7), and the climate in which Bottoms and McWilliams proffered their 'new theoretical framework for probation practice – the non-treatment paradigm' (Feaver and Smith, 1994: 381). One broad plank of their argument defined crime as having social, rather than pathological, causes. A consequence of this was that social work with offenders was in part defined as the provision of 'appropriate help' in respect of issues brought to the attention of the probation officer by the client. There was no place for practitioner-led strategies which might influence the behaviour of individuals (because 'nothing worked') and thus no consideration of individual offence-focused work (Raynor and Vanstone, 1994: 396–9). A parallel aim of this new framework for practice emphasized the diversion from custody of appropriate offenders and the development of alternatives to custody in a community setting; prison was fundamentally damaging and patently unable to stop re-offending; any approach which kept people out of prison could almost be viewed as an end in itself.

It is this latter aim of diversion from custody which appeared to attract the most visible practitioner energy and innovation in the 1980s, lending legitimacy to the developing concept of 'punishment in the community' as projects had increasingly to stress their restrictive, and hence punitive, characteristics at the expense of their rehabilitative ones in order to persuade sentencers of their credibility. Paradoxically, in terms of the 'non-treatment paradigm' offered by Bottoms and McWilliams, the interventions being devised within the context of diversion from custody have tended to focus on the direct confrontation of offending behaviour, rather than on associated social phenomena and, importantly for the subsequent development of sex offender work, were often being employed in an intensive group-work setting. Behind this front line, however, it has to be said that the general content of probation orders remained fairly eclectic, and a reading of the *Probation Journal* in the late 1980s indicates that contributions from practitioners discussed structural issues of poverty, unemployment and poor housing, alongside issues of empowerment and masculinity: the difficulties and implications of creating a truly anti-oppressive practice alongside problems associated with the administration of the criminal justice system; and specific techniques for working directly with clients about their offending, including cognitive-behavioural initiatives.

Sex Offender 'Treatment' and the Probation Service

Before continuing to look at how work developed with sex offenders in this setting, some comment must be made about the then current styles of intervention with those whose offences were sexual in nature. Thus, until the 1980s, the conventional approach to the treatment of people who had committed sexual offences was based on a medical/psychiatric model, and the work that was undertaken directly with offenders largely took place in National Health Service settings. The causes of sexual offending were perceived to be rooted in an individual's 'biological malfunctioning' or 'abnormality', treatment was based on concepts of 'disease' and hence of 'cure', and such an approach placed intervention beyond the scope of criminal justice professionals and most social workers. Interestingly, however, one of the earliest recorded Probation Service initiatives involved a probation officer in Essex administering a libido suppressant drug, in collaboration with a general practitioner, to sex offenders under his supervision. While group work was employed to foster positive attitudes towards the drug, an additional support group worked with offenders and their families on wider issues. The importance of this initiative is summarized by Leah Warwick (1991: 27–8):

> Firstly, it shows the benefits that might be gained from the probation service working closely with medical practitioners. Secondly, it suggests that sex offenders are amenable to treatment and that groupwork is a feasible approach. Thirdly, it reveals that the courts may be more prepared to consider probation supervision as an alternative to custody when a clear treatment plan is available. Finally, it demonstrates the fragility of projects dependent upon the sustained interest and initiative of a single probation officer.

Growth in the reporting of the physical abuse of children and subsequently of sexual abuse encouraged social workers to focus on the family context of abuse, and led to the adoption of a 'family dysfunction' approach in which abuse is seen as a symptom of what is wrong with the way the family operates, rather than the fault of the offender within it. Although this approach, by definition, could not account for non-familial offending, nevertheless it gained some orthodoxy among social workers trained in systems theory and struggling against an individual pathology model of behaviour, and appears to have been advocated as the standard model of intervention by a wide range of organizations and individuals (MacLeod and Saraga, 1991: 110–14).

Although the 'family dysfunction' approach has been documented as forming one of the techniques used by Probation Service practitioners in the early 1980s, and provided a useful example of inter-agency working (Warwick, 1991: 28), the general response to this as an analysis of behaviour was fairly muted, not least because it failed to address the problem of non-familial offending. Additionally, the broader approaches to offending suggested by the 'non-treatment paradigm' and the 'nothing works' philosophy outlined above also appeared to be insufficient responses to the problem of sexual offending. While the concept of the social generation of offending was familiar to most probation officers, the developing critique of the causes and nature of sex offending rested fairly and squarely on an individual pathology model of behaviour and it is this which delineated the methods of intervention.

Research conducted by Dr Li, a clinical psychologist with the East Suffolk Health Authority in the late 1980s, supported this viewpoint. He undertook a survey of professionals concerned with child sexual abuse, the largest number of respondents being probation officers. From this, he concluded that feminist and family system insights, despite their prominence in the literature, had little influence on practitioners compared with the assumption that the treatment of the adult perpetrator – whether to deal with individual pathology or social skills deficits – should form an important part of professional intervention (reported in *Probation Journal*, 3, 1989: 138). My own experience as a semi-specialist worker with a

Probation Service sex offender project, and anecdotal evidence from former colleagues, suggests that a primary motivation in engaging in work with sex offenders is that the focus can be on that individual's specific behaviour within a framework that acknowledges the responsibility of each offender for his actions and his consequent ability to amend his behaviour. While more sophisticated analyses concerning how an individual makes his choices within the constraints and conventions of a wider social structure can, and should, develop, the starting point for most practitioners is that they can have an impact on the particular behaviour of a specific individual.

A further comment on motivation is relevant here. In a frank article, published in the *Probation Journal* in December 1990 entitled 'Confrontative work with sex offenders: legitimized nonce-bashing?', Michael Sheath speculates that what is attracting male workers towards working with sex offenders is the style of confrontational interviewing being sanctioned, as this encourages a worker to challenge the distortions and justifications being used by offenders in a fairly aggressive manner. Sheath suggests that sex offenders in prison, having being given the 'nonce' label, 'perform a vital function as scapegoats. Male prisoners are able to affirm their own healthy heterosexuality by "giving the beasts a hard time" . . . Since nonce bashing was denied to me, I learnt the technique of the confrontational interview' (Sheath, 1990: 159–60). He goes on to illustrate the point by reference to his own practice at that time, concluding that his approach was counter-productive and that there was a need for a much more gradual, sensitive and indirect approach. This is an important observation and worthy of further consideration in a more detailed analysis of gendered motivation in respect of working with sex offenders.

The implication that probation officers were choosing to focus on the specific behaviour of individual offenders does not indicate a uniformity of intervention either in terms of strategy or rationale. However, the late 1980s witnessed the rapid spread and assimilation into practice of theories and techniques from North America which stressed the need for a multi-factor, rather than a single-factor, model as an explanation of offending and highlighted the importance of cognitive-behaviourist methods in working with the offender to reduce the risk of re-offending. While these have developed into an orthodoxy for practitioners in this area, they are less well established among other professionals, even those who are only slightly removed from the subject. For example, as a probation officer I had the opportunity of discussing the contents of a report I had prepared on a man convicted of sexual offences with the sentencing judge a short time after he had imposed a sentence of imprisonment on the offender. At the time of sentence, the judge had taken exception to my analysis of the man's behaviour, i.e. that as an adult having sexual intercourse with a 14-year-old girl, he shared certain characteristics with other abusers of children; and consequently no elaboration of my argument or proposed intervention had been possible in open court. In private discussion it was clear not only that the judge viewed offending of this nature against a 14-year-old as quite distinct from offending against younger children (which is at least arguable), but that the intervention he considered appropriate for a 'paedophile' was derived from a medical model analysis of sex offending. The language and concepts of what I perceived to be an accepted and uncontroversial cognitive-behaviourist perspective were alien to him.

Theoretical Developments

The treatment of sexual offenders is an area of intervention in which workers are consciously attempting to relate their practice to theoretical initiatives; indeed, one of the intentions of the Home Office's inspection of work being undertaken with sex offenders by the Probation Service was to ascertain 'the theoretical knowledge base which informed the development of local policy and practice' (Home Office, 1991b: 31). Among those who are working directly with people who have committed sexual offences, Wolf (1984) and Finkelhor (1986) have made especially influential contributions, both offering multifactorial models to describe how someone develops the motivation to abuse sexually, and the process via which an offence takes place. I am not offering a comprehensive critique of either model at this point; however, it is important to outline the main features of each in order to explain why they are now so universally employed by Probation Service practitioners.

Wolf's model stresses the importance of someone's early history and the impact this has on the development of a particular type of personality, which is believed to be characteristic of sex offenders generally: 'egocentricity, a poor self-image, defensiveness, distorted thinking, being ruminative to the point of becoming obsessive in thoughts and behaviour, socially alienated and sexually preoccupied.' Additionally, he 'has a tendency to blame external factors for things which go wrong and has a strong need for tightly structured social situations in which he can exercise control and thus lessen anxiety' (Fisher, 1994: 17–18).

The process of offending is explained by using a 'cycle of offending', viewing behaviour as circular, rather than linear, in order to emphasize the repetitive nature of the conduct. Thus an offender typically has a poor self-image, expects rejection and withdraws into himself, using sexual fantasies to compensate for the feelings of isolation. The offender's personality development means that these fantasies are deviant in some way and may be reinforced through masturbation. The fantasy develops into the rehearsal of the future offence, a victim is targeted, and 'groomed' to accept the forthcoming assault, possibly over a long period of time, before the assault takes place. Once the sexual excitement of the actual offence or subsequent masturbation has passed, the offender slides into guilt at the reality of his behaviour, this reinforces his low self-esteem and these feelings can only be dissipated by a repeat of the process of fantasy, leading again to assault.

The model of a cycle of offending is not necessarily applicable to all offenders; for example, adolescent sex offenders may not have established a repetitive pattern of behaviour. The importance of the model is that if an offender can learn to identify the elements of behaviour which make up his own specific cycle, then he can identify the points at which he is able to control and divert his thoughts and actions and consequently avoid offending. An individual may, on occasions, travel through his cycle in the space of a few hours, or it may take days or even years for someone to reach the point of re-offending. The principle, however, remains the same; the earlier in the cycle that an offender can recognize the offence-inclined nature of his thoughts and his behaviour, the more likely he is to be able to take the responsibility for undertaking aversive action.

Finkelhor's model list four factors explaining why adults may be specifically interested in children:

> (1) emotional congruence – why the adult has an emotional need to relate to a child; (2) sexual arousal – why the adult could become sexually aroused by a child; (3) – why alternative sources of sexual and emotional gratification are not available; and (4) disinhibition – why the adult is not deterred from such interest by normal prohibitions. (Finkelhor, 1986: 117)

All these contribute to motivating someone to abuse, the starting point of the process which leads to an offence taking place. Finkelhor terms his analysis of this process as the Four Preconditions Model of Sexual Abuse; the initial motivation to abuse sexually is not sufficient for an offence to take place, and must be accompanied by an offender's willingness to overcome internal inhibitors in respect of offending by using individual disinhibitors, such as alcohol or more social or culturally based rationales, such as the ideology of patriarchal prerogatives for fathers. External environmental inhibitors to offending have then to be surmounted in terms of, for example, manipulating or taking advantage of a situation in which a child is not receiving the usual amount of supervision; finally, the child's own resistance to abuse has to be undermined (Finkelhor, 1986: ch. 5). The particular benefit of using this model is that it allows the process of an offence to be analysed in detail, moving an offender on from asserting that his behaviour 'just happened' to an understanding of the thoughts, feelings and conscious manipulation of people and events which he undertook before the offence could take place.

Both models employ the technique of 'cognitive restructuring' which necessitates the offender examining the various distortions and excuses he has used to justify his behaviour; both have been used in a particularly confrontational way as indicated above, though this is not the only style of intervention these models suggest. Neither is completely satisfactory, for example in the lack of consideration given to female offenders, but both mark a considerable sophistication of previous analyses of the reasons for, and the process of, sexual offending.

Impact on the Probation Service

It is these theoretical developments which have had a particular resonance for field workers in the Probation Service, and which are partly responsible for the growth in sex offender projects as detailed above. The Probation Service areas responding to Warwick's survey in 1991 indicated a similarity in approach and methods and were generally basing their intervention on the multifactorial models advocated by Wolf, Finkelhor and Ray Wyre (Wyre, 1987), whose pioneering work at the Gracewell Clinic, a residential centre for the treatment of sex offenders, did much to disseminate the American research in Britain. Within a broad perspective of cognitive restructuring, social skills training and behavioural control techniques, the main features of the Probation Service programmes were: 'the use of group dynamics to confront offending behaviour and denial, understand the offence cycle and how to break it, explore power differentials between victim and perpetrator, examine damage done to victims, build internal and external controls to prevent relapse, improve relationship skills and provide sex education' (Warwick, 1991: 35).

Recent research evaluating six probation programmes indicates that the behavioural component, defined as techniques for reducing arousal to deviant fantasies and skills with which to develop appropriate relationships, was the least developed component of the intervention. While skills training was in evidence in the long-term programmes, it is likely that input in respect of the distinct techniques for reducing deviant arousal was omitted because of the specific psychological knowledge and training needed to utilize them. Additionally, this style of work is more suited to one-to-one contact rather than group work (Beckett et al., 1994: 28–51; Fisher, 1995: 3).

In general terms, I would suggest that the reasons these models of intervention gained such rapid popularity is that, unlike the earlier endeavours using drugs or family therapy, these 'new' techniques seemed exactly to match the personal initiatives and the practice experience of officers working with a range of offenders in terms of the type of input which appeared to be successful in encouraging offenders to amend their behaviour. Notwithstanding the pervasiveness of the 'nothing works' ideology, probation officers individually and collectively were developing specifically cognitive approaches to their work with clients, alongside more optimistic conclusions about the rationale, aims and effectiveness of probation input. It would seem logical that field officers conversant with some of these ideas were already beginning to transfer this approach to working with sex offenders, or at the very least starting to think about whether the transference of techniques was possible.

Credit is given to a major US survey conducted by Abel and his associates (Abel et al., 1987), for promoting the development of work with sex offenders. It has been described as 'a watershed in the knowledge base about sex offenders' (Fisher, 1994: 6), due to the new information it revealed about offenders, principally in the disclosure of the huge amount and variety of offending which was taking place across offence categories. The previous assumption had been that offenders were offending within one offence category, and had a specific gender preference in choosing a victim. This survey demonstrated that 23.3 per cent of respondents offended against both family and non-family victims; 20 per cent offended against both sexes and 26 per cent indulged in both contact and non-contact behaviours.

The importance of the study in research terms is that it provided evidence which contradicted one of the fundamental tenets of the 'family dysfunction' school of thought in that some offenders chose to offend against both family and non-family members. However, I would question its impact at the time of publication on the majority of field workers in Britain. Social work practitioners' awareness of research can be patchy and their acceptance of conclusions capricious; the existence of a particular set of research findings does not necessarily guarantee an impact on practice. While conferences, the commitment of individual practitioners, and the work of organizations such as NOTA (National Association for the Development of Work with Sex Offenders) all assist in the dissemination of ideas and research findings, it is simplistic to describe either the research or the dissemination of findings as the cause of the growth in working with sex offenders. If a multifactorial model is applied to an analysis of how research impacts on practice, the starting point has to be in the attitudes and perceptions of practitioners, i.e. the belief that probation officers should work with and can influence the behaviour of all offenders. The environmental or external factors of an explanatory framework and methods of working could not in themselves ensure an influence on practice. The interrelatedness of the process should not be overlooked; clearly, the emergence of new theoretical tools assists in encouraging a practitioner that particular interventions are possible and reinforces existing understanding. However, the acceptance and assimilation of specific models and methods has to be because these reflect the real-life practice experience of real-life practitioners. Thus the methods of working with sex offenders were credible, and the accompanying multifactorial model concerning the causes of offending mirrored a truth, if not a truism, known to most probation officers, that offending rarely has a single cause and that a full analysis of the origins of someone's offending requires the balancing of individual, family, environmental and societal factors.

Organizational Context

It is fair to say that the initiatives in developing work with sex offenders have been practitioner-led, but that from the late 1980s onwards this has been with the increasing support of Probation Service managers, employers (in the form of local Probation Committees who have to authorize certain local developments) and policy-makers and imple-menters at the Home Office, leaving to one side the experience of one project which operated successfully for 14 years on a voluntary basis, only to fold, albeit on a temporary basis, during the formalization of its arrangements by management (Barker and Morgan, 1991). This single example illustrates that the transition from the voluntarily staffed project to the integrated, resourced and managed programme is not straight-forward; however, problems in respect of implementation do not diminish the importance of the fact that the Home Office has clearly sanctioned the validity of undertaking work, in both a custodial and a community setting, with men who have committed sexual offences.

In June 1991, a major initiative was announced in respect of the assessment and treatment of adult male offenders in prisons, and two main treatment programmes were to be established, a 'core programme' and an 'extended programme' for men considered to be a higher risk, to be introduced at a total of 14 prisons with additional complementary pro-grammes to be run at three other institutions (Sabor, 1992: 14–15). Training, planning and piloting all took place before the formally evaluated programme was implemented in late 1992, targeting all inmates serving four years or more; both men who have abused children, and men who have abused women are candidates for the group-work programme. Additionally, the community-based programmes are receiving recognition in terms of local management including sex offender group work as part of divisional plans and taking cognizance of the need to staff them adequately following on from some fairly erratic managerial responses to the practitioner-generated projects (Morrison, 1992: 122–8). Given the degree of central control demonstrated by the Home Office over what had previously been relatively autonomous probation areas (Jones, 1993), such community-based approaches implicitly had the approval of central government.

The custodial and non-custodial developments are worthy of separate consideration and, while the fine detail of both are beyond the scope of this chapter, some comment should be made about the prison service initiative. Various kinds of offence-focused work had been undertaken in prison establishments for years, the difference now being that a coordinated programme devised centrally by the Home Office was being introduced, although a major qualifying point has to be that the programme was to be financed out of the prisons' existing budgets with no provision to increase staffing levels (Sabor, 1992: 16).

Sentencing trends for the 1980s were demonstrating that an increasing percentage of sex offenders were being sentenced to immediate custody, though this was in line with other indictable offences, the peak year for incarceration as the judicial and magisterial response to offending being 1987. The difference in respect of sexual offending was that in this year someone convicted of a such an offence was twice as likely to receive a prison sentence as six years previously (1981, 18 per cent; 1987, 37 per cent), a growth not replicated in other offence categories. While by the end of the decade imprisonment for non-sexual offences had dropped back, or even fallen below, the 1980 level, sexual offending was still attracting a 34 per cent imprisonment rate. Further to this, the average length of sentence was also increasing (Home Office, 1991a) with the consequence that more sexual offenders were entering the prison system for longer periods of time. Prison statistics demonstrated that, while 4.7 per cent of sentenced male prisoners in custody in 1980 had been convicted of sexual offences, by 1989 the figure was 7.5 per cent (Barker and Morgan, 1991); it would be reasonable to assume that the consequences of this increasingly punitive response was causing some disquiet in the Home Office, given the expressed government intention of reducing the prison population.

The late 1980s also witnessed discussions about changes in sentencing policy which culminated in the Criminal Justice Act of 1991. Under the terms of the Act, those convicted of sexual offences could be required to attend specific offence-focused projects for longer periods than other offenders, could receive sentences of imprisonment which were longer than the seriousness of their offence would justify if they were considered to be a serious risk to the public, and were singled out for a longer period of post-custodial supervision if this had been indicated by the judge at the time of sentence. Arrangements for the early release of prisoners changed significantly for all prisoners and a particular distinction was drawn for those sentenced to four or more years, exactly the group who were being targeted in the prison service programme for the treatment of sex offenders. The possibility that the Home Office was undertaking some future planning is further evidenced by the commissioning of research at the Bristol Centre for Criminal Justice into Probation Service practice with sex offenders, which was 'in the context of the Criminal Justice Act 1991, to assist with planning for the increasing amount of supervision of sex offenders likely to be required' (Barker, 1991: 3). The Home Office projection of prison discharges was that 1,700 sex offenders would be released from custody annually, 700 of whom would have received a sentence of four years or more and whose period of supervision by the Probation Service was likely to be lengthy, amounting in all cases of up to a quarter of the original term (Sabor, 1992: 18).

Conclusion

The above discussion outlines contradictory developments, some of which were apparent from the outset, but whose implications are only just beginning to emerge. Thus, in the 1980s, custody was increasingly used for this group of offenders and the Criminal Justice Act specifically identified violent and sexual offenders as meriting harsher punishment on the grounds of public protection, yet the same legislation authorized greater community provision. The rehabilitative nature of work with offenders is understood and sanctioned in both prison and community settings, yet the contemporary political rhetoric in respect of offenders is undoubtedly punitive; public acceptance and understanding of the need to work with any offender from a rehabilitative perspective is minimal, still less a sex offender.

The irony of practitioner interest is that it was a response to an essentially qualitative perception about the problems associated with work with sex offenders, but work is now being developed in an increasingly restrictive and redefining climate in respect of the funding and role of the Probation Service which may call into question the appropriateness of such resource-intensive input. A review of the literature on sanctions for serious or persistent offenders in general (McIvor, 1990) suggests that what does, in fact, appear to work is offence-focused inputs, based on a cognitive-behaviourist model with a clearly structured programme and trained staff. Other research literature suggests that results are inconclusive in respect of sex offenders, particularly when the men are assessed on the basis of type of offences committed (Marshall and Barabee, 1990: 363–82) or the level of deviancy demonstrated (Beckett et al., 1994: 78). This in turn raises the question of whether sex offenders, or at least child abusers, can be treated as an homogeneous group in terms of intervention, which the current programmes would seem to imply. Workers in the projects are beginning to grapple with the issue of whether an offender can, in fact, learn to maintain control over his actions in a truly cognitive-behaviourist manner if the broader issues of socially constructed images of men and acceptable male behaviour are not addressed.

While the importance of working with sex offenders in a rehabilitative manner is unquestioned by practitioners and has been a major practice shift in social work in the past decade, the parameters of the intervention are still uncertain, and comprehensive evaluation is still in its early stages. All the areas listed above need both further consideration and further resourcing in order to achieve the breadth and depth of response that the issue of child sexual abuse requires.

References

Abel, G.G., Becker, J., Cunningham-Rathner, J. and Routeau, J. (1987) 'Self-reported sex crimes of 561 non-incarcerated paraphiliacs', *Journal of Interpersonal Violence*, 2 (6): 3–25.

Barker, M. (1991) *A Survey of Probation Practice with Sex Offenders*, Bristol Centre for Criminal Justice.

Barker, M. and Morgan, R. (1991) 'Probation practice with sex offenders surveyed', *Probation Journal*, 38 (4): 171–6.

Beckett, R., Beech, A., Fisher, D. and Fordham, A.S. (1994) *Community-based Treatment for Sex Offenders: an Evaluation of Seven Treatment Programmes*, London: Home Office.

Blagg, H. and Smith, D. (1989) *Crime, Penal Policy and Social Work*, Harlow: Longman.

Feaver, N. and Smith, D. (1994) 'Editorial introduction', *British Journal of Social Work*, 24 (4): 379–86.

Finkelhor, D. (1986) *A Sourcebook on Child Sexual Abuse*, London: Sage.

Fisher, D. (1994) 'Adult sex offenders', in T. Morrison, M. Erooga and R.C. Beckett (eds), *Sexual Offending against Children*, London: Routledge.

Fisher, D. (1995) 'The therapeutic impact of sex offender treatment programmes', *Probation Journal*, 42 (1): 2–7.

Gocke, B. (1991) *Tackling Denial in Sex Offenders*, Norwich: Social Work Monographs.

Home Office (1991a) *Criminal Statistics of England and Wales*, London: HMSO.

Home Office (1991b) *The Work of the Probation Service with Sex Offenders: Report of a Thematic Inspection*, London: Home Office.

Jones, C. (1993) 'Auditing criminal justice', *British Journal of Criminology*, 33: 187–202.

Kennington, R. (1994) 'Northumbria's sex offender team', *Probation Journal*, 41 (2): 81–5.

McIvor, G. (1990) *Sanctions for Serious or Persistent Offenders: a Review of the Literature*, Stirling: Social Work Research Centre.

MacLeod, M. and Saraga, E. (1991) 'Child sexual abuse: challenging the orthodoxy', in M. Loney, R. Bocock, J. Clarke, A. Cochrane, P. Graham and M. Wilson (eds), *The State or the Market*, London: Sage.

Marshall, W.L. and Barabee, H.E. (1990) 'Outcome of cognitive-behavioural treatment programmes', in W.L. Marshall, D.R. Laws and H.E. Barabee (eds), *Handbook of Sexual Assault*, New York: Plenum Press.

Morrison, T. (1992) 'Managing sex offenders: the challenge for managers', *Probation Journal*, 39 (3): 122–8.

Morrison, T., Erooga, M. and Beckett, R.C. (eds) (1994) *Sexual Offending Against Children*. London: Routledge.

Northamptonshire Probation Service (n. d.) *Working with Perpetrators of Sexual Abuse: Course Papers*.

Raynor, P. and Vanstone, M. (1994) 'Probation practice, effectiveness and the non-treatment paradigm', *British Journal of Social Work*, 24 (4): 387–404.

Sabor, M. (1992) 'The sex offender treatment programmes in prison', *Probation Journal*, 39 (1): 14–18.

Sheath, M. (1990) 'Confrontative work with sex offenders: legitimised nonce-bashing?', *Probation Journal*, 37 (4): 159–62.

Warwick, L. (1991) *Probation Work with Sex Offenders: a Survey of Current Practice*, Norwich: Social Work Monographs.

Wolf, S.C. (1984) 'A multifactor model of deviant sexuality', Paper presented at the Third International Conference on Victimology, Lisbon.

Wyre, R. (1987) *Working with Sex Abuse*, Oxford: Perry.

PART IV

GENERATION AND GENDER

10

Violence, Gender and Elder Abuse

Terri Whittaker

The past 25 years have witnessed a mass of research and intervention targeted at child abuse and, more latterly, domestic violence. Only recently however, have policy-makers and academics begun to show an interest in the phenomenon of elder abuse. This is not to say that abuse of old people is new. Mistreatment of older people, whether in domestic or institutional settings, has been around for a long time and has been manifested in various forms (Murphy, 1931; Thomas, 1978; Stearns, 1986). However, the significance attached to elder abuse and the degree of public and/or private concern expressed about it has varied greatly over time in line with historically and politically specific conflicts about resources and what constitutes acceptable domestic violence and appropriate responses to it (George, 1989).

The past decade has seen a flurry of research and academic publications, mainly coming from the USA, focused on the modern phenomenon of elder abuse (Sengstock and Liang, 1982; Eastman, 1984; Phillips, 1986; Pillemer and Wolf, 1986; Quinn and Tomita, 1986; Godkin et al., 1989; Bennett and Kingston, 1993; Decalmer and Glendenning, 1993). However, even with new momentum in research interest and an almost obsessive concern with definitions and numbers, very little is known about what Ogg and Bennett (1992a) call 'another iceberg phenomenon' and feminists have been slow to register an interest in this area. Within the literature on elder abuse there is a curious absence of discussion as to why it occurs and a suspicion that this can only mean one thing – an avoidance of the most glaring feature of elder abuse as something that overwhelmingly men do to old women (McCreadie, 1991). This is especially so in relation to physical and/or sexual abuse (Pillemer and Wolf, 1986; Holt, 1993). The systematic failure to address the fact that the majority of abusers are male is the clearest example of a feminist analysis being screened out of public discussion.

The men come from every social class and from all kinds of families and cultures. Very little attention has been paid to studying them as men. Instead, the focus of frantic study has shifted from an initial concern with the characteristics of the 'victims' to growing attention to the stresses and characteristics of 'carers'. More recently, the discourse on elder abuse is moving towards an orthodoxy in which the complex social and political problems inherent in the phenomenon are located in various models of 'family violence' or 'family pathology' which look set to achieve the status of 'common sense'.

Elder Abuse: Definitions, Prevalence and Incidence

Definitions

The first stage in developing any adequate form of policy or practice among those involved in elder abuse necessitates reaching agreement about what it is, how common it is, why it happens and how best to respond to it. The runaway success of the Women's Movement in theorizing and responding to child abuse is a testimony to the fact that practice has to be born of theory and the success in establishing child sexual abuse as the public scandal it always has been is a credit to those who had the courage to acquire orthodox knowledge and transform it.

A review of available USA and UK research reveals that the process of reaching agreement about elder abuse is fraught with difficulties and that professionals and academics have been almost obsessively involved in debates about definitions, incidence and prevalence at the expense of adequate theorizing. The way that elder abuse is experienced and under-stood by victims themselves and by those working in the field will be heavily reliant upon the way that these events are conceptualized and categorized.

The main problems seem to centre around which criteria to include or exclude in various definitions of abuse and around whether or not elder abuse is different from other forms of 'family violence'. The 1980s gave rise to growing anxiety about the changing nature of the family and to fierce debate about the resourcing of an ageing population (Phillipson, 1993). In this context, there was a flurry of academic and research interest in elder abuse with many different definitions being proposed and a subsequent recognition that they lacked clarity and precision (Decalmer and Glenden-ning, 1993).

These difficulties have been attributed to differences in emphasis and perspective among investigators and a tendency to distinguish between typologies and conceptualizations of elder abuse and neglect. This 'defini-tional disarray' and failure to reach consensus is a major thread throughout the published literature. It is mainly the Americans who have sought to clarify our understanding of the abuse and neglect of older people. But, as Decalmer and Glendenning (1993:10) note, 'the case material is perfectly recognisable elsewhere. American investigators have been largely concerned with domestic abuse.'

Most definitions of elder abuse include the following categories:

- physical abuse
- sexual abuse
- psychological abuse (emotional and verbal abuse and harassment)
- financial or material abuse and exploitation

Common features in the majority of definitions are physical assault, sexual abuse, involuntary isolation and confinement, financial exploitation, emotional and verbal abuse including threats, deprivation of items necessary for daily living (food, warmth, shelter, glasses, dentures, money) and inappropriate medication. There appears to be no attempt to include the victim's subjective experience of abuse as part of the definitional debate and very little attention is paid to issues of inequalities of power between victim and perpetrator other than to stress that old women are not children and that dependency exists as a two-way process within relationships between them and their abusers (Ogg and Bennett, 1992a).

How far this definitional chaos is related to the assumption that theory derives from definition, rather than the reverse, is a question which needs to be posed. The obsessive and lengthy conflict and concern with finding correct definitions has diverted attention from the real issue. Most abusers know exactly what they are doing and are well aware that actions ranging from verbal abuse to incest are abusive.

Prevalence and Incidence of Elder Abuse

The obsession with the numbers of old people who are abused appears to be another false trail. As yet we cannot say exactly how common elder abuse is. However, as more research has been done and as more people have begun to listen to the findings, there is now growing acceptance of the fact that elder abuse is more common than was previously imagined. There has been no major study of the prevalence or incidence of elder abuse in Britain. 'Prevalence' indicates the number of cases in a given population at one time, while 'incidence' means the number of new cases occurring in a given population within a defined period of time (Victor, 1991: 4–5). Evidence from the USA indicates that 10 per cent of elders supported by family members are at risk (Eastman, 1982: 12).

In Britain, Hocking (1988) pioneered a study of non-accidental injury and claimed that one in 10 is at risk and one in 1,000 suffers physical abuse. Ogg and Bennett (1992a: 63) have translated American figures to arrive at an estimate of 'eight elderly people who are subjected to abuse or inadequate care within a patient register of 200'. Other investigators have commented upon the methodological problems pertaining to much of the

American research relating to prevalence/incidence (Decalmer and Glendenning, 1993: 12), while others point to difficulties inherent in the fact that much elder abuse is hidden and unreported (McPherson, 1990: 360).

Hairsplitting discussions about what elder abuse is and how common it is, obscures the fact that a significant number of old women are exposed to unacceptable forms of violence from adult men in particular and detracts from thinking about why it happens. Much more important than establishing an agreed definition or a prevalence rate is agreeing a set of rules about what is permissible or not and ensuring that old people in general and old women in particular are protected as and when necessary and/or appropriate. Preventing elder abuse must be achieved through the promotion of safe dependence for old people, whereas preventing spouse abuse must involve the promotion of safe independence for women.

Victims and Perpetrators

Until recently, most research attention has been focused on the characteristics of the 'victims' of elder abuse and on the production of a stereotypical picture of the nature of old age. The 'classic' victim of elder abuse has been painted by various British, Canadian and American researchers as:

- female aged over 75
- living at home with adult carer/s
- physically and/or mentally impaired
- roleless – lost previous roles as wife/mother/caregiver
- isolated, fearful

(Horrocks, 1988; Tomlin, 1989; Ogg and Bennett, 1992b)

This profile of the 'victim' of abuse has run parallel with liberal explanations of elder abuse concentrated on depicting a straight correlation between biological ageing and dependency (Phillips, 1986: 198). The situational or 'carer stress' model, in which elder abuse is persistently explained in these terms, has had huge appeal for professionals who, while not condoning abuse as such, have been able to empathize with this picture of old age and the strain of caring. In so doing, there has been a tendency to downplay the gender significance of elder abuse and to look for victim-related sources of stress, thereby falling into the 'victim blaming' trap and colluding with various forms of institutionalized ageism and sexism (Traynor and Hasnip, 1984).

Recently, a more complex picture of victims and perpetrators has begun to emerge which indicates that old men are also victims of elder abuse while women are also perpetrators. Though all studies agree that the overwhelming majority of abusers are men and the majority of victims are old women, research does demonstrate the fact that frail, vulnerable old men are also victims of abuse and that some of their abusers are women

(Pillemer and Wolf, 1986). However, there are some methodological problems associated with these findings and we should recall that they are revealed in the context of an overall increase in the number of elder abuse cases being discovered (Decalmer and Glendenning, 1993).

Within newer research there is a suggestion of gender-specific differences in the forms and types of abuse which occur (Homer and Gilleard, 1990; Holt, 1993). Miller and Dodder (1989) separated physical abuse from neglect and discovered a statistically different sex bias in that men were more likely to physically abuse while women were more likely to neglect the old person in their care. They point to the high rates of reported neglect by women and emphasize that this may create the appearance of large numbers of female abusers when in fact the nature and extent of physical or sexual elder abuse by men is as yet unknown and there is much more resistance to disclosure of abuse of this type. Holt (1993), investigating 90 cases of elder abuse discovered a female to male victim ratio of 6 : 1 and that all but two abusers were male. Holt hypothesized that the common denominator between male and female victims of abuse was physical and mental frailty and their consequent vulnerability to abuse by those in positions of power and authority.

Orthodox research, underpinned by liberal notions of old age as dependency and a concern with preserving the 'family', has generally failed adequately to examine the significance of gender as a centrally important feature of elder abuse. This may account for the shift in research focus away from the characteristics of predominantly female victims towards the characteristics and circumstances of perpetrators and a concern with the 'dynamics' of their interpersonal relationships. In this context, the resistance to the idea that elder abuse is predominantly a male problem has been manifested in various forms, including a search for an increasing number of female abusers and the claim that women are also perpetrators of elder abuse. In this way, the 'experts' justify refusing to engage with feminist analysis and fail to recognize or acknowledge men's power in the world and in the family.

Women are, of course, quite capable of abusing power and trust and of exploiting old people to fulfil their own emotional and material needs. However, it seems they rarely resort to physical and/or sexual abuse. This does not imply that women are morally superior but suggests that if we refuse to consider gender-specific behaviours, we may lose important clues as to why elder abuse occurs.

The Perpetrators and their Characteristics and Circumstances

In recent years, the focus of attention in elder abuse has shifted from 'granny battering'. New research has drawn on theories of family pathology to challenge the idea of a close association between abuse and the physical and/or mental state of the 'victim', suggesting that the characteristics and circumstances of the perpetrators may be more important risk indicators (Pillemer and Wolf, 1986; Homer and Gilleard, 1990). The notion of 'inadequate care', which is underpinned by a model of a pathological abuser, has been introduced to facilitate this shift (Fulmer and O'Malley, 1987). Various attempts have been made to identify the predisposing factors leading to abuse, and researchers have emphasized the dependency of 'carers' on victims and on drugs or alcohol as significant factors.

As a result, earlier ways of seeing and thinking about elder abuse which drew on the experience of those working in the field and were conceptualized as a form of 'granny battering' have been dismissed. What is called 'the initial stereotyped plot' (Bennett and Kingston, 1993) is set aside in favour of a new orthodoxy in which it is held that elder abuse is much more complex, consisting of a varied set of characteristics and relationships which occur within the context of the relationship between the victim and the 'carer'.

From a feminist perspective, there is some irony in the continued use of the word 'carer' and the deliberate misuse of gender-neutral language to mask gender-specific behaviour. Language such as 'carers', victims, perpetrators, abusers, abused, are all used to obscure the gender significance of data. This, together with information relating to the inadequate personality types of the 'carers', forms the basis for 'compassion' as opposed to 'control' philosophies of assessment and intervention (Bennett and Kingston, 1993).

The Relationship Between Elder Abuse and 'Family' Violence

There has been a growing interest among researchers in the nature and extent of the relationship between elder abuse and other forms of family violence. Elder abuse is said to occur in a context of family relations and therefore, it is argued, more attention needs to be paid to the literature relating to child and spouse abuse (Pillemer and Suitor, 1988). Some writers have argued that elder abuse should be seen as a part of the spectrum of domestic abuse which affects all ages (Department of Health, 1992), while others have sought to establish a special category for elder abuse and associated programmes of assessment and intervention (Finkelhor and Pillemer, 1988).

The growing interest in domestic violence in general and child abuse and spouse abuse in particular looks set to dominate the discourse on elder abuse. However, as with early research and debates on child abuse, the interest is confined to certain liberal and conservative theories of family violence which are often not made explicit. In this context, the growing interest in 'the family' is not about making the gender significance of research data more explicit or about exposing the problems of sexual politics inherent in elder abuse. Instead, the research reflects a growing anxiety about the nature of 'the family' and a concern to enshrine and safeguard 'normal' family relationships.

Five major explanations rooted in theories of family violence are examined at various points in the research. They are:

1 Pathology of abuser – intra-individual dynamics
2 Cycle of violence – violence transmitted between generations
3 Dependency – of abused and/or abuser
4 Isolation – limited social networks/denial of access
5 External stress – unemployment, bereavement, inadequate community care, low income, poor housing

Pillemer and Suitor (1988: 143), reviewing the literature associated with these themes, argue: 'These factors may directly precipitate domestic violence against the elderly. That is *families* that have one of these characteristics may be at greater risk of elder abuse' (italics added).

What is crucial here is the focus on the 'family' rather than particular individuals who may have abused or been abused. Indeed, the literature is now beginning to be peppered with references to *'abusive families'* (Godkin et al., 1989) as 'systems' or sets of interrelationships which are not functioning properly. Thus elder abuse becomes a *symptom* of what is wrong within the *family* and the personality traits and behaviour of both victims and abusers become fair game however widely they vary. Discussion of the complex gender issues and sexual politics inherent in the relationship between them is completely avoided and there is no attempt to explain why it is mostly men who abuse. Instead, we are prompted towards compassionate responses as we learn that 'carers' have histories of psychosocial disorder, are addicted to drugs or alcohol, and are pathetically dependent upon the predominantly frail and vulnerable old women they are supposed to 'care' for.

> Elders (*mostly women*) mistreated by spouses (*mostly male*) were more apt to suffer from physical abuse, to be in poorer emotional health and to be more dependent on them for companionship, financial resources, management and maintenance of property. The perpetrators were more likely to have both recent and long term medical complaints and to have experienced a recent decline in physical health . . .They were also more likely to have a history of mental illness and alcoholism. (Wolf and Bergman, 1989; italics added)

Another twist to the tale of the 'problem relative' (Finkelhor and Pillemer, 1988) lies in the notion of the 'cycle of violence'. Here, some commentators argue that elder abuse is directly related to the fact that perpetrators were themselves products of domestic violence which had become learned behaviour and normative for them (Fulmer and O'Malley, 1987). The child abuse literature has shown how dangerous these ideas are and pointed to the way they feed myths about 'pathological' families and fuel class and race stereotypes to the point where abusers have been known to tell their victims that abuse is quite normal (Nelson, 1987: 48).

The idea that 'perpetrators' abuse because they were themselves abused says nothing about the number of perpetrators who were abused in childhood who do not go on to abuse young or old women or about the number of women who were abused in childhood but have not married or had relationships with men who abused them at any point in their lifespan. There has been no attempt to describe or confirm a causal link between childhood or family abuse and adults who abuse old people, yet it is important not to underestimate the strength of these ideas. Not only do they have a spurious liberal appeal by saying that individual men are not to blame, but they are also internalized by all of us and their effect is to prompt compassionate and therapeutic responses and to absolve the abuser of responsibility by inferring that *he* is a victim too!

From Anger to Analysis: Towards a Feminist Analysis of Elder Abuse

There is scope for growing anger as one reads the annals of academic enquiry into elder abuse. However, if we are to move from the suspicion of conspiracy towards a better understanding of why elder abuse occurs and to an adequate examination of the complex gender, social and political issues therein, we must move beyond rage and 'problem families'.

Ageing society is primarily a female society. It is well known that women generally outlive men and that ageism and sexism combine to produce a socially constructed dependency in old age in which the feminization of poverty is a key feature. These social processes are so pervasive that it is but a small step from here to justify the discrimination and disadvantage which old women experience and to render them and their experiences invisible. McDonald and Rich (1983) note that for older women, invisibility is symbolic of the process and politics of ageing and point to the way this extends to the feminist movement which, until recently, has given very little thought to the position of older women in the family. Any adequate analysis of elder abuse must take account of the social structural position of old women in our society and how this relates to their position within the family and the resources they have at their disposal to resist abusive behaviour.

In this context, it is perhaps not so extraordinary that the high levels of severe physical abuse experienced by old women who rely on their 'carers' for financial, practical and emotional support are explained by reference to demographics, longevity and variations in reporting elder abuse (Johnson et al., 1985; Pillemer and Wolf, 1986). The sexual, social and economic politics which underpin their relationships with men within the 'family' are not explored. Does this mean, as Schecter (1982) suggests, that we are indifferent to the pain and danger in old women's lives or that we prefer to hide behind principles of autonomy and self-determination rather than get involved?

Feminist analysis starts with gender. In looking at why elders get abused we are not looking at some psychopathological abuser or dependent, provoking or controlling old woman who 'initiates' abuse (Penhale, 1993). Nor are we looking at problems of 'inadequate caregiving' or even at 'dysfunctional families'. A feminist analysis will consider problematic sexual and adult–child politics and take account of the growing marginalization of old people in general and old women in particular within our society. In this context, elder abuse is not the product of a pathological family but of a patriarchal family in which men have access to and power over those less powerful and more vulnerable than themselves and regard them as their property. In so doing they are protected by societal norms which uphold the sanctity and privacy of 'home' despite it being the prime site of women's oppression.

From this perspective, the references in the literature to the provoking and controlling characteristics and behaviours of 'non-compliant' dependant victims (Straus and Yllo, 1981), where 'the caregiver is seen as being driven to a sense of helplessness, rage and frustration' (Decalmer and Glendenning, 1993: 15), can be seen as attempts by old women to struggle against and resist the power and control of men over their lives. However, all too often these behaviours are seen universally as indicators of carer stress and used to explain and justify abusive behaviours and prompt compassionate responses which absolve the abuser from responsibility. Instead of making the biology of old age and associated vulnerability and dependency problematic, feminists consider the socially constructed aspects of dependency which women young and old experience (albeit differently) and look for answers to male rage and abuse in the cultural representation of masculinity, femininity and sexuality.

As yet the voices of 'survivors'of elder abuse have not been heard above those of 'experts' in the field, so we know very little about the strategies or tactics employed by victims to resist or cope with abuse. The difficulties inherent in helping old women to talk and tell, due to fear of stigma, institutionalization or physical and mental frailty can be overcome (Feil, 1993). There is a need to build up a body of knowledge based on old women's experiences of abuse and to learn about what is helpful from this. Feminist policies for tackling abuse must therefore be concerned with advocacy and empowerment and with increasing the resources that old women have available to them to empower themselves and help them resist male violence.

Feminist theory holds that elder abuse is just one part of a spectrum of male hatred and violence against women and that it is a mistake to separate off any particular manifestation or to see it as a special case. This is not to argue against the complexity of elder abuse or to suggest that feminist theory, with its focus on gender, is the only dimension for analysis and theorizing about the phenomenon. It is, however, an argument against those who insist that elder abuse deserves a special category because of the dependency or vulnerability of victims or because of the difficulties inherent in locating responsibility, due to the fact that old women are legally autonomous beings.

The argument about legal autonomy is a spurious one. Everything we know about male violence to women tells us that their legal status as adults

156 Generation and gender

offers little in the way of the protection women say they want from the men who abuse them (Kelly, 1987). Equally, the argument for special categories and programmes, due to the dependency and vulnerability of old women, is at best misguided paternalism and, at worst, another example of resistance to feminist analysis. While the orthodox insistence on separation of elder abuse from the spectrum of other forms of male violence remains unchallenged, thinking and theorizing about elder abuse will continue to be powerfully constrained and woefully inadequate. One of the lessons learnt from child abuse work, which is transferable, is that the answer to why the majority of abusers are male will not be found in studying their victims or in gender-blind studies of their personal inadequacies or those of their families.

From Analysis to Practice

A feminist challenge to orthodox approaches to elder abuse will tackle notions of old women as burdensome, controlling and provoking individuals who initiate their own abuse by stressed-out carers within dysfunctional families; or as legally autonomous adults who cannot be protected because of their right to say 'no'. No matter how scientifically and academically respectable orthodox thinking on elder abuse is, the first aim of feminist practice must be to develop and argue an alternative theory which recognizes abuse for what it is – a crime against the person. It is well known that the 'family' is filled with many different forms of male violence and oppression and that violence is perpetrated on old and young alike (Dobash and Dobash, 1992). Feminists must develop analyses of elder abuse which acknowledge the social and cultural construction of abuse and locate causation outside of the personality traits and characteristics of either abuser or abused. There is an urgent need for feminists to grasp the nettle with regard to elder abuse. The fact that they have yet to do so is a reflection not only of the powerfully constraining effects of orthodox thinking and the resistance to feminist analysis, but of deeply entrenched ageism within the movement.

From a different analysis and meaning arise different policies and practice. It is apparent that the ideological and methodological debates within elder abuse are mirroring those which occurred in the child protection area, and that elder abuse has been claimed by 'experts' in family violence (Penhale, 1993). It is thus not surprising that many agencies attempting to deal with elder abuse have looked for guidance to the experiences of the child abuse orthodoxy which, unlike elder abuse, has been successfully challenged by feminist thinking and practice. Child abuse procedures based on normative versions of the 'family' are not, as various writers have noted, transferable wholesale to the area of elder abuse (Decalmer and Glendenning, 1993; Penhale, 1993). There is a need for much more research, debate and discussion before an adequate theory, policy or practice of elder abuse is articulated or implemented.

There is an urgent need, however, for feminists to contest the hold of family violence 'experts' on elder abuse terrain. Elder abuse has to be located within a feminist analysis of 'the family', and dominant ideologies about old women and 'dependency' within the family have to be challenged. Feminists have to press for changes at the policy level which will place more resources at the disposal of old women to enable them to resist various forms of abuse by 'families' in old age. Some feminists have pointed to the feminization of poverty in old age and recognized economic independence as a crucial form of self-care and empowerment for old women. This is certainly a crucial element in any successful preventative strategy (Groves, 1983; Groves and Finch, 1983).

It is well documented that most 'victims' want to remain in their own homes and families, so moves to enable the exclusion of abusive men and to find alternative forms of 'care' in the community would be important elements in a feminist policy/practice framework, as would the development of 'safe places' for old women who need respite from abuse and do not want to be placed in a residential home. This is particularly challenging in the context of changes in community care legislation and policy which are forcing more and more old people to rely on already overstretched and under-resourced systems of 'family' or 'informal' care. This can only increase the risk of abuse, especially for the very old and frail who are predominantly women (Department of Health, 1992).

Various writers have pointed to the inadequate legal framework which exists in terms of elder abuse and to the need for balance between protection and intrusion upon adult status and autonomy (Griffiths et al., 1992). Feminists will be concerned with finding such a balance and ensuring that old women are not infantilized but do get the protection from abuse they need. This means working with a range of agencies to improve collaboration and coordination and arguing for forms of intervention which locate responsibility where it belongs and acknowledge the risks of abuse which old women are exposed to. The growing 'professionalization' and 'medicalization' of old age in general and elder abuse in particular should be treated with caution. The focus on inadequate personality types and on producing 'profiles' of abusive families as risk indicators is problematic if a feminist analysis of elder abuse leads to the conclusion that it is a product of the social and cultural construction of the family, old age, masculinity and sexuality.

The child abuse literature demonstrates the fact that therapeutic or compassionate philosophies of assessment and intervention which obscure the complex gender and power issues around abuse have done very little to reduce risk (Nava, 1988). Feminists will be aware of the need to work for changes in police theory and practice in relation to elder abuse and to press for changes in the law which are appropriate. This means contesting orthodox notions of 'the family' and the tendency to reduce domestic violence to 'system' faults. The family is clearly not a monolithic structure which serves everyone's needs equally. The inequalities of power and the conflicts of interest and struggle for scarce resources within families have to be acknowledged. This is not an argument for no intervention but for wider and more adequate theorizing about causation.

What is to be Done about Abusers?

The literature on elder abuse has virtually nothing to say about abusers beyond the production of their psychosocial profiles as risk indicators. Whether the abuser is mentally ill, dependant on drugs or alcohol, prone to violence or isolated and unemployed, there is no discussion of the links between the abuse and the social and cultural construction of elder abuse. In Britain at any rate, there is certainly no real debate about the criminal aspects of elder abuse. Attempts by some lawyers to guide practitioners on how the law can be used to pursue criminal proceedings (Griffiths et al., 1992) are widely ignored and there is an almost unspoken assumption fuelled by compassionate philosophies of assessment and intervention that the criminalization of elder abuse is inappropriate.

A feminist analysis and practice of elder abuse will have to question whether or not criminal proceedings are the most appropriate way of dealing with offences. Arguments against criminalization come from those who believe that abuse is a 'family' matter; from those who believe it punishes and blames the victim still further; from those who argue that labels such as 'abuse' and associated proceedings prevent disclosure; and from those who believe that prosecution and prison will not change the man whereas therapy might. Feminists will argue that the decriminalization of elder abuse and the reluctance to consider 'control' forms of assessment/intervention are misguided because a very clear message is thereby given to society at large and men in particular that there is nothing very serious or wrong about abusing old women. It is also a way of supporting the idea that abusers are over-stressed, pathetic, dependent or disturbed characters and certainly not responsible for their actions.

Elder abuse, like other forms of abuse, must be seen as a crime against the person; anything else is unjust. While it is clear that prison is not successful at reforming anyone, to abandon it as a possibility is to collude with those who want to see elder abuse as a separate category of behaviour and abusers as not responsible for it. As long as the orthodoxy perpetuates the ideology of abusers being 'driven' to it by provoking, controlling, non-compliant, burdensome, old women, abusers will internalize it for themselves and statutory workers will concur. The argument that involving the police only increases victims' feelings of self-blame is an important one, but experience of working with other survivors indicates that victims are ambivalent about their feelings and that one way of helping is for society to say quite clearly 'He is responsible.' What is clear is that arguments about what should be done should not come from denial and an inability to face up to and accept the reality and seriousness of elder abuse.

Until and unless the complex gender issues inherent in elder abuse are addressed as a product of dominant ideologies about 'the family', about old age, masculinity and sexuality, there can be no adequate theory or practice. Attempting to begin the difficult task of posing an alternative explanation of elder abuse and thereby giving it a different meaning is an essential part of the wider political struggle towards real prevention and change. Feminists have a wealth of experience and knowledge to bring to the task at hand. Their expertise and commitment is needed urgently.

References

Bennett, G. and Kingston, P. (1993) *Elder Abuse: Concepts, Theories and Interventions*, London: Chapman and Hall.

Decalmer, P. and Glendenning, F. (1993) *The Mistreatment of Elderly People*, London: Sage.

Department of Health/Social Service Inspectorate (1992) *Confronting Elder Abuse: an SSI London Region Survey*, London: HMSO.

Dobash, R. and Dobash, R. (1992) *Women, Violence and Social Change*, London: Routledge.

Eastman, M. (1982) 'Granny battering', *Geriatric Medicine*, November: 11–15.

Eastman, M. (1984) *Old Age Abuse*, Mitcham: Age Concern England.

Feil, N. (1993) *The Validation Breakthrough: Simple Techniques for Communicating with People with Dementia*, Baltimore, Md: Health Professions Press.

Finkelhor, D. and Pillemer, K.A. (1988) 'Elder abuse: its relation to other forms of domestic violence', in G.T. Hotaling, D. Finkelhor, J.T. Kirkpatrick and M.A. Strauss (eds), *Family Abuse and its Consequences: New Directions in Research*, Newbury Park, CA: Sage.

Fulmer, T. and O'Malley, T.A. (1987) *Inadequate Care of the Elderly*, New York: Springer.

George, L. (1989) *Heroes of their own Lives: the Politics and History of Family Violence*, London: Virago.

Godkin, M.A., Wolf, R.S. and Pillemer, K.A. (1989) 'A case-comparison analysis of elder abuse and neglect', *International Journal of Ageing and Human Development*, 28 (3): 207–25.

Griffiths, A., Roberts, G. and Williams, J. (1992) *Sharpening the Instrument: the Law and Older People*, Stoke on Trent: British Association for Service to the Elderly.

Groves, D. (1983) 'Members and survivors: women and retirement pensions legislation', in J. Lewis (ed.), *Women's Welfare, Women's Rights*, London: Croom Helm.

Groves, D. and Finch, J. (1983) 'Natural selection: perspectives on entitlement to the invalid care allowance', in D. Groves and J. Finch (eds), *A Labour of Love: Women, Work and Caring*, London: Routledge and Kegan Paul.

Hocking, E.D. (1988) 'Miscare – a form of abuse in the elderly', *Update*, 15 May: 2411–19.

Holt, M. (1993) 'Elder sexual abuse in Britain: preliminary findings', *Journal of Elder Abuse and Neglect*, 5 (2): 16–18.

Homer, A. and Gilleard, C. (1990) 'Abuse of elderly people by their carers', *British Medical Journal*, 301: 1359–62.

Horrocks, P. (1988) 'Elderly people: abused and forgotten', *Health Service Journal*, 22: 1085.

Johnson, T.F., O'Brien, J.G. and Hudson, M.F. (1985) *Elder Abuse: an Annotated Bibliography*, Westport, Conn.: Greenwood Press.

Kelly, L. (1987) 'The continuum of sexual violence', in J. Hanmer and M. Maynard (eds), *Women, Violence and Social Control*, London: Macmillan.

McCreadie, C. (1991) *Elder Abuse: an Exploratory Study*, London: Age Concern, Institute of Gerontology, King's College.

McDonald, B. and Rich, C. (1983) *Look Me in the Eye: Old Women, Ageing and Ageism*, London: Women's Press.

McPherson, B. (1990) *Ageing as a Social Process*, Toronto: Butterworths.

Miller, R.B. and Dodder, R.A. (1989) 'The abused–abuser dyad: elder abuse in the State of Florida', in R. Filinson and S.R. Ingman (eds), *Elder Abuse: Practice and Policy*, New York: Human Sciences Press.

Murphy, J. (1931) 'Dependency in old age', *Annals of the American Academy of Political and Social Science*, 154: 38–41.

Nava, M. (1988) 'Cleveland and the press: outrage and anxiety in the reporting of child sexual abuse', *Feminist Review*, 28: 103–21.

Nelson, S. (1987) *Incest: Fact and Myth*, Edinburgh: Stramullion.

Ogg, J. and Bennett, G. (1992a) 'Screening for elder abuse in the community', *Geriatric Medicine*, February: 63–7.

Ogg, J. and Bennett, G. (1992b) 'Elder abuse in Britain', *British Medical Journal*, 24 October: 998–9.

Penhale, B. (1993) 'The abuse of elderly people: considerations for practice', *British Journal of Social Work*, 23 (2): 95–112.

Phillips, L.R. (1986) 'Theoretical explanations of elder abuse', in K.A. Pillemer and R.S. Wolf (eds), *Elder Abuse: Conflict in the Family*, Dover, Mass.: Auburn House.

Phillipson, C. (1993) 'Abuse of older people: sociological perspectives', in P. Decalmer and F. Glendenning (eds), *The Mistreatment of Elderly People*, London: Sage.

Pillemer, K.A. and Suitor, J. (1988) 'Elder abuse', in V. van Hasselt, R. Morrison, A. Belack and M. Hensen (eds), *Handbook of Family Violence*, New York: Plenum Press.

Pillemer, K.A. and Wolf, R.S. (eds) (1986) *Elder Abuse: Conflict in the Family*, Dover, Mass.: Auburn House.

Quinn, M.J. and Tomita, S.K. (1986) *Elder Abuse and Neglect: Causes, Diagnosis and Intervention Strategies*, New York: Springer.

Schecter, S. (1982) *Women and Male Violence: the Visions and Struggles of the Battered Women's Movement*, London: Pluto Press.

Sengstock, M.C. and Liang, J. (1982) 'Identifying and characterising elder abuse', unpublished manuscript, Wayne State University.

Stearns, P. (1986) 'Old age family conflict: the perspective of the past', in K.A. Pillemer and R.S. Wolf (eds), *Elder Abuse: Conflict in the Family*, Dover, Mass.: Auburn House.

Straus, M. and Yllo, K. (1981) 'Interpersonal violence among married and cohabiting couples', *Journal of Family Relations*, 30 (3).

Thomas, K. (1978) *Religion and the Decline of Magic*, London: Weidenfeld and Nicolson.

Tomlin, S. (1989) *Abuse of Elderly People: an Unnecessary and Preventable Problem*, London: British Geriatrics Society.

Traynor, J. and Hasnip, J. (1984) 'Sometimes she makes me want to hit her', *Community Care*, August: 20–1.

Victor, C. (1991) *Health and Health Care in Later Life*, Milton Keynes: Open University Press.

Wolf, R. and Bergman, S. (eds) (1989) *Stress, Conflict and the Abuse of the Elderly*, Jerusalem: Brookdale Institute.

11

Organized Abuse: Themes and Issues

Brid Featherstone and Elizabeth Harlow

In recent years the questions raised by individual sexual abuse cases appear to have been further complicated by the discovery of forms of abuse which include large numbers of adults and children and/or involve strange rituals or ceremonies. In the wake of each 'case' of such abuse, fast and furious debates have ensued in the popular and social work press. Such debates have been at their sharpest when suggestions of ritual or satanic abuse have been aired.

In this chapter we will explore what has become known as the phenomenon of 'organized abuse'. We will address, in the first instance, definitional issues. Such issues have historically been of considerable importance in the child abuse literature and are no less so in this area. We will identify what we feel are the key themes which have emerged from the debates, themes of silence and disbelief. Such themes are, of course, familiar to professionals who have worked with children who have been subjected to sexual abuse and are related to fundamental questions about families, sexuality and power. They do, however, appear to take on a heightened focus in cases such as those we will be discussing in this chapter. Finally, we will be exploring some of the issues for professional intervention and practice which have been raised and we hope to bring together some of the lessons that workers in a variety of agencies appear to have learned, particularly in relation to therapeutic interventions. We are, however, conscious of this being a new area of study and see this chapter as an exploration of some of the themes and issues rather than a definitive exposition.

What's in a Name?: Constructing Reality

With its recent inclusion in the official guidance on inter-agency co-operation, 'organized abuse' appears to have become the reality of official discourse. In this document, organized abuse is defined as 'a generic term which covers abuse which may involve a number of abusers, a number of abused young children and often encompasses different forms of abuse. It involves to a greater or lesser extent, an element of organization' (Home Office, 1991: 38). This definition is notable for what it omits as well as what it includes. The omission of any reference to ritual abuse reflects continuing battles about this phenomenon. These battles have split, among others, professional networks, agencies, feminists and the courts. The adoption of the term 'organized abuse' is, for some, an attempt to side-step the issues and to avoid engaging with the necessary debates (Clapton, 1993). The definitional issues also key into a current debate about who has the right to be heard, and the reliability of women (social workers particularly) and children. They open up what counts as truth and whose definition is most influential.

To complicate matters further, competing definitions are not just part of a process of creating and validating phenomena. They are also used to distinguish between phenomena. For example, as a result of the exposure of a range of abusive situations, Corby (1993) differentiates between organized abuse, ritual abuse and institutional abuse. The last encompasses any form of abuse and can take place in a school or residential setting, for example, the Pindown regime in Staffordshire (Levy and Kahan, 1991) and the case of sexual abuse in residential establishments in Leicestershire (Kirkwood, 1993).

More fundamentally still, the term 'organized abuse' is undoubtedly problematic as it is all encompassing and vague. Kelly (1993), for example, points out that all sexual abuse involves a high degree of organization. Attempts at greater clarity have been made, for example, by Burgess (1984) who suggested the following typology: 'solo rings' involving an adult alone with a small group of children; 'transition rings' where the adult may be involved with others and certainly has links with other abusers; and, finally, 'syndicated rings' which involve large numbers of children and adults. Burgess's research conducted in the United States was primarily concerned with the links between sex rings and pornography. As a result of cases both in Britain and in the United States, Kelly (1993) has suggested the following categories of organized abuse which both helpfully build on Burgess's work and address some of the issues which have been raised most recently.

1 *Family sexual abuse rings* Within this category there may be a number of forms. For example, sexual abuse extending through generations or where a primary abuser, frequently the father, offers his children for the sexual use of others.
2 *Local sexual abuse rings* Either one or more abusers target children in one particular locality. While pornography may be produced, it is for the abusers' own use rather than to generate income.
3 *Commercial sexual exploitation rings* The abuse of children occurs through pornography and prostitution.
4 *Ritualistic sexual abuse rings* More than one abuser is usually involved and ceremonies associated with the occult may be enacted.

Kelly (1993) also notes the following distinctions which were drawn by Finkelhor et al. (1988). Cult-based abuse occurs where the abuse may serve other purposes such as induction rather than being an end in itself. In pseudo-ritualistic abuse more emphasis is placed on the sexual abuse with the ritual serving mainly as a means of intimidation and control. In a word of warning about her typology, Kelly adds that individual abusers might also use some of the above strategies. Thus caution has to be exercised about making any rigid claims for the definition of abuse rings. Unlike Corby (1993), Kelly has not entirely separated organized sexual abuse from ritual abuse. She sees ritual abuse as one particular type of organized sexual abuse.

Clearly attempting to define organized abuse is problematic. The term itself is still relatively young and has already been the subject of much scrutiny. In this respect it echoes debates of the past; arguments around definition have been a recurrent feature of political and professional agendas in the area of child abuse. As further research and social work and other professional practice are carried out in this area a greater under-standing of the specific forms of organized child abuse may be reached. There appears already to have evolved a greater clarity around the different kinds of organized sexual abuse and ritual abuse as evidenced above. However, the process of dispute will continue, echoing as it does, long held concerns about families, power and sexuality. In the next sections we will look at some of the recent cases and identify some recurrent themes. In doing so we concentrate on the area of organized sexual abuse, where necessary using Kelly's definitions.

Some Examples of Organized Sexual Abuse

It is not possible here to identify all the known cases of organized sexual abuse. Certainly some cases have become particularly well known, for example, the McMartin case in America. This case involved the systematic and organized long-term abuse of children within day care by professional workers (Crewdson, 1988). Other cases in the UK include the Brent case involving paedophiles and young boys and the Nottingham case where what appeared initially to fall within Kelly's definition of a family sex ring later became a case involving allegations of ritualistic sexual abuse (Dawson and Johnston, 1989). Cases in Rochdale (Department of Health/ SSI, 1990) and the Orkneys (Scottish Office, 1992) followed on from Nottingham. Others, less publicized, have occurred in Manchester, Ayr and Humberside.[1]

It does appear that allegations of ritual abuse lead to controversy. It is important to remember, however, that this is not always the most crucial ingredient for ensuring publicity or indeed controversy. The presence of well-organized parents groups and cohesive communities also contribute in a significant way. Allegations of ritual abuse do appear to have a number of functions, however. They often polarize the professionals involved and they are used to cast doubt on both the professionals' (mainly the social workers') judgement and the children's veracity. In our study of the literature, we have identified silence and disbelief as central features in the debates on organized sexual abuse. Silence and disbelief often, paradoxically, lead to women and children being both central to the debate but at the same time ignored and marginalized.

The Sound of Silence: Whose Voice Matters?

While there is now far more professional knowledge, awareness and openness about child sexual abuse than has been the case in the recent past,[2] silence remains a significant component particularly for the individuals directly involved. Neither victim nor abuser are usually eager to disclose the secret. Secrecy and silence is essential for the abuser to continue his or her practices and to avoid detection given what that might entail. The child may be fearful of breaking the silence following threats of punishment or murder from the perpetrator. Children may also remain silent because they may love the perpetrator, despite the abuse, and fear the disruption of the relationship, the possible punishment of the perpetrator and the break-up of the family (Reid, 1992). Close family ties may be a means of perpetuating silence, but where those ties do not exist then other methods of maintaining silence may be drawn upon. The rituals in pseudo-ritualistic abuse may serve such a purpose (Eaton, 1991). Seduction (engaging the child), cultivation (ensuring the child returns) and hooking (the threat of violence) are all methods which Bibby (1991) suggests are used by the perpetrators of organized sexual abuse for ensuring the child's compliance and silence. Where a child or young person has acted as perpetrator as well as having been victim, then disclosure is even more difficult. Bibby argues that the amount of energy required to maintain the secret is a particular characteristic of organized abuse. He also points out that even where one part of a 'web' of organized abuse gets broken it can continue to function and develop.

One of the difficulties for practitioners, then, is not only that visible signs of sexual abuse are unlikely to be seen without medical investigation but also that those involved are likely to take great care in ensuring that the secret is maintained. This inevitably leaves professionals with great difficulties in making investigations. This may, for example, have contributed to the Orkney social workers' decision to concentrate on the disclosures of children rather than on interviews with adults. While it is recommended in the Orkney report (Scottish Office,1992) that enquiries should be made of adults in an attempt to investigate allegations, adults may in practice offer little assistance due to the aforementioned aspects of secrecy. Where social work practitioners are gathering certain kinds of information in connection with organized abuse then they themselves may be confined to silence by their managers as in the Nottingham case (Kelly and Scott, 1991). Although there were successful prosecutions in the

Nottingham case, according to Campbell (1991) the prosecution were relatively silent on the ritualistic aspects of the abuse and the police tried to silence social workers once children began to name people outside of their own deprived family (Campbell, 1990a). Hopkins (1991) suggests that successful prosecutions may be more likely where social workers remain silent on ritualistic components of a case but let 'the facts speak for themselves'. Silence therefore is a factor which impinges upon social workers in their practice in all cases of sexual abuse but which may have a specific importance in organized sexual abuse.

Disbelief

Closely related and indeed intertwined with silence is disbelief. Silence may either result from the fear of being disbelieved or it may be a consequence of disbelief. While the occurrence of sexual abuse which requires some degree of organization and planning (Kelly, 1993) may now be generally accepted, the existence of organizations which are purpose-fully structured around the exploitation of vulnerable young people and children may, for some, be more difficult to contemplate. This may be particularly hard to accept when those who are identified as abusers do not 'fit' with the conventional image of an abuser. For example, in the Orkney case a local religious leader was alleged to be an abuser and two of the families were noted in the report to be of a particular religious faith – one Quaker and one Jewish. The suggestion that individuals with a commit-ment to an accepted religious belief may be implicated in organized ritualistic sexual abuse may be particularly difficult for some to accept. The significance of such 'mind sets' might to some extent account for the difficulty in accepting some accounts of organized abuse which include women or care staff as perpetrators. Where someone has been identified as 'caring', whether as a result of their gender or of their particular occupation, it might be more difficult to accept that they are capable of ruthless abuse.

The difficulties are, of course, multiplied when allegations of ritual abuse are made. As Clapton (1993) notes, both the popular and the social work press have been dominated by debates about whether such abuse exists or not. Non-believers have suggested that fundamentalist Christians have fuelled and exaggerated claims of satanic or ritualistic practices while others, such as Dawson and Johnston (1989), imply that non-believers may be exhibiting classically Freudian symptoms of denial. Clapton (1993) himself suggests that it is not the influence of fundamentalism which is at fault but the Christian principles which have historically influenced social workers. These, he argues, were drawn upon to facilitate the acceptability of such claims. Feminists have also disagreed with each other. Writers such as Wilson (1990) have argued that the issue has been a tactic to divert attention away from sexual abuse within the family and from male power, while others such as Campbell (1990b) argue that it was the moving of the debate away from conveniently deprived and depraved families which caused the problems of belief.

There are a number of possible ways of accounting for the phenomenon of disbelief. These are dependent to some extent on particular theoretical and political stances, although as we have seen there is not unanimity among those who might ordinarily share a political belief system, for example, feminists. As previously indicated, social workers have drawn on the psychoanalytic tradition to explain disbelief and have seen it as an aspect of the defence mechanism denial. Woodhouse and Pengelly (1991) have looked at the role anxiety plays in skewing relational dynamics inside and between agencies. They note from an examination of the report following the Cleveland controversy (Butler-Sloss, 1988) that individuals have particular difficulty in coming to terms with the existence of sexual abuse and that those who struggled to raise awareness of its existence were resisted. For example, they note the following submission to the enquiry.

> Somehow sexual abuse touches a part of the individual which perhaps physical abuse does not. Most of us can see how we could quite easily hit a child in a moment of stress . . . and emotional abuse, again I think we can all understand the damage that is done by it . . . sexual abuse has an effect on the person which is an individual response depending on perhaps your own knowledge, your own background experience, and some people find it extremely difficult to listen to us talking about it. I have sometimes had to go back and repeat training I have given because they found it so painful . . . .(quoted in Woodhouse and Pengelly, 1991: 243)

According to Woodhouse and Pengelly, the Cleveland report suggests that it was as difficult for people to accept the possibility of sexual abuse in the 1980s as it had been for them to accept the existence of physical abuse in the 1960s. If this is the case then the difficulty in accepting the existence of organized sexual abuse and organized ritualistic sexual abuse may be part of the same phenomenon. The implication, from this particular theoretical perspective, may also be that in time the occurrence of organized sexual abuse and organized ritualistic sexual abuse may be more generally accepted.

Psychoanalytic theory is, of course, not the only tradition which can be used to explore issues of belief or disbelief. Reder et al. (1993) use insights from systemic theories to explore why communication problems bedevil child abuse cases. Their insights could be adapted to explore the many breakdowns in communication which have occurred in ritual abuse cases and to assess the processes which lead people to fixed positions whereby they are unable to consider the possibility that ritual abuse might have happened.

In the meantime social workers and other professionals face serious challenges if they wish to pursue allegations or draw attention to the phenomenon. Furthermore, disbelief and its frequent attendant ridicule may have serious consequences, for example voluntary agencies may feel unable to draw attention to their work with survivors of organized sexual abuse without risking their funding (Scott, 1991). In the next sections we look at some of the implications for professional practice and draw together some of the lessons which have been learned by those working in this field.

The Disclosure of Children: Fact or Fiction?

One of the key issues that has arisen in organized ritualistic sexual abuse is whether children's disclosures are reliable. Even if the possibility that children might deliberately mislead is rejected, the possibility might still remain that they may confuse fact with fiction or waking reality with dreams. Those who are sceptical about the 'disclosures' of ritual abuse argue that children's healthy imaginations, fuelled by literature, television and videos, are in part responsible for the accounts. Responsibility also lies, for the sceptics, with social workers who jumped on the bandwagon of ritual abuse and were determined to find evidence of it. Thus interviews were seen as inappropriate and leading questions were put to suggestible and vulnerable children. Furthermore, the questioning was often so intensive that the children eventually succumbed and agreed to the social workers' suggestions. This argument is presented by Reid (1992) in relation to the procedures followed in the Orkneys. For Reid the belief that children always tell the truth is a problematic aspect of current child care practice. He argues that children are, in fact, suggestible and their disclosures should always be considered contextually. Westcott (1992) suggests that children are not inevitably suggestible,

> [suggestibility] is a situational factor which can be exacerbated by stress, pressurised questioning and the ambiguity of the witnessed event. Children are more likely to be suggestible when they have been a bystander witness, rather than a participant in the event, and regarding peripheral rather than central details. They are also more likely to be suggestible about descriptions of people, than descriptions of events. (Westcott, 1992: 7)

The Memorandum of Good Practice for Video Recorded Interviews with Child Witnesses (MOGP), which accompanies the Criminal Justice Act 1991, has been specifically designed to deal with the concerns which have been raised. It recommends a phased approach to interviewing similar to the technique of statement validity analysis (Farr and Yuille, 1988). Social workers are now being trained to use these interviewing techniques and video equipment. Hopkins (1991), however, suggests that planned structured interviews may not always be appropriate. As the experience of the Nottingham social workers and foster parents would indicate, allegations of such abuse might emerge over a long period of time in an unplanned way. This argument is supported by others (Hartmann et al., 1984). This highlights a fundamental issue for practitioners working in the field of child protection: the contradiction between interviewing children as a means of gaining evidence for court proceedings and working with the child at the child's pace for therapeutic purposes (Mason, 1991). A further series of issues is raised when therapeutic work is undertaken.

Power and Powerlessness in Abuse and the Implications for Therapy

Those working therapeutically with survivors of organized sexual abuse have become aware of the specific issue that survivors may not only have been victims of the abuse but also perpetrators (Scott, 1991). This blurs the distinction between the dichotomized subject positions of the powerful abuser and the powerless victim. It therefore forecloses therapeutic approaches which have emphasized that the survivor reject feelings of guilt and legitimately express anger at the perpetrator who is solely responsible. This is also a particular issue for feminists who have relied on an analysis that places men as abusers and women as victims of sexual abuse. Women who have been the victims of organized sexual abuse may also have been perpetrators. Matthews (1993) does not address the involvement of women in organized abuse specifically but her case study of Helen is relevant here. Helen's involvement as a child in 'cult' parties led her to pair anger and sex and to gain a confused and conflicted relationship with her own sexual power. 'At the age of 9 she was no longer the object of abuse . . . It was her job to get the victims quieted down by persuading them to drink Kool Aid laced with tranquillizers' (Matthews, 1993: 70). When Helen became an adult abuser herself she knew from her own experience how to inflict pain and also how awful it was to be hurt. The therapeutic approach described by Matthews (1993) encourages clients such as Helen to acknowledge that acting out sexually gives them feelings of power and importance. According to Matthews, this fantasy of power and importance should not be stopped but clients should be helped to face the consequences of their actions.

According to Belitz and Schacht (1992), the experience of power and powerlessness is also pertinent to the analysis of why boys become involved in abusive group satanic activities and to the therapeutic approaches with them. Belitz and Schacht looked at the treatment of 10 boys aged 12–17 years who had been voluntarily involved in satanic groups and who were admitted to child and adolescent inpatient psychiatric facilities over a three-year period. As a result of their experience of abuse within their own families the boys had learned that bad equalled powerful and good equalled powerlessness and victimization. They found it safer to identify with the aggressor than the victim. Furthermore, they began to see themselves as bad in order to understand why they deserved such abuse. For these boys, 'magical means of asserting power and taking revenge were particularly appealing' (Belitz and Schacht, 1992: 858). Satanic groups offered these boys an opportunity to play out the victimizer role.

Therapeutic intervention meant for these boys: (a) a reframing of the satanic involvement as learned abusive behaviour which allowed for the replication and communication of rage about their familial abuse; (b) an opportunity to explore the range of needs being met by the involvement in satanic groups; (c) an exploration of the identification with the aggressor; and (d) an opportunity for the therapist to offer a model of an adult who is both powerful and non-abusive.

In their work with young people who have been involved in sex rings, Hartmann et al. (1984) reiterate the significance of understanding power relationships. The young people they worked with did not see themselves as victims, and initially contact with them was made on their own territory as this provided them with some degree of power within the interaction. Relationships of power appear to be significant not only for the subject's experience of the abuse but also the practice and effectiveness of therapeutic interventions with 'victim/perpetrators'.

Conclusion

In this chapter we have attempted to explore some of the issues which have been highlighted in recent organized sexual abuse cases. The whole issue raises questions of such complexity that it is small wonder it has often resulted in fixed and rigid positions being taken, particularly in the cases where ritual abuse has been alleged. Organized sexual abuse often confounds long-cherished belief systems about the goodness of communities, families or women and refutes easy categories of victims or villains. It is profoundly uncomfortable and distressing, and it is these features that future theorizing and intervention must address.

Notes

1. For a brief résumé of each case, see Eaton (1991).
2. According to Linda Gordon (1988), the current discovery of child abuse, including child sexual abuse, is in fact a rediscovery. Early feminists and reformers were concerned with these problems at the end of the nineteenth century.

References

Belitz, J. and Schacht, A. (1992) 'Satanism as a response to abuse: the dynamics and treatment of satanic involvement in male youth', *Adolescence*, 27 (108): 855–72.
Bibby, P. (1991) 'Breaking the web', *Social Work Today*, 3 October: 17–19.
Burgess, A. (ed.) (1984) *Child Pornography and Sex Rings*, Lexington: Lexington Books.
Butler-Sloss, E. (1988) *Report of the Inquiry into Child Abuse in Cleveland 1987*, Cmnd 412, London: HMSO.
Campbell, B. (1990a) 'Hear no evil', *New Statesman and Society*, 19 October: 10–11.
Campbell, B. (1990b) 'Children's stories', *New Statesman and Society*, 5 October: 15.
Campbell, B. (1991) *The Guardian*, 20 February.

Clapton, G. (1993) *The Satanic Abuse Controversy: Social Workers and the Social Work Press*, London: University of North London Press.

Corby, B. (1993) *Child Abuse: Towards a Knowledge Base*, Buckingham: Open University Press.

Crewdson, J. (1988) *By Silence Betrayed: Sexual Abuse of Children in America*, Boston: Little, Brown and Company.

Dawson, J. and Johnston, C. (1989) 'When the truth hurts', *Community Care*, 30 March: 11–13.

Department of Health/SSI (1990) *Inspection of Child Protection Services in Rochdale*, Manchester: SSI.

Eaton, L. (1991) 'Ritual abuse: fantasy or reality?', *Social Work Today*, 26 September: 8–12.

Farr, U. and Yuille, J. (1988) 'Assessing credibility: preventing sexual abuse', *Preventing Sexual Abuse*, 1 (1): 8–13.

Finkelhor, D., Williams, D. and Burns, N. (1988) *Nursery Crimes: Sexual Abuse in Day Care*, Beverly Hills, CA: Sage.

Gordon, L. (1988) 'The politics of child sexual abuse: notes from American history', *Feminist Review*, 28, January.

Hartmann, C., Burgess, A. and Powers, P. (1984) 'Treatment issues with children involved in pornography and sex rings', in A. Burgess (ed.), *Child Pornography and Sex Rings*, Lexington: Lexington Books.

Home Office (1991) *Working Together under the Children's Act: a Guide to Arrangements for Inter-agency Co-operation for the Protection of Children from Abuse*, London: HMSO.

Hopkins, J. (1991) 'Trial and error', *Social Work Today*, 17 October: 21.

Kelly, L. (1993) 'Organised sexual abuse: what do we know and what do we need to know?', in Child Abuse Studies Unit (ed.), *Abuse of Women and Children: a Feminist Response*, London: University of North London Press.

Kelly, L. and Scott, S. (1991) 'Demons, devils and denial', *Trouble and Strife*, 22: 33–5.

Kirkwood, A. (1993) *The Leicestershire Inquiry 1992*, Leicestershire: Leicestershire County Council.

Levy, A. and Kahan, B. (1991) *The Pindown Experience and the Protection of Children: the Report of the Staffordshire Child Inquiry 1990*, Staffordshire: Staffordshire County Council.

Mason, M.A. (1991) 'The McMartin case revisited: the conflict between social work and criminal justice', *Social Work*, 36: 391–5.

Matthews, J. K. (1993) 'Working with female sexual abuse', in M. Elliot (ed.), *Female Sexual Abuse of Children: the Last Taboo*, Essex: Longman.

Reder, P., Duncan, S. and Gray, M. (1993) *Beyond Blame: Child Abuse Tragedies Revisited*, London: Routledge.

Reid, D.H.S. (1992) *Suffer the Little Children: the Orkney Child Abuse Scandal*, St Andrews: Napier Press.

Scott, S. (1991) 'The challenge to feminists and feminist services', Paper presented at the Conference: Towards a Feminist Understanding and Approach to Organised Sexual Abuse, North London Polytechnic, 13 December.

Scottish Office (1992) *Inquiry into the Removal of Children from Orkney in February 1991*, Edinburgh: HMSO.

Westcott, H. (1992) 'The 1991 Criminal Justice Act: research on children's testimonies', *Adoption and Fostering*, 16 (3): 7–12.

Wilson, E. (1990) 'Immoral panics', *New Statesman and Society*, 31 August: 18–19.

Woodhouse, D. and Pengelly, P. (1991) *Anxiety and the Dynamics of Collaboration*, Aberdeen: Aberdeen University Press.

12

Issues of Race and Culture
in Child Abuse

Melody Mtezuka

the day to day problems facing black women are interpreted as the result of cultural differences, or even at worst, cultural inferiority. Where cultural differences are reinterpreted as deficits, black women as mothers may be identified as the bearers and transmitters of these deficits. The twists and turns of this approach mean that black women are open to blame whatever they do, and racist stereotypes about their lives and their relationships with men and their children are reaffirmed.

L. Day, 'Women and oppression: race, class and gender', 1992 p. 17

It is my intention to examine the 'twists and turns' referred to above by focusing on child abuse within the black family, as well as attempting to address the themes of violence, gender and social work. Throughout this chapter I shall confine myself to sexual abuse of black female children. This is not to suggest that boys are not vulnerable to sexual violence. However, my personal work experience has largely involved female children. Also girls are more likely than boys to be sexually abused within black families: 'there is little doubt that boys are victimised by sexual abuse, but I would argue that it is not nearly to the same extent, and if it were the attitudes surrounding it would not be so casual, nor the silence so complete' (Wilson, 1993: 210). In addition, my writing style for this paper appears to lend itself to the single sex. The subject matter is complex enough – race, violence and sexual abuse – without complicating issues further by appearing to cover fairly the two sexes through the usage of he/she.

The term 'black' is used here in its political sense. It refers to people who share a common experience of colonialism, immigration to Britain, and racial oppression. It therefore refers to the people from different countries, cultures and races who are in Britain today, and they are mainly from Africa, the Caribbean (including South America and Guyana) and Asian sub-continents. In looking at child abuse among black families, issues around race need to be examined within the context of a society which defines normality from a particular monocultural value base. The black family is perceived as 'different' and negative connotations are ascribed to this difference.

While black children, especially those of African-Caribbean descent, appear frequently before professionals such as social workers and teachers for what are termed behavioural difficulties, the professionals are less likely than with white children to consider sexual abuse as a possible underlying cause. Instead, the child's behaviour is judged against a distorted white view of family and social relationships within the black culture. Black families are stereotyped as having unpleasant characteristics which derive directly from their blackness (Droisen, 1989). For example, African-Caribbean families are said to mete out over-harsh physical punishment when disciplining their children. The reality is quite different. All societies have boundaries of acceptable and non-acceptable behaviour as well as recognizable responsibilities of parenting adults towards children. Children should be disciplined but *not maltreated* (Obikeze, 1986; Hampton, 1987). The notion of accepting another culture or viewing that culture from a particular, negative position without close scrutiny leaves black children unprotected.

Stereotypical views of women in black families can compound the problem, certainly in Britain. For example, there is the view that the Asian mother is 'passive' and that the African-Caribbean mother is 'over-disciplinarian' (Dominelli and McLeod, 1989). The distorted perception of Asian women ignores the history of Asian people's migration to Britain. The colonial past is bound up with the migration of Asian men primarily to the cotton and wool textile mills notably in the north of Britain. Once the men were well established here, the women were able to join them. This two-stage process in migration may well have contributed to the existing gender inequalities or produced new inequalities in that the men became more familiar with the various British institutions such as housing departments, the then Department of Health and Social Security etc. The contacts with some of these institutions by the men left a sizeable number of women ignorant of some of the services available to them and their children. Thus, in cases of child abuse, sexual abuse in particular, 'Asian women were in the main not used to bureaucracies, such as the Department of Social Security (DSS), and were perhaps less confident about approaching these services in order to gain any measure of autonomy for themselves and their children' (Mtezuka, 1989-90: 256).

The sequential impact of slavery, colonialism and migration should not be underestimated. Yet, we are given a picture of the African-Caribbean mother who, while described as over-disciplinarian, is expected to be 'coping'. Black women are thus expected to have the capacity to cope with a variety of hardships at the expense of their emotional needs (Lawrence, 1992). This picture of the coping black woman is vividly demonstrated in the report on the circumstances surrounding the death of Tyra Henry in 1987. In commenting on Tyra's grandmother's financial and material position, the authors of the report were perplexed by the fact that the white social worker involved in the case had herself worked in Jamaica. In her written statement to the inquiry the social worker had mentioned that one of the reasons for working in Jamaica was that she wished to study the dynamics of West Indian families living in the West Indies. She found that the experience helped her to get in touch with the parents of West Indian children in Britain. Nevertheless, the social worker's own understanding of the dynamics of West Indian families was to have dire consequences for Tyra Henry. The report looks critically at the grandmother's capacity to care for Tyra.

> Even allowing for hindsight, we are struck by the failure to see the inherent contradictions and risks of the arrangements . . . in our view the placement should not have been embarked upon *at all unless and until* Beatrice Henry had been provided with the wherewithal to cope. (London Borough of Lambeth, 1987: 30; italic added)

Tyra's grandmother was not offered the opportunity to act as foster parent for her grandchild, which would have helped to relieve some of the financial stresses she was under. This status would also have enabled her to call on the usual help and support from the Social Services department. In addition, the foster mother status would have offered Tyra some legal security and would have perhaps speeded up the resolution of the housing crisis. But, instead, Beatrice Henry was seen as 'coping' in the stereotypical way most black women are viewed.

Violence within black families tends to receive the familiar stereotypical focus. The basic concern for most black women seeking help is whether their situation will be understood by the white majority (Mama, 1992; Hampton, 1987). The dual dimensions of racism and sexism add to their difficulties. It has to be appreciated that not all black female–male relationships are troubled or are in turmoil. Moreover, some of the criticisms levelled at black female–male relationships need to be examined within the context of living in a white (and class) dominated British society (Bryan, 1992).

The Effects of Racism

Black children from an early age experience racism – in the nursery class, primary school and so on through society at large. The 'positive images' they are surrounded with are of white females. 'They are taught the ABCs of racism and anti-Semitism. Black and/or Jewish children are taught that they are inferior, guilty of some quality that marks them unworthy and somehow dirty' (Droisen, 1989: 160). Cushioning the effects of racism is usually undertaken within the family network. If the child is abused within her own home, it becomes almost impossible for her to disclose to outsiders what is happening to her as this would amount to a confirmation of the unworthiness of her race. Also, with so much secrecy and denial surrounding sexual abuse within black families themselves, mainly because of the absence of discussions about sexual activity generally and through the absorbed messages about the sexual behaviours of black families from a white perspective (Mtezuka, 1989-90), it is not surprising that children can get confused about what is happening or has happened to them. 'Black children who are sexually abused are subject to racialised images of sexual abuse that may make the process of disclosure even more difficult' (Hudson, 1992: 141). The child finds herself in a position where she has to consider the consequences of the abuse not only for her family, but also for the community (Mtezuka, 1989–90). One of these consequences, apart from betrayal of the race, is the real possibility of disintegration of the family unit. The intervention of the various welfare state apparatus and immigration controls carries with it the ultimate danger of deportation of the main carer (Cohen, 1981; Mama, 1992). This additional ingredient in child abuse investigations makes it even more complex for the black child to disclose abuse compared with her white counterpart.

Investigation and Assessment

The burden of responsibility shouldered by the child is compounded by professionals who insist upon using Western theoretical models for the detection, investigation and assessment of child abuse cases (Department of Health, 1988; Home Office/Department of Health, 1992). Thus the black child is left unprotected and feeling even more betrayed. The difficulties she is experiencing, the violence through sexual abuse, are going to be outside the remit of the professionals who may themselves hold stereotypical images about black families. In trying to be 'culturally sensitive', it is unfortunate that professionals can end up by bending over backwards to such an extent that they do not wish to be seen to be racist. Alternatively, they may approach the black male as an intrinsically violent person or the adult black female as an overly sexual being. Cultural sensitivity and anti-discriminatory practice can lead to a child being left unprotected. Violence within domestic households should not be mini-mized; what is abhorrent is the reductionist view of violence within black families.

> The number one issue for most of our sisters is violence – battering, sexual abuse. Same thing for their daughters, whether they are twelve or four. We have to look at how violence is used, how violence and sexism go hand in hand, and how it affects the sexual responses of females. We have to stop it because violence is the training ground for us. (Avery, 1988, quoted in Wilson, 1993: 208)

With regard to the police, while joint Social Services department/police investigations are applauded as a step in the right direction in reducing the stress faced by children when recounting their sexual abuse experiences, a critical look at these new arrangements is called for in the case of the black child. The child's perception of contacts with the police is shaped by her community's experiences with the police. We have mentioned elsewhere that immigration and nationality laws tend to come into play during investigations of child abuse. Furthermore, from previous experiences and commentary from the community, there might be added fears for the child that should the perpetrator of the abuse be black he would incur higher penalties under the criminal justice system. These fears are critical when considering that a higher proportion of black people are either tried or sentenced in the Crown Courts which have greater sentencing powers than the lower Magistrates Courts (Gordon, 1992).

Similar traumas are faced by the black woman in her contacts with the police. In her study on domestic violence, Amina Mama found that black women are reluctant to call the police, even in life-threatening situations; that the police are reluctant to intervene and 'most disturbingly . . . that the police themselves perpetrate crimes against black women' (Mama, 1992: 95). It is against this backcloth of racism and welfare state intervention that the black child has to find the energy to divulge the abuse in her family. Unfortunately, the various helping agencies are constructed in such a way that the black child (and her family) is further abused. 'The older the child, the greater the likelihood that they will be aware of the potential repercussions of police involvement and the greater the reluctance to disclose abuse' (Hudson, 1992: 142).

Intervention Strategies

Although some local authorities are attempting to be imaginative and creative about where a child is placed following removal from home, the general picture is that the child is placed within a white foster home. Scant knowledge is demonstrated of the principles of the Children Act 1989 regarding a child's cultural background. This apparently protective environment can be damaging to a child, largely because it confirms for her that her own people are not worthy as a race. Under the Children Act 1989, when a child is removed from home efforts should be made to seek out a member of the child's extended family, and one who clearly has the capacity to protect the child. This measure would help to relieve the additional stress of secondary abuse for a black child – racism.

Among Asian families, bigger challenges face the child in terms of the stigma attached to the whole family within the community. Comments have been made that some of the values adhered to within the Asian community could lead to a situation whereby a violated female child has 'no future prospects regarding marriage'. In addition, not only are the children no longer marriageable but there is the danger that subsequent generations could be stigmatized as well (Mtezuka, 1989–90). Helpful intervention strategies are the ones where the child is removed to trusted members of the family, even if they live hundreds of miles away.

Conclusion

The Eurocentric value base which continues to underpin theory and practice in child abuse/child protection is damaging to the black child. The so-called 'Orange Book' (Department of Health, 1988) confirms this value base. Although critiqued in social work circles through the work of MacDonald (1991), we continue to hear about examples of inappropriate assessments and interventions.

Cultural differences must be explored within the context of our socialization (racism and sexism). Strengths within the black family, particularly those of collectivity and shared responsibility rather than individualism, should be given greater attention when intervening in abused children's lives. Also important is the need for a systematic collation of data on black children who have been abused. For example, the often-quoted study by Baker and Duncan (1985) is detailed in its analysis of the incidence of sexual abuse in Britain. Comparisons are made between boys and girls across a range of age groups. Detailed information is given about the social class position of the abused persons as well as their home district whether urban, mixed or rural area. Nowhere does the study comment on the racial mix of the sample. A recent British publication adds to the despair about the dearth of research. Gillham (1994), unlike some of his English-speaking Northern American counterparts, finds it difficult to stratify British society by race.

Furthermore, social work as a profession should engage in a critical analysis of theory and practice in child abuse issues as they affect black families, and not depend solely on black professionals. Finally, black men should examine and cease their exploitation of women and children. Black men cannot assert that they are 'unaccountable because of the extenuating circumstances of race, poverty and economic disadvantage' (Wilson, 1993: 210).

References

Baker, A.W. and Duncan, S.P. (1985) 'Child sexual abuse: a study of prevalence in Great Britain', *Child Abuse and Neglect*, 9: 457–67.

Bryan, A. (1992) 'Working with black single mothers: myths and reality', in M. Langan and L. Day (eds), *Women, Oppression and Social Work*, London: Routledge.

Cohen, S. (1981) *The Thin End of the White Wedge: the New Nationality Laws – Second Class Citizenship and the Welfare State*, Manchester: Voluntary Organisations and Local Student Union.

Day, L. (1992) 'Women and oppression: race, class and gender', in M. Langan and L. Day (eds), *Women, Oppression and Social Work*, London: Routledge.

Department of Health (1988) *Protecting Children: a Guide for Social Workers Undertaking a Comprehensive Assessment*, London: HMSO.

Dominelli, L. and McLeod, E. (1989) *Feminist Social Work*, London: Macmillan.

Droisen, A. (1989) 'Racism and anti-racism', in E. Driver and A. Droisen (eds), *Child Sexual Abuse: Feminist Perspectives*, London: Macmillan.

Gillham, B. (1994) *The Facts about Child Physical Abuse*, London: Cassell.

Gordon, P. (1992) 'Black people and the criminal law: rhetoric and reality', in P. Braham, A. Rattansi and R. Skellington (eds), *Racism and Anti-racism: Inequalities, Opportunities and Policies*, London: Open University/Sage.

Hampton, R.L. (1987) *Violence in the Black Family: Correlates and Consequences*, Massachusetts/Toronto: Lexington Books.

Home Office/Department of Health (1992) *Memorandum of Good Practice on Video Recorded Interviews with Child Witnesses for Criminal Proceedings*, London: HMSO.

Hudson, A. (1992) 'The child sexual abuse "industry" and gender relations in social work', in M. Langan and L. Day (eds), *Women, Oppression and Social Work*, London: Routledge.

Lawrence, M. (1992) 'Women's psychology and feminist social work practice', in M. Langan and L. Day (eds), *Women, Oppression and Social Work*, London: Routledge.

London Borough of Lambeth (1987) *Whose Child?: the Report of the Public Inquiry into the Death of Tyra Henry*, London: Lambeth Borough Council.

MacDonald, S. (1991) *All Equal under the Act?*, London: NISW.

Mama, A. (1992) 'Black women and the British state: race, class and gender analysis for the 1990s', in P. Braham, A. Rattansi and R. Skellington (eds), *Racism and Anti-racism: Inequalities, Opportunities and Policies*, London: Open University/Sage.

Mtezuka, E.M. (1989–90) 'Towards a better understanding of child sexual abuse among Asian communities, *Practice*, 3 and 4: 248–60.

Obikeze, D.S. (1986) 'Child maltreatment in non-industrialised countries: a framework for analysis', in Z. Bankowski and M. Carballo (eds), *Battered Children and Child Abuse*, CIOMS.

Wilson, M. (1993) *Crossing the Boundary: Black Women Survive Incest*, London: Virago.

13

Victims or Villains? Women who Physically Abuse their Children

Brid Featherstone

As an area of study women's violence towards their children occupies a paradoxical position in that it is simultaneously over-scrutinized and neglected. This is scarcely surprising given how often women are either idealized or denigrated in contemporary Western society. Ambivalent and contradictory processes operate to position women, particularly mothers, on the one hand, as the source of all the harm children suffer or as their only source of protection and, on the other, as powerless victims themselves. Attempts to understand women's violence towards children reflects such a counterposition frequently investing the women concerned with total power or total powerlessness. Men, by contrast, are either invisible or the source of all violence.

This chapter will initially explore some of the methodological and definitional difficulties involved in research in this area. It will then go on to identify some of the central themes arising out of the research that has been carried out, paying particular attention to issues of mothering and power.

Competing Definitions: Competing Realities

How is violence to children defined? Whose definitions become influential and why? This whole area has been identified as problematic by a host of writers (see, for example, Besharov, 1981; Parton, 1985; Gordon, 1989; Corby, 1993). Parton (1985) and Gordon (1989) both point to the political nature of the process by which particular definitions become accepted. Parton highlights, for example, the process by which 'the battered baby syndrome' became the subject of media and professional attention in the 1960s and 1970s and the way in which particular professional interests were served by such a definition. Gordon, in a study which looks at all aspects of violence within the family, points out that 'the very definition of what constitutes unacceptable domestic violence and appropriate responses developed and then varied according to political moods and the force of certain political movements' (Gordon, 1989: 3).

Currently, definitions range from those which stress what happens to individual children, for example 'a battered child is any child who receives a non accidental physical injury or injuries as a result of acts (or omissions) on the part of his parents or guardians' (Kempe and Helfer, 1980, quoted in Corby, 1993: 41) to those which stress the gaps between optimal living conditions and children's actual conditions thereby highlighting questions of social and structural abuse (Gil, 1975). Definitions also refer to the intent of the actor/actress, the effect on the child and the judgements of the professional involved (Gil, 1970; Corby, 1993). Indeed, the disparity in definitions is such that Corby (1993) argues that the only safe definition is that it is a judgement reached by a group of professionals.

Unlike sexual abuse, questions about the relationship between gender and definition have not been central. Hearn does make such a link by defining all forms of child abuse 'as a matter of men's violence to babies, children and young people' (Hearn, 1990: 64). Gordon argues that the gender politics of family violence issues are central to any debates around definition 'not only when women or girls were the victims of men but also when women were the abusers' (Gordon, 1989: 5). Family violence is, for her, bound up with gendered and generational conflicts over resources and benefits. Such contests are not solely attributable to personal aspiration but also refer to changing social norms and conditions. Gordon's perspective is, however, unusual in that she poses gender as a social relation and does not see it solely as a question of men's wrongdoing and women's or children's victimization. Her understanding of gender opens up the possibility of locating women who abuse within a framework which sees gender as a central category of analysis. This is especially important in the current situation where the discovery, for example, that a minority of women sexually abuse has led some to argue that gender is no longer a useful or relevant category (see Hooper, 1989).

To summarize, battles over definition are political battles in themselves and serve as a guide to central debates. In terms of definitions of physical abuse, these battles indicate some degree of preoccupation with individual versus social explanations which are often gender blind, a concern with the role of professionals and professional judgements and little concern or debate about how or whether gender should be a category of analysis.

The Issue of Prevalence

Given the definitional difficulties outlined, it is hardly surprising that there is no consensus about the size of the problem of women's violence to their children. Debates around prevalence are not 'innocent' debates located outside power relations. The possibility of women's involvement in violent activity towards their own or other children opens up painful and difficult issues particularly for feminists. The fear that any such debates would allow men to abdicate responsibility for their disproportionate share in violence may have partly contributed to their relative silence in this area (Gordon, 1986).

At the same time there has also been a tendency by others to over-identify and scrutinize women in child abuse cases and to ignore men (Allan, 1978; Martin, 1983; Milner, 1993). A typical example of this is provided by Korbin (1989). In a paper entitled 'Fatal maltreatment by mothers: a proposed framework', she accepts as unproblematic that in her sample of nine women, the male companion had been, according to the mother, the sole perpetrator in three cases. While recognizing that mothers in such situations might minimize their role, it is interesting that she does not exercise a degree of caution about both the title of the study and the question of how judgements around responsibility key into gendered expectations. Kelly (1988), Hearn (1990) and Forbes (1993) have all raised issues about the ways in which the official identification and prosecutions of child abuse are themselves gendered. Forbes (1993), for example, documents the case of Sally Emery who was sentenced to four years' imprisonment for failure to protect her baby. Her conviction was not for harming her daughter but for 'allowing' her to be harmed by the man involved.

Wise (1991) has attempted to develop a picture of women's involvement in physical abuse by analysing the statistics provided by the National Society for the Prevention of Cruelty to Children (NSPCC). She points out that, until recently, in the absence of officially collected government figures, such statistics had an added importance. She found it impossible to produce a full picture of men and women's involvement in physically abusive activity on the basis of the figures provided. For example, no information was provided on gender except in relation to birth mother and birth father. The other categories used were non-gender specific. Wise requested further information from the compiler of the statistics, Susan Creighton, and was able on the basis of this information to develop a clearer picture. Creighton's original information suggested that women were the perpetrators in 28.4 per cent and men in 28.9 per cent of cases. However, this information only related to birth parents. On the basis of the additional information received, Wise was able to show a prevalence rate of 48 per cent for men and 31 per cent for women with 21 per cent unspecified (Wise, 1991).

As Wise notes, we cannot hope for an improved information base for the future. The information which is now being collected by the Association of Directors of Social Services (ADSS) and the Department of Social Security (DSS) does not include information on the sex of perpetrators. Moreover, there has also been a consistent problem in Britain with developing some sense of prevalence rates in relation to black communities (Singh, 1993). The NSPCC did not collect information on race or ethnicity. Asbury (1993) has looked at research on the relationship between race, ethnicity and the physical abuse of children carried out in the United States. She argues that the research has been dominated by attempts to estimate how frequently 'minority' children are abused in comparison with European American children. Accordingly, there has been little 'within group' research.

Gelles has argued, on the basis of data from the Second National Family Violence Survey conducted in the United States, that the rates of severe violence towards children (such acts were classified as aggressive acts with a high probability of causing physical injury) are similar for mothers and fathers in homes with two adults; 110 per 1,000 children for mothers and 97 per 1,000 for fathers. However, the rate of severe violence for single fathers was substantially higher than the rate for single mothers; 189 per 1,000 as against 130 per 1,000 (quoted in Carlson, 1992). Other commentators appear to agree that when the disparity between the amount of time men and women care for children is taken into account, then men are much more likely to abuse children physically (Finkelhor, 1983; Pagelow, 1984; Hearn, 1990). However, this still leaves us with some degree of certainty about the fact that 'women commit a great deal of physical child abuse' (Carlson, 1992: 103). Recent research on children who are murdered would also indicate that the involvement of mothers, in particular, is quite significant (Morris and Wilczynski, 1993). They analysed data on 474 child homicides in the UK between 1982 and 1989 and found that mothers had committed almost half the child killings attributed to parents in that period.

As I indicated earlier, discussions around prevalence are not 'innocent'. Equally, decisions to study women who are violent or to ignore them are related to very fundamental questions about how we understand the role of mothers and, most importantly, how we view the operation of power relations in and around families.

Mothering and Child Abuse: Some themes from the Literature

A number of names recurs when any examination of the dominant influences on research into child care and child abuse in the UK is undertaken. Bowlby and Kempe are usually recognized as significantly influencing the direction of policy and practice. Bowlby's work stressed the importance of secure attachments for children and posited abuse as the most extreme expression of a parent's incapacity to form an attachment. His work has led to a series of papers and studies on the relationship between early separation experiences, with the consequent failure to develop bonding, and child abuse (for example, Lynch and Roberts, 1977; Hyman, 1978; Argles, 1980; Egeland and Vaughn, 1981). Such studies have emphasized the role of mothers and have often solely studied the relationship between mother and child. Bowlby himself was clear that, although it did not have to be the mother who was the primary caretaker, the early years of a child's life were vital and that 'either mother looks after them herself or she has to have a reliable stable person to do it for her' (Bowlby et al., 1986: 51).

Certainly many studies have seen the mother as central. When examining who gets researched, Martin (1983) found that studies on mothers alone made up 41 per cent of the sample. Only two of the 76 works reviewed dealt exclusively with men. Furthermore, within this perspective, even when mothers are not the subject of study, 'mothering' has a hegemonic position as a paradigm of caretaking. For example, Steele (1976), a close associate of Kempe, the originator of the term 'the battered baby syndrome', argues 'During the last fifteen years of working with parents who neglect or abuse their children we have been led to the conviction that the basic ingredients of their behaviour have their origin in the very earliest part of the parent's life and predominantly in relation to the lack of "empathic mothering" ' (Steele, 1976: 13). This is more significant than any other single factor such as gender, socioeconomic status or living conditions. Steele argues that the term describes a variety of less than ideal responses by the caretaker, usually the mother. It often begins with insufficient bonding which leads to subsequent interactions being orientated more to the needs of the caretaker than the child. Parent's own experiences of being parented and of being children are centrally important here: 'When men and women become parents, two kinds of memories are activated, often largely unconscious; the memories of what it was like to be a child, and the recollections of how one's parents cared for one in the earliest years' (Steele, 1976: 14).

The criticisms of the above approaches are extremely wide ranging and it is beyond the scope of this chapter to engage with them fully (see, for example, Parton, 1985; Dale et al., 1986, for two very different critiques). The approaches are criticized for their exclusive focus on individual families, the neglect of socioeconomic factors and the promotion of a disease model of child abuse. Hilary Graham (1980), in one of the earliest attempts by feminists to address this area, introduces a theme which has recurred in the debates. She argues for a move away from seeing child abuse as a reflection of individual pathology and for the development of a sociological perspective. She also contests the way in which the context and the constraints of contemporary motherhood are ignored in accounts such as those of Steele.

In some of the subsequent contributions (for example, Parton, 1985) mothering, or indeed fathering, as a subject of study disappears completely, in favour of explorations which study the social processes by which problems become defined as problems and the way in which individual families become the subject of scrutiny rather than the social and economic system.

The few feminist analyses of physical abuse which have been carried out have followed Graham (1980) in stressing the way in which motherhood as an institution oppresses women and the lack of support that women receive either financially or emotionally (see, for example, Ong, 1985; Parton, 1990). They have tended to express concern at attempts to explore individual mother–child dynamics and, indeed, the received feminist wisdom appears to be that attempts to explore explanations at an individual level lead to a pathologizing of the woman or child concerned.

Within these analyses, women are primarily positioned as victims, although there is an acknowledgement of the complexity involved. The attribution of victim status has interesting consequences particularly in Ong's (1985) analysis which is a study of a specific group of women attending a family centre. For example, she fails to develop the workers' observations that the women sometimes beat their children to get their own way. She reframes their refusal to conform to the requirements of the professionals and engage in work around their relationships with their children as evidence of their powerlessness and oppression. She does not explore the possibility that the women may occupy a range of subject positions which shift. They may be victims in one situation, for example in relation to their husbands, but in relation to the family centre worker or their children they may be in a position of power for a variety of reasons. They can therefore be both victim and victimizer and these positions themselves shift; for indeed children grow up, workers move on, agency policy changes.

Gordon (1989) is critical of what she terms the 'victimization paradigm' which she argues dominates feminist work in this area. She sees this operating in at least two ways. One relates to the conceptualization of social control as a 'top down' phenomenon which is neither requested nor resisted by its recipients. Secondly, she contests the notion that there are clear-cut victims or villains who are readily recognizable. She argues that much family violence is interactional and involves battles over scarce resources. While her analysis is very clear on the significance of socio-economic factors and ethnicity, she also argues for the importance of incorporating an understanding of interactional factors and 'personality' (Gordon, 1989). Consequently, she does not repeat the counterposition of individual and structural explanations so often evident. Equally, her focus on the significance of interactional explanations is unusual. Theories which stress the interactional nature of family violence have tended to be heavily criticized. Such approaches abolish 'both the criminality of the attacker and the innocence of the victim' (Jackson and Rushton, 1982: 25). Their analysis, alongside that of others (Stark and Flitcraft, 1988), argues that violence to children cannot be separated from violence to women and both cannot be understood outside the context of male power.

Kelly (1991) and Carlson (1992) have argued that it is time for feminists to take the issue of women's violence towards their children more seriously than hitherto. Kelly argues that the failure to do so means that we are failing women and children who have and continue to suffer at the hands of other women. They have both emphasized from rather different perspectives that this means a reappraisal of the question of power. Before turning to address the shape such a reappraisal might take, it is important briefly to locate the discussion on women's violence within the context of feminist theory as a whole.

Like all social theories, feminism is marked 'by ambivalence, omissions and gaps' (Flax, 1990a: 179). Currently the gaps would appear motivated by contradictory feelings about women's capacity to be aggressive, their sexuality and motherhood. Anxiety and the need to split off or deny the contradictions and ambivalences are revealed in intolerance and overly coherent theories (Flax, 1990a).

Women's violence towards their children is both anxiety provoking and a challenge to theories which have identified violence as male. As we have seen earlier when the question has been raised, the assumption is, often, that changing the social circumstances in which women mother will address the problem. This assumes that the interests of mothers and children automatically coincide (Riley, 1983). A lack of attention by feminists to child-rearing as distinct from childbearing has allowed this assumption to go unchallenged. As Flax (1990b) notes, feminists still write social theory in which everyone is assumed to be adult and mothering as a relation between persons is not generally discussed.

Doane and Hodges (1992) argue that many current writings, in particular feminist psychoanalytic writing, promote an idealized notion of mothering for women to live up to. Others, while still recognizing the helpful possibilities of this tradition, agree, arguing that a sanitized version has been promoted which obscures, denies, represses women's anger, autonomy and agency (Flax, 1990a). In trying to develop understandings that do integrate women's anger and violence, we need to be aware of the dangers of (re) producing analyses that are assumed to be of universal applicability. Such 'grand narratives' disregard and marginalize those who do not fit and maintain their coherence by suppressing difference and uncertainty (Sawicki, 1991). They also universalize aspects of the theorist's own situation and are insufficiently self-critical in terms of questioning their own location.

In moving debates forward, a number of key issues would appear to be both important and controversial. These include the refinement of the question of power, and the analysis of relational dynamics and responsibility.

A Question of Power

The issue of power, particularly men's power, has been central to feminist thought and practice. The position of women in the world is the result of asymmetrical power relations. Consequently, analyses of women's lives are undertaken bearing that fundamental truth in mind. More recently, the recognition that there are differences between women, and that these differences may also constitute power relations, has meant that the issue of power has been recognized as more complex than perhaps hitherto thought.

In particular, the increased understanding that white women may occupy simultaneously differing positions *vis à vis* white men, black men and black women has led some feminists to attempt to develop a more nuanced understanding of power and powerlessness. This has led to questioning on a number of levels. How does power operate? Is it a hierarchy? Is it fixed? Is it a possession?

Many feminists have found the work of Michel Foucault useful as a way of exploring issues of power (Sawicki, 1991). Foucault attempted to explore notions of power which stress that it is not absolute, or a possession or fixed. It is not located in one place or in one group (for example, in men or the state). Power is understood here as contextual and shifting. Foucault's approach can therefore encompass the possibility that an individual woman may be positioned differently in relation to her husband, her children and other women.

Foucault emphasized the importance of exploring the 'how' of power relations rather than the 'why'. He advocated a cautious experimental approach and was wary of generalizations and totalizing impulses, a wariness that has been shared by those from within what has been termed post-modernist/post-structuralist perspectives. Although Foucault's emphasis on the 'micro-politics' of power has been perceived as compatible with feminist understandings of the politics of the everyday, his work has not been accepted uncritically. In particular, concern has been expressed about the political dangers of posing such a diffuse view of power. Emphasizing the shifting nature of power can obscure how often there are limits to the shifts and lead us to an unhelpful celebration of limitless possibilities.

However, this emphasis on context and the concern with how power relations operate in particular practices could, in relation to the concerns of this chapter, be helpful in moving debates away from abstract free-floating mothers and children. It could lead us to an exploration of differing mothering practices and the role that physical violence plays in either the assertion of control or as a manifestation of the loss of control. By moving away from grand abstract theories which assert how power operates, space could be provided for mothers, themselves, to explore how they locate themselves in relation to their children, their partners and the range of agencies within our society who are involved in pronouncing on motherhood. This might also enable the question of difference to be posed in a way which has not occurred hitherto, as not just a question of differences between and among mothers, important as they are, but also in terms of differences within women. Thus we might begin to gain some understanding of '[their] inconsistencies and complex allegiances' (Doane and Hodges, 1992: 79).

Furthermore, such explorations might ensure that children are no longer rendered invisible. Important issues could therefore be addressed. Are particular children powerful at particular times? How do differences between boys and girls manifest themselves? How do children negotiate between and with mothers and fathers? How do they negotiate and manage interactions with those outside the family?

Clearly, any such explorations would have to investigate the relationship between power in intimate relations and power in other areas of life. Goldner (1991) argues that a consequence of studying 'the ambivalent paradoxical expressions and meanings of power in intimate relationships have led most feminists away from simplistic characterizations of victims and victimisers towards more complex views of power as a relational arrangement buttressed by the larger socio-political context of gender inequality but not reducible to it' (Goldner, 1991: 64-5). Others, as we have seen earlier, are less convinced, pointing to the way in which men's violence in particular operates to ensure that power relations in the private are a reflection of those in the public (Stark and Flitcraft, 1988). The case of Lisa Steinberg highlights the continuing debate and lack of unanimity around this issue. Lisa's death in the late 1980s at the hands of her father split American feminists, with some arguing that her mother as a middle-class woman should have used the support networks available to her to prevent her daughter being killed and others arguing that as a woman who had been consistently battered she was as much a victim as her daughter.

Developing contextual understandings of women in such situations might enable us to move from characterizing such women as either abstract victims or villains and help us to identify what factors are implicated in specific women's decisions to stay with or leave violent men.

Relational Dynamics and Responsibility

A further area of some controversy and complexity is uncovered when we move from considering whether and how women exercise power them-selves to a consideration of their relationship to men's power. Benjamin (1990) is one of a range of writers who have turned to psychoanalytical perspectives in order to develop understandings of power which move away from simple notions of 'doer' and 'done to'. She argues that traditional gender divisions offer an escape from the all-powerful mother as perceived by the infant. In opposition to Freud, who suggested that the mother would be seen as weak by her children, Benjamin suggests that, on the contrary, because the mother is largely responsible for the day-to-day care of infants she appears all powerful. The boy child recognizes in paternal difference the chance to escape from this power. For the girl child the external and different power of the father also offers the possibility of escape and the possibility of recognition by someone who represents the excitement of the outside in contrast to the mother whose 'capacity to recognize her daughter's agency is limited by her cultural articulation as OBJECT of male desire rather than as subject who owns her own desire' (Wright, 1992: 21). Both the girl and the boy seek recognition from the father but only the boy has this identification confirmed by someone who recognizes him as being like him. This sense of identification is missing for the girl and she is left both with the wish to be chosen and idealizing the father who represents power to her. As a result contemporary arrange-ments mean boys identify with power and girls hand it over (Coward, 1993). Many feminists, of course, view such accounts and indeed the whole psychoanalytic enterprise with deep suspicion.

Others, like Temperley (1984: 25), go on to argue that

> If we [women] are to improve our society we need to take proper cognizance of our own investment in it. Jean Baker Miller's contention is that men have conveniently rid themselves of certain uncomfortable experiences, such as vulnerability and dependence, by obliging women to carry them on men's behalf. She fails, to my mind, to see the reciprocity in this system, ie that women are thereby relieved of conscious knowledge and experience of the violence and competition that men express for us.

Lawrence (1992) makes a similar point specifically in relation to child abuse when she argues that social workers must at least consider the possibility that some women do sometimes allow men to hold and express the hostility they unconsciously feel towards their children. She is very clearly arguing, however, that this is not a conscious decision but that the unconscious split-off part of the woman may find expression in the abuse of the child.

For many women this feels suspiciously like mother-blaming yet again and highlights a continuing dilemma around the pairing of responsibility and blame. By this is meant the way in which attempts by women to take responsibility for issues often become reframed in this particular culture in terms of blame. A further difficulty with the above is that it can be used in a universalist way to explain all situations. This may only serve to reproduce current theoretical difficulties whereby a singular set of meanings is attached to mothering or power.

Despite these concerns, it is important that we move to exploring gender as a social relation rather than posing it as dichotomous and oppositional. By this is meant developing, for example, understandings of how masculinity and femininity operate in a dynamic and changing relationship rather than as fixed and clear cut.

Goldner et al. (1990) have attempted in their work as feminist systemic therapists to develop what they call 'both-and' positions rather than either/or positions (either/or referring specifically to those of victim or villain) in relation to the men and women they work with. Equally, in attempting to explore explanations for violent behaviour, they also attempt to avoid dichotomizing approaches. They argue 'that one level of description or explanation does not exclude another. To say that violence, domination, subordination and victimization are psychological, does not mean they are not also material, moral or legal' (Goldner et al., 1990: 345).

Extending such approaches, combined with an appreciation of the dangers of universalizing and a focus on context to women's relationships with children, would enable mother's, father's and children's positions to be interrogated in a way which addressed the complexity of the relations involved and acknowledged the different levels at which problems exist – economic, political, psychological. It would further explore how gender and generational conflicts operate in concrete situations.

Conclusion

It has been noted that a difficulty with current debates in relation to gender and child abuse is the way in which explanations are posed as if they are mutually exclusive (Stevenson, 1989). Furthermore, such explanations are assumed to apply to all within their ambit and, as a consequence, differences between women, men and children are therefore often not adequately explored.

This chapter has made a plea for research which explores the complexity of women's lives, in particular, and facilitates the process of integrating children as agents into analyses. Such research would eschew uncritical generalizations and explore the 'particular' in a way which links it but does not reduce it to the whole.

References

Allan, L.J. (1978) 'Child abuse: a critical review of the research and the theory', in J.P. Martin (ed.), *Violence and the Family*, Chichester: Wiley and Sons.

Argles, P. (1980) 'Attachment and child abuse', *British Journal of Social Work*, 10: 33–42.

Asbury, J.E. (1993) 'Violence in families of color in the United States', in R. Hampton, T. Gullotta, G. Adams, E. Potter and R. Weissberg (eds), *Family Violence: Prevention and Treatment*, California: Sage.

Benjamin, J. (1990) *The Bonds of Love: Psychoanalysis, Feminism and the Problem of Domination*, London: Virago.

Besharov, D. (1981) 'Towards better research on child abuse and neglect: making definitional issues an explicit methodological concern', *Child Abuse and Neglect*, 5: 383–90.

Bowlby, J., Figlio, K. and Young, R. (1986) 'An interview with John Bowlby on the origins and reception of his work', *Free Associations*, 6: 36–64.

Carlson, B. (1992) 'Questioning the party line on violence', *Affilia*, 7 (2): 94–111.

Corby, B. (1993) *Child Abuse: towards a Knowledge Base*, Buckingham: Open University Press.

Coward, R. (1993) *Our Treacherous Hearts: Why Women let Men get their Way*, London: Faber and Faber.

Dale, P., Davies, M., Morrison, T. and Waters, J. (1986) *Dangerous Families: Assessment and Treatment of Child Abuse*, London: Tavistock.

Doane, J. and Hodges, D. (1992) *From Klein to Kristeva: Psychoanalytic Feminism and the Search for the 'Good Enough' Mother*, Ann Arbor: University of Michigan Press.

Egeland, B. and Vaughn, B. (1981) 'Failure of bond formation as a cause of abuse, neglect and maltreatment', *American Journal of Orthopsychiatry*, 51: 78–84.

Finkelhor, D. (1983) 'Common features of family abuse', in D. Finkelhor, R. Gelles, G. Hotaling and M. Strauss (eds), *The Dark Side of Families: Current Family Violence Research*, California: Sage.

Flax, J. (1990a) *Thinking Fragments: Postmodernism, Feminism and Psychoanalysis*, Oxford: University of California Press.

Flax, J. (1990b) 'Postmodernism and gender relations in feminist theory', in L. Nicholson (ed.), *Feminism/Postmodernism*, London: Routledge.

Forbes, J. (1993) 'Female sexual abusers: the contemporary search for equivalence', *Practice*, 6 (2): 102–11.

Gil, D. (1970) *Violence against Children*, Cambridge, Mass.: Harvard University Press.

Gil, D. (1975) 'Unravelling child abuse', *American Journal of Orthopsychiatry*, 45: 346–56.

Goldner, V. (1991) 'Sex, power, and gender: a feminist systemic analysis of the politics of passion', *Journal of Family Therapy*, 3 (1–2): 63–83.

Goldner, V., Penn, P., Sheinberg, M. and Walker, G. (1990) 'Love and violence: gender paradoxes in volatile attachments', *Family Process*, 29 (4): 343–64.

Gordon, L. (1986) 'Feminism and social control: the case of child abuse and neglect', in J. Mitchell and A. Oakley (eds), *What is Feminism?*, Oxford: Basil Blackwell.

Gordon, L. (1989) *Heroes of their own Lives*, London: Virago.

Graham, H. (1980) 'Mothers' accounts of anger and aggression towards their babies', in N. Frude (ed.), *Psychological Approaches to Child Abuse*, Guildford: Billing.

Hearn, J. (1990) 'Child abuse and men's violence', in Violence against Children Study Group (ed.), *Taking Child Abuse Seriously*, London: Unwin Hyman.

Hooper, C. (1989) 'If women do it too', *Community Care*, 16 November: 26–7.

Hyman, C. (1978) 'Some characteristics of abusing families referred to the NSPCC', *British Journal of Social Work*, 8 (2): 629–35.

Jackson, S. and Rushton, P. (1982) 'Victims and villains: images of women in accounts of family violence', *Women's Studies International Forum*, 5 (1): 17–28.

Kelly, L. (1988) 'What's in a name?: defining sexual abuse', *Feminist Review*, 28: 65–73.

Kelly, L. (1991) 'Unspeakable acts', *Trouble and Strife*, 21: 13–20.

Korbin, J. (1989) 'Fatal maltreatment by mothers: a proposed framework', *Child Abuse and Neglect*, 13: 481–9.

Lawrence, M. (1992) 'Women's psychology and feminist social work practice', in M. Langan and L. Day (eds), *Women, Oppression and Social Work: Issues in Anti-discriminatory Practice*, London: Routledge.

Lynch, M. and Roberts, J. (1977) 'Predicting child abuse: signs of bonding failure in the maternity hospital', *British Medical Journal*, 1: 624–6.

Martin, J. (1983) 'Maternal and paternal abuse of children: theoretical and research perspectives', in D. Finkelhor, R. Gelles, G. Hotaling and M. Strauss (eds), *The Dark Side of Families: Current Family Research*, California: Sage.

Milner, J. (1993) 'A disappearing act: the differing career paths of fathers and mothers in child protection investigations', *Critical Social Policy*, 38: 48–68.

Morris, A. and Wilczynski, A. (1993) 'Rocking the cradle: mothers who kill their children', in H. Birch (ed.), *Moving Targets: Women, Murder and Representation*, London: Virago.

Ong, B. (1985) 'Understanding child abuse: ideologies of motherhood', *Women's Studies International Forum*, 8 (5): 4–18.

Pagelow, M. (1984) *Family Violence*, New York: Praeger.

Parton, C. (1990) 'Women, gender oppression and child abuse', in Violence against Children Study Group (ed.), *Taking Child Abuse Seriously*, London: Unwin Hyman.

Parton, N. (1985) *The Politics of Child Abuse*, Hampshire: Macmillan.

Riley, D. (1983) *War in the Nursery: Theories of the Child and Mother*, London: Virago.

Sawicki, J. (1991) *Disciplining Foucault: Feminism, Power and the Body*, New York: Routledge.

Singh, G. (1993) 'Research findings on race and child protection', Paper presented at Day Conference on Research and Child Protection, Bradford Metropolitan Council Training Unit, 25 March.

Stark, E. and Flitcraft, A. (1988) 'Women and children at risk: a feminist perspective on child abuse', *International Journal of Health Services*, 18 (1): 97–118.

Steele, B. (1976) 'Violence within the family', in R. Helfer and C.H. Kempe (eds), *Child Abuse and Neglect: the Family and the Community*, Cambridge: Ballinger.

Stevenson, O. (1989) 'Reflections on social work practice', in O. Stevenson (ed.), *Child Abuse: Public Policy and Professional Practice*, Hertfordshire: Harvester Wheatsheaf.

Temperley, J. (1984) 'Our own Worst Enemies: Unconscious Factors in Female Disadvantage', *Free Associations*, Pilot Issue: 23–38.

Wise, S. (1991) *Child Abuse: The NSPCC Version*, Manchester: Feminist Praxis.

Wright, E. (ed.) (1992) *Feminism and Psychoanalysis: a Critical Dictionary*, Oxford: Basil Blackwell.

Index